Reneau Z. Peurifoy, M.A., M.F.C.C. has a private practice in Sacramento, California. He first specialized in anxiety-related problems in 1981. He was selected to present his treatment approach at the Ninth (1988), Tenth (1990), Eleventh (1991), and Twelfth (1992) National Conferences on Phobias and Related Anxiety Disorders presented by the Anxiety Disorders Association of America and co-sponsored by Massachusetts General Hospital and Harvard Medical School. He has spoken to groups and conducting training seminars on treating anxiety-disorders nation-wide.

In addition to his work with anxiety-related problems, Mr. Peurifoy also works with couples, and problems with school age children. He has designed and conducted educational programs on anxiety, anger, assertiveness, stress management, and other topics in a wide variety of settings. He has a special commitment to teaching effective parenting skills and has worked with over two thousand parents in the various parenting classes he has taught.

Mr. Peurifoy spent five years as a teacher before deciding to go into counseling. Two of those years were spent in Japan teaching science at St. Joseph's College, an all boys school in Yokohama. Mr. Peurifoy met his wife, Michiyo, in college. They were married in 1974 and together they have two children, Audric born in 1979 and Monique born in 1983.

SECOND EDITION

ANXIETY, PHOBIAS AND PANIC

Taking Charge and Conquering Fear

Reneau Z. Peurifoy MA, MFCC

LIFE SKILLS

Note: The ideas, procedures, and suggestions contained in this book are not intended as a substitute for consulting with either a physician or psychotherapist. You should regularly consult a physician in matters relating to your health and particularly in respect to any symptoms that may require diagnosis or medical attention. Likewise, if you feel desperate and are unable to cope with stressful events, you are urged to seek help from a qualified psychotherapist.

Library of Congress in Publication Data

Peurifoy, Reneau Z.
        Anxiety, phobias & panic: taking charge and conquering fear: a step-by-step program for regaining control of your life/by Reneau Z. Peurifoy. — 2nd ed.

        p.   cm.
        Includes bibliographical references and index.
        ISBN 0-929437-13-6: $12.95
        1. Anxiety—Problems, exercises, etc. 2. Relaxation—Therapeutic use. 3. Mental discipline. I. Title. II. Title: Anxiety, phobias, and panic.
        BF575.A6P45 1992
        152.4'6—dc20   91-42115
                                                                                          CIP

Printed in the United States of America

Acknowledgements

There are many people who have made this book possible. First, I would like to thank the clients who have worked with me. Through their struggles with anxiety, they helped perfect the program outlined in these pages. Next, I would like to thank the people who read the various drafts of the manuscript for the first edition. Kris Baxter, Carole Sabo, Joyce Herman, Dorothy Lambert, and Jann McCord labored through the first drafts and offered many suggestions on both content and format.

After the first drafts were revised, Alissyn Link, Lucille De Rose, Jane Fry, Mary Ann Kinyon, Linda Kenney and my mother, Clara Peurifoy all made extensive suggestions on style and format. Kim and Kevin Thompson managed the actual page layout and production of the first edition. Alissyn Link, Dr. Frank Capobianco, Jane Fry, Nancy Morris-Struben, and Kaaren Smith all helped with the revisions for the second edition. I would also like to thank Shirley Green, founder of ABIL (Agoraphobics Building Independent Lives) which is a large self-help organization in Richmond, Virginia, who has offered much encouragement and support.

Finally, I would like to thank my wife, Michiyo. Without her support this book would not have been possible. Because her love and companionship have helped sustain me, I dedicate this book to her.

Contents

Preface

The evolution of this book began a little over a decade ago when I was beginning my career as a therapist. I heard two people on the radio who suffered from what was then called agoraphobia but is now known as panic disorder. Their story intrigued me. I soon discovered that there were not many people who were working with agoraphobia at that time. I found a group in another city working with agoraphobia and spent a week there studying their approach. This included visiting support groups they had organized for agoraphobics.

Upon returning to Sacramento I held two lectures where I shared my new found knowledge and was surprised to find that enough people attended to enable me to begin two therapy groups of my own. Within two weeks it became evident that the approach I had studied was woefully inadequate. This is when I began developing the program that has evolved into the one described in this book.

I went to a local university and reviewed all of the current research on agoraphobia. This was relatively easy as the explosion of research that is available today had not yet begun. There were also not that many good books written on the subject. After my research I took what I had found and combined it with material from several workshops I had conducted and put together a set of twenty lessons. After several years of refining this material I wrote the first edition of *Anxiety, Phobias & Panic* which was published in 1988.

It was gratifying to see not only individuals, but self-help groups and therapists across the nation use the book as the basic text for their groups and report back how well it was working. This new edition includes many suggestions made by groups using the first edition as well as new insights I have gained while using the original work with my own clients.

As with any author, my work and ideas are an extension of work done by many people. My main goal while writing this book was to produce a practical manual that would help people struggling with anxiety live full and satisfying lives. As a result of this goal I have not used extensive footnotes to credit my sources as I felt it would detract from that my overall purpose. Instead, I will discuss a little of my background and acknowledge those sources of inspiration who have most directly influenced this work. Those who want detailed references relating to the topics in this edition can find them in the books written specifically for therapists and researchers listed in the recommended reading.

As a child, my family had a dog, several cats, and a parrot. I raised chickens and rabbits and collected insects. By the time I entered high school, a keen interest in animal behavior had developed. I was especially fascinated by the work of Konrad Lorenz, the founder of modern ethology (the study of animal behavior). In college I majored in biology and graduated with minors in chemistry and math minors. I then studied to be a teacher and taught junior high and high school science and math for five years before deciding to become a therapist. During the time when I trained to be a teacher, self-directed learning modules were in vogue. Both this training and my experience as a teacher are reflected in the organization of this work. During this time I was also actively involved in what was then referred to as the human potential movement. Many of the exercises that are included in the recommended activities evolved out of things I learned during this period.

When I began my training to be a therapist, I was especially interested in hypnosis and the techniques of Neurolinguistic Programming. However, as my training progressed I was introduced to theory and techniques from most of the major schools of psychology. This opened up many new doors for me. In my work as a therapist, I draw from many different schools of psychology. The strongest source of influence for this work comes from the ideas developed by cognitive psychologists such as Albert Ellis and Aaron Beck. Adlerian psychology provides a strong secondary source of inspiration.

In closing I would like to add that I have always been involved in teaching in one form or another. One of my greatest thrills has always been when a struggling student, a person in therapy, or a workshop participant grasps a new concept or skill that opens up new vistas for that person. My sincere hope is that this work will help you master ideas and skills that will enable you to travel *The Path To Freedom.*

Reneau Z. Peurifoy, M.A., M.F.C.C.

The Path To Freedom

by Reneau Z. Peurifoy

As each day passes,

I am better able to embrace and love myself,
all of myself,
and to more fully embrace and love others;

I am better able to understand
that feelings are friendly,
and this understanding allows them to flow freely
through me;

I am better able to think rationally and realistically,
to look at life as a series of choices
and to stop and look before choosing;

I am better able to know
that perfection is a direction rather than a place,
and to laugh at my mistakes and imperfections;

I am better able to be patient with time
and face my world with courage,
knowing that each day
I take another step on The Path To Freedom.

Getting Started

This book describes a self-help program that has been used successfully by many people. For good results, the program has to be used correctly. The following guidelines describe how to achieve the most success possible.

Do not read the book from front to back quickly like a novel. Instead, spend at least one week on each lesson. Since each lesson builds on the ones before, do not skip around. If you wish to preview the program, read the contents. This will give you a general idea of the book's format and the areas in which you will be working.

When you start a new lesson, read the headings to get an overview of the material. Then read it word-by-word at your usual reading rate. Read each lesson at least three times, more if you find the information difficult. The second and third readings will increase your understanding of the material and reveal ideas that were missed during the first reading.

Overcoming anxiety-related problems requires more than a general understanding of ideas. Your goal is to internalize the information and skills presented in each lesson, to make them a natural and automatic part of your behavior. The recommended activities play a key role in this process. The more time and energy you spend on them, the more successful you will be.

There may be times when you could spend several weeks on a lesson. While it is important to be thorough, it is also important to keep your momentum going. Spend no more than two weeks on a lesson and do as many of the recommended activities as possible. After completing the program, you can spend additional time on those areas where you feel more work is needed.

This may sound like a lot of work; it is. But keep in mind that it took all your life to develop the behaviors and thinking patterns that produced your condition. It will take time, energy, and commitment to learn new and effective ways of thinking and acting. If you work through the material in the manner outlined, chances are excellent that you will be as successful as the many others who have used this program to overcome severe anxiety.

Lesson

What, Why, and How

Congratulations! You are about to start a journey along the path to freedom. During this journey you will meet many people just like yourself. Like most who traveled this path before you, your first questions are probably: "What has happened to me?" "Why me?" and "How can I overcome these anxiety-related problems?" This lesson answers the first two questions and starts you on the path that leads to freedom from anxiety-related problems.

☐ *Anxiety and Fear*

Anxiety and *fear* are normal responses to a perceived threat. For the purposes of this program, anxiety and fear are considered as opposite ends of a spectrum. Anxiety is usually triggered by a vague or ill-defined threat while fear is usually triggered by a well-defined threat, such as a car skidding on wet pavement. This relationship between anxiety and fear can be diagrammed as follows:

| Anxiety —————————————————— Fear |
| Vague or ill-defined threat   Well-defined threat |

Both anxiety and fear trigger unpleasant mental symptoms such as a sense of helplessness, confusion, apprehension, worry, and repeated negative thoughts. Both also trigger physical symptoms ranging from simple muscle tension to a pounding heart. The full range of possible symptoms is listed in the description of panic attacks.

☐ *Panic Attacks*

A panic attack is an intense state of fear that occurs for no apparent reason and is characterized by four or more of the following symptoms.

1

- Shortness of breath (dyspnea) or smothering sensations.
- Dizziness, unsteady feelings, or faintness.
- Palpitations or accelerated heart rate (tachycardia).
- Trembling or shaking.
- Numbness or tingling sensations (paresthesias) usually in the fingers, toes or lips.
- Flushes (hot flashes) or chills.
- Chest pain or discomfort.
- Fear of becoming seriously ill or dying.
- Fear of going crazy or of doing something uncontrolled.
- Sweating.
- Choking.
- Nausea or abdominal distress.
- Feelings of unreality (depersonalization or derealization).

An attack with fewer than four of the above symptoms is called a limited symptom attack. Panic attacks can build gradually over a period of several minutes or hours or strike very suddenly. While they can last from a few minutes to several days, most do not last longer than a half hour.

When anxiety or panic is felt regardless of where one is, it is called spontaneous anxiety or spontaneous panic, depending upon the degree of intensity. If the anxiety or panic occurs only in a particular situation, it is called situational or phobic anxiety or panic. If anxiety or panic is triggered simply by thinking of a particular situation, it is called anticipatory anxiety or anticipatory panic.

☐ *"Medical" Causes of Anxiety*

The first step in overcoming any anxiety-related problem is to rule out possible "medical" causes by having a complete examination by a a physician. Examples of medical conditions that can cause one or more of the symptoms associated with anxiety include cardiovascular problems, asthma, seizure disorder, diabetes, hypothyroidism, and problems with the inner ear. Medications such as stimulants, thyroid supplements, cold medications, tranquilizers, sleeping pills, certain blood pressure medications, steroids, and, ironically, antidepressants can also cause anxiety symptoms. Sometimes, anxiety symptoms are due to unsupervised experimentation with or withdrawal from some medications. Finally, the common legal and illegal "recreational" drugs, such as caffeine, alcohol, and marijuana, provide yet another potential source of anxiety symptoms.

☐ *Seven Types of Anxiety-Related Problems*

People with anxiety-related problems often feel that they alone suffer from this problem. Nothing could be further from the truth. The National Institute of Mental Health (NIMH) ranks anxiety disorders as the most common mental-health problem in the United States. During any given six months, about 9% or 16 million[1] people in the U.S. suffer from one of the anxiety-related problems described below. During the course of their lives, anxiety-related problems will affect about 14.6% or 26 million people. Two studies[2] found that of those asked, one third reported having at least one panic attack in the last year. While not all of these developed the problems described below, it is clear that anxiety-related problems are very common. The name used for each of the seven main types of anxiety-related problems described in the following is the one most generally recognized by mental health professionals working with anxiety problems.

Generalized Anxiety Disorder

A person with generalized anxiety disorder has experienced unrealistic or excessive anxiety and worry about two or more life circumstances for at least six months. For example, worry might center on possible misfortune to a child who is in no danger, or finances which also are in no real danger. In addition, at least six of the following symptoms are often present when anxious. These symptoms must also *not* be due to some medical condition such as hyperthyroidism or caffeine intoxication.

Motor Tension

- Trembling, twitching, or feeling shaky
- Muscle tension, aches, or soreness
- Restlessness
- Easy fatigability

Autonomic Hyperactivity

- Shortness of breath or smothering sensations
- Palpitations or accelerated heart rate (tachycardia)
- Sweating or cold, clammy hands
- Dry mouth
- Dizziness or lightheadedness
- Nausea, diarrhea, or other abdominal distress
- Flushes (hot flashes) or chills
- Frequent urination
- Trouble swallowing or "lump in throat"

Vigilance and Scanning

- Feeling keyed up or on edge
- Exaggerated startle response
- Difficulty concentrating or "mind going blank" because of anxiety
- Trouble falling or staying asleep
- Irritability

Panic Disorder

The key feature of panic disorder is the presence of unexpected panic attacks occurring for no apparent reason. No reasonable external threat is present nor are any of the factors described in the section on "medical" causes of anxiety present. People with panic disorder do not avoid places or situations associated with anxiety or panic. Some people with panic disorder never develop avoidance behaviors. Unfortunately, without effective treatment most find they eventually begin to associate various activities or situations with the panic attacks and begin to avoid these activities or situations. When this occurs, they now have *panic disorder with agoraphobia.*

Panic Disorder With Agoraphobia[3]

People with panic disorder often develop agoraphobia—the tendency to avoid places or situations where escape might be difficult or embarrassing or where help might be unavailable in the event of a panic attack. While the types of places or situations avoided vary greatly from person to person and sometimes even from time to time, a definite pattern is usually present. A person with this condition may need a companion, called a support person, when traveling away from home or into new or frightening areas. A support person ensures the availability of help.

The agoraphobic avoidance can range from mild to severe. Agoraphobic tendencies can also appear and disappear. Common situations that might be avoided include being outside of the home alone, traveling beyond a "safe" distance from the home, being in a crowd or standing in a line, being on a bridge, using an elevator, using public transportation, making a left turn that requires the car to be in a turning lane, driving on the freeway, or going to a theater or restaurant.

Social Phobia

Social phobia is characterized by a fear of embarrassing or humiliating oneself in social situations. As a result of this fear, situations are avoided where one must "perform" and be under the scrutiny of others. In one sense, social phobia is an extreme form of "performance anxiety." For some people, just thinking about feared situations can produce severe anxiety and even panic attacks.

Mild forms of social phobia are very common. The fear of public speaking, sometimes referred to as "stage fright" by actors and musicians, is probably the most common social phobia. Other common forms include difficulty in using public bathrooms, fear of writing or signing one's name in the presence of others, difficulty in eating or drinking in public, and the fear of blushing.

Obsessive-Compulsive Disorder

An obsession is a persistent idea, thought, image, or impulse that is senseless or repulsive and intrudes on a person's consciousness. Common obsessions involve thoughts of harming others, violating social norms such as swearing or exhibiting unacceptable sexual behavior, producing contamination or infection in oneself and others, and doubt about whether some action has been performed.

A compulsion is an action repeated in a ritualistic fashion. The action may be done with the intent to produce or prevent some future event or situation, even though the compulsion has no realistic bearing on the event or situation it is meant to effect. Compulsions can also be normal, rational activities performed in a clearly excessive manner. Compulsions are usually done in response to an obsession. For example, a person fearing contamination (the obsession) might engage in ritualistic or excessive handwashing. The most common compulsions are handwashing, counting, checking, and touching. Mild obsessions and compulsions are common and are only considered a problem when they interfere with normal activities, cause mental or emotional distress, or when a person lacks control over them.

Research that is still in the very early stages as of this writing suggests that Obsessive-Compulsive Disorder (OCD) may be the result of biological factors. It is thought by some that OCD is a sort of neurological "hiccup" where the brain becomes stuck while performing a normal checking or grooming activity. One particularly strong source of support for viewing OCD as primarily a biological problem comes from the fact that OCD is associated with several diseases of the basal ganglia such as epilepsy, Sydenham's chorea, toxic and vascular lesions of the basal ganglia, and postencephalitic Parkinsons's disease. The basal ganglia is a portion of the brain that plays a major role in fixed-action patterns, such as grooming in animals.

Simple Phobia

Simple phobias, also called specific phobias, can involve objects or situations such as animals, insects, flying, closed spaces, heights, darkness, elevators, or bridges. A simple phobia differs from agoraphobia in that anxiety is focused on a specific external object or situation and is present only when that object or situation is encountered. Simple phobias are common and do not usually create major problems in life since one simply avoids the feared object or situation. A simple phobia becomes a problem only when the feared object or situation cannot easily be avoided or is important to one's work or personal life.

Post-Traumatic Stress Disorder

Post-traumatic stress disorder, or PTSD, is severe stress resulting from a traumatic event such as rape, assault, a natural disaster, major surgery, wartime combat duty, experiencing a serious accident, or observing a serious accident. A person with PTSD can experience recurring images of the traumatic event, a feeling that the traumatic event is occurring in the present, recurring distressing dreams of the trauma, or intense physical discomfort when exposed to events that symbolize or resemble an aspect of the traumatic event. A person with PTSD may avoid places or things associated with the trauma or experience a general numbing. This numbing can range from avoidance of thoughts or feelings associated with the trauma to a general feeling of detachment or estrangement from others. At least two of the following types of body arousal will also be present:

- Difficulty falling or staying asleep
- Irritability or outbursts of anger
- Difficulty concentrating
- Hypervigilance
- Exaggerated startle response

- An excessive physical reaction when exposed to events that symbolize or resemble an aspect of the traumatic event—for example, a person who was rear-ended in an automobile accident becomes very anxious whenever a car approaches from behind.

☐ *The "High Anxiety Personality"*

People with anxiety-related problems share many of the same personality traits. This set of traits will be referred to as the "high anxiety personality." As you read the following list of traits, you may feel that some do not apply to you, or that they describe people you know who do not suffer from anxiety-related symptoms. However, you probably will find that many do accurately describe you. The presence of many, if not all, of these traits is what creates the high anxiety personality. Check those that you feel apply to you.

❑ High Level of Creativity/Imagination

People suffering from severe anxiety tend to be very creative with the ability to imagine things vividly. Unfortunately, this creativity is the force behind two self-defeating activities. The first, negative anticipation or "what if" thinking, is the tendency to think of many frightening things that could occur in a given situation. The second is the tendency to imagine vividly these frightening possibilities.

❑ Rigid Thinking

Rigid thinking is the tendency to perceive life as a series of either/or alternatives. Events are either right or wrong, fair or unfair. Another characteristic of this type of black-and-white thinking is the presence of many rigid rules. There is usually a "correct" way to do things, and it is upsetting when things are not done in that correct way. In addition, there are often many things that "should", "must", or "can't" be done by oneself or others.

❑ Excessive Need for Approval

The excessive need for approval is often referred to as low self-esteem or low self-acceptance. A person with this trait depends on others for a sense of self-worth. This creates a fear of rejection that results in a heightened sensitivity to criticism and difficulty in saying "no" to the demands of others. An excessive need for approval can also create the tendency to take responsibility for the feelings of others and to be overly sensitive to others needs. A person with this trait often makes it his or her responsibility to keep friends and relatives happy.

❑ Extremely High Expectations of Self

There is often the expectation from oneself of a much higher level of performance and accomplishment than would ever be expected from others.

❏ Perfectionism

Perfectionism is actually a combination of three things: the excessively high expectations mentioned above; the tendency to use all-or-nothing thinking when evaluating one's actions; and a tendency to focus on small flaws and errors rather than on progress or overall achievement. This causes the perfectionist to consider any less-than-perfect achievement as a failure that is personalized so that both the task and the person become failures. One common way in which this is expressed is the "but" habit. A perfectionist often says things such as, "This project was done pretty well, *but*...." The perfectionist then dwells on what was wrong.

❏ Competent, Dependable "Doer"

The interaction of all of the above often creates a person who is not only competent, capable, and dependable, but one who is a real "doer" and is skilled at getting jobs done and done well.

❏ Excessive Need to Be in Control

A person with this trait places a high value on being calm and in control. Often there is also a need for events to be predictable. Unexpected changes in a predetermined schedule cause distress because it is harder to be in control when one is not sure what will happen. There may also be a tendency to try to control the feelings and behavior of others. This is not done with the intention of hurting others, but out of fear of losing control.

A person with the need to be in control can experience fairly intense anxiety symptoms but appear normal to the casual observer. Since a person like this usually presents a "proper" image to the world even when there is tremendous self-doubt and turmoil inside, he or she may be considered to be very strong by friends and relatives.

❏ Suppression of Some or All Negative Feelings

A person with the above traits often suppresses feelings that "shouldn't" be felt because they might cause loss of control or disapproval from others. Pride and anger are two common examples.

❏ Tendency to Ignore the Body's Physical Needs

This trait is commonly reflected in the attitude that the body is unimportant. Signs from the body indicating it is tired or hurting and needs rest or care are ignored or given low priority. A person with this trait is frequently only aware of fatigue when the symptoms of exhaustion are present.

It needs to be emphasized that the above traits are not necessarily undesirable. When used in a positive fashion, creativity is the source of all effective problem solving. The need for approval is shared by all and makes fulfilling relationships possible. A moderate degree of perfectionism, high personal expectations, and dependability creates a valuable member of society. The ability to maintain control of oneself and one's emotions helps a person function well during emergencies and in the midst of chaos. As with any given traits a person can possess, there is a healthy range for each of the above. Some people will be at the low end of this range for some traits and others at the high for others. People with anxiety-related problems tend to be at the high end for this group of traits. This creates problems only when several of the traits become exaggerated and are outside of this healthy range.

The key to success is learning how to moderate these traits and tap into them only during times when they are appropriate. Learning to use them in this way and minimizing them during the times they interfere with your life, transforms these traits into valuable assets. In the weeks that follow, much of your time will be devoted to accomplishing this task.

☐ *The "Roots" of the High Anxiety Personality*

Your personality developed from the interaction of the following seven factors: 1) the values and beliefs of the family in which you were raised; 2) the methods of discipline used to train and socialize you; 3) the role models presented by the adults in your life when you were young; 4) your place within the family constellation (your birth order, the sex of your siblings; and whether or not you had siblings that died, were handicapped, or joined the family as a result of remarriage or adoption); 5) the social and cultural influences present while you were growing up; 6) your biological inheritance; and 7) the meaning you gave to each of the above while growing up.

There are many ways in which these seven factors can interact to produce the high anxiety traits. Experiences and events commonly found in the childhood background of people with severe anxiety are listed below. It only takes the presence of a few of these factors to produce the high anxiety traits. Check the ones that apply to you.

❑ Alcoholism in the Family

Much has been written recently about adult children of alcoholics (ACAs). Many similarities exist between traits given in materials describing ACAs and the traits described in the previous section. This does NOT mean all ACAs develop severe anxiety or that all people with severe anxiety are ACAs. It simply means the traits listed in the previous section can contribute to a wide range of problems and be generated in many different ways. Alcoholism in a brother, sister, or other relative is also sometimes a factor.

❑ Child Abuse

There are six types of child abuse.

Physical abuse: Any non-accidental injury of a child. This is usually the result of being hit, pushed, whipped, bitten, punched, slapped, or burned.

Sexual abuse: Any kind of sexual contact with a child by either an adult or child through the use of coercion, threat, or force.

Neglect: The failure to provide basic necessities such as clothing, shelter, medical attention, or supervision.

Cruel and unusual punishment: A punishment that is extreme or inappropriate for a child's age or ability to understand. Examples include corporal punishment that results in injury, locking a child in a closet, forcing a child to toilet train at six months, and sitting a child in a corner for hours at a time.

Emotional neglect: Failure by a parent to be emotionally available to take an interest in, talk to, hold, or hug a child.

Psychological abuse: Any form of recurring communication that causes extreme and unnecessary mental suffering. Examples include name calling or belittling, blocking a child's efforts to accept himself, and threats of abandonment.

Adults who have experienced child abuse are referred to as adult survivors. Like adult children of alcoholics, adult survivors share many of the high anxiety personality traits described in the pervious section. If you experienced severe child abuse, you may find it helpful to join an adult survivors self-help group.

❏ Anxious Parental Role Model

When a parent suffers from severe anxiety or has many of the high anxiety personality traits, the child can develop many of those traits by modeling after the parent.

❏ Critical Parent or Family Member

Excessive criticism often comes from a perfectionistic parent with unrealistic expectations. A parent like this often demands adult behavior and capabilities far beyond the child's ability. Sometimes excessive criticism or teasing can come from a jealous brother or sister.

❏ Rigid Family Rules

Growing up in an environment characterized by many rigid rules can set up a pattern of black-and-white thinking that continues into adulthood. Usually the rigid rules in such an environment are imposed by parents, older brothers or sisters, or other family members. A child in a family where there is chaos due to illness, alcoholism, abuse, or some similar factor, may develop rigid rules in order to create a sense of security amid the chaos or may need them simply to survive.

❑ Rigid Belief System

It is very common for the parents of a person with severe anxiety to have a fairly rigid set of values and beliefs. Often, these values and beliefs are based on the cultural background or religious affiliations of the parents and are expressed in a black-and-white fashion. A rigid belief system can produce the rigid rules discussed above and can also become a major model for rigid thinking which is passed on to the child.

❑ Emphasis on Appearances or "Proper" Behavior

A rigid belief system can create a perfectionistic model of a "proper" person and demand for the child to always act properly. A rigid belief system can also generate a feeling that either the family is or should be better than others. Failure to live up to this ideal image of a perfect person or meet the family's rigid standards can cause the child to feel inadequate and worthless.

❑ Overprotective Parent

An overprotective parent usually attempts to shield the child from life's adversities in the mistaken belief that the child is fragile. Sometimes overprotection is the result of the parent's need to have someone who is dependent. Unfortunately, even when given with the best of intentions, overprotection tends to encourage the belief that taking risks is dangerous and should be avoided. It also keeps the child from learning how to handle adversity and learning that taking risks is a natural part of life.

❑ Suppression or Denial of Feelings

A child can be taught to suppress feelings directly by being told things such as, "Don't cry," "You shouldn't feel that way," or "Don't be angry with me." A child can also be taught indirectly by watching parents who suppress and deny feelings. Another way to learn that feelings are not important is to have them discounted. This can be done by ignoring a child when feelings are expressed, telling the child the feelings being expressed are not important, or denying the feelings by saying something like, "You're not really angry." When the expression of feelings triggers violence or abuse in others, a child may need to suppress feelings in order to survive.

❑ Lack of Information about Bodies and Emotions

Many children grow up in families where there is little information about how bodies, emotions, and thoughts are interconnected. This often plays a major role in developing unrealistic expectations about what one should be able to do.

❏ Performance-Related Approval

Sometimes a child only receives approval when something is accomplished such as household chores, high grades at school, or the development of a talent. This type of strict performance-related approval occurs when a parent fails to distinguish between the child's actions and the child's value as a person. Pleasing behaviors are labeled "good." Displeasing behaviors are labeled "bad."

This is a common experience for people both with and without anxiety-related problems. Strict performance related approval encourages the mistaken belief that a person has value only when doing something valuable. The negative impact of this experience is increased when there is a perfectionistic parent who not only requires the child to perform in order to be loved, but who also demands a level of competence beyond the child's ability.

❏ Anxiety about Separation or Loss

A child can experience much anxiety when separated from a parent for a prolonged time. This is especially true when the child doesn't understand the reason for the separation. Common situations where this can occur are when a parent works out of town, a prolonged hospitalization, divorce, or death. A parent who is physically present but ignores a child can also cause separation anxiety and a feeling of abandonment.

❏ A Reversal of Parent/Child Roles

When a parent is sick, busy, or absent, a child sometimes assumes the role of a parent in some way. This can range from managing the house to just trying to keep things calm so the parent won't become angry, abusive, or distressed. A child who is required to assume adult responsibilities for which he or she is not ready often needs to develop a rigid set of rules in order to survive. This rigid approach to life is usually carried into adulthood, contributing to black-and-white thinking, the suppression of feelings, the need to be in control, and high expectations of self.

❏ A Family Secret

Sometimes a lot of a family's energy is used to keep a family secret hidden. This secret can be something simple or involved such as a premarital pregnancy, alcoholism, legal wrongdoing by a family member, or a family member in a mental institution. This type of family behavior generates the mistaken belief that certain types of feelings are wrong and must be suppressed or hidden from others. Family secrets can also contribute to the creation of an excessive need for approval.

Before going on, take a moment to look at the personality traits you checked in the previous section, and the childhood experiences you checked in this one. You will find that the development of the traits you checked was essential for your survival during childhood. Unfortunately, some of the traits which helped you function during childhood are no longer helpful to you as an adult.

Fortunately, people have a tremendous capacity to learn and adapt to new situations. You can learn to modify those traits causing your anxiety-related problems. In fact, you have already taken the first step by gaining some insight into what these traits are and how they developed.

☐ *The "Fight or Flight Response"*

Your nervous system is divided into two parts: the voluntary nervous system and the autonomic nervous system. The *voluntary nervous system* controls actions which require thought, such as raising your arm. The *autonomic nervous system* controls all activities that do not require thought, such as breathing. The autonomic nervous system is itself divided into the *sympathetic* and *parasympathetic* divisions as diagrammed below:

Autonomic Nervous System ↗ Sympathetic division—regulates your "fight or flight" response
↘ Parasympathetic division—regulates the "resting" functions in your body such as growth, digestion, relaxed breathing, etc.

When triggered, the sympathetic division of the autonomic nervous system suspends all nonessential activity in the body and increases activity in any system necessary to either fight or flee from an external *physical* threat. This response involves many complex reactions in the body. Some of the most noticeable changes that take place include the following:

Accelerated heartbeat: This pumps more blood to the muscles for the impending struggle.

Deeper and more rapid breathing: This insures a large supply of oxygen and is the basis of the "pant" of strong excitement.

Increased muscle tension: This prepares the muscles for the upcoming action they will be taking.

"Cold sweat": This is in preparation for the warm sweat of actual muscular activity.

Constriction of peripheral blood vessels near the surface of the body: This raises blood pressure and is the basis of "blanching with fear."

Shivering and raising of hairs: This conserves heat and protects the body from the increased threat of cold caused by the constriction of the peripheral blood vessels.

Dilation of the pupils: This permits a better view of threatening dangers and is the basis of having "eyes wide with fear."

Suspension of digestive activity: This provides additional blood for the motor muscles.

Dry mouth due to decreased flow of saliva: This accompanies the decreased flow of gastric juices in the stomach as digestive activity is suspended.

Tendency toward voiding bladder and bowels: This frees the body for strenuous activity.

When the fight or flight response is triggered, it releases increased amounts of adrenalin (epinephrine) and related chemicals into the bloodstream. This response provides the added strength, stamina, and ability to respond quickly that help soldiers survive in battle, athletes perform better, and people facing dangerous situations respond more effectively. Fortunately, in our modern technological world, we face fewer physical dangers requiring strenuous action than did our ancestors.

The most common threats we face today are *psychological* threats such as the loss of love, status, prestige, or one's sense of belonging and significance. Usually, these losses do not require an immediate physical response. Unfortunately, our bodies respond to any threat as if the threat requires an immediate physical response. So, when a person is embarrassed and feels threatened by what others think, the person's body triggers the fight or flight response and begins gearing up to physically run away or to fight. A person experiencing a panic attack in this situation is actually experiencing an overreaction of the fight or flight response. If you compare the above responses to the list of symptoms of a panic attack given earlier, you will see that each of the symptoms characteristic of a panic attack is simply an exaggeration of one or more of the normal body responses triggered by the fight or flight response. The reasons for this excessive reaction are discussed in the next section.

□ *How Panic Disorder Develops*

There are several theories that explain how and why people develop panic disorder with or without agoraphobia. Detailed discussions of the theories can be found in the books listed in the Recommended Reading at the end of the book. The model that offers the best explanation of the currently known facts sees panic disorder developing as the result of a series of steps. Let's follow Brian as he goes through this process.

The first step is an episode of unpleasant physical sensations that are frightening and for which the cause is not understood. These sensations can be any combination of the ones listed in the description of a panic attack at the beginning of the lesson. For Brian this occurred while he was at work. Suddenly, he experienced his heart pounding and found it difficult to breath. The sensations only lasted for ten minutes but left him shaky and frightened for the rest of the day. Like most people, Brian attributed the physical symptoms to some physical illness and left work to seek a diagnosis from a physician.

The next step in the process is the lack of an acceptable explanation for the mysterious symptoms. At the doctor's, Brian was told that he was fine and that the symptoms were just "nerves." Many people at this stage would be reassured by the doctor and quit thinking about what had happened. However, Brian had most of the high anxiety personality traits listed earlier in the lesson (These traits will be referred to as *HAP traits* for the rest of the lesson.). Like most people with the HAP traits, Brian had a high need to be in control of himself, to appear normal, and to avoid anything that might cause the disapproval of others. He began to worry that the mysterious and frightening symptoms would recur and again produce that terrible sense of being out of control.

This fear caused Brian to become very aware of internal sensations such as his heartbeat and rate of breathing. This increased awareness of the body is called *internalization* or *body scanning*. Brian also began to worry about what might happen if the frightening sensations were to occur in various situations. This worry is called *negative anticipation.* The combination of not understanding what had happened, internalization, and negative anticipation caused the development of an *anxiety/panic cycle*, which can be diagrammed as follows:

A normal reaction in the body	→	The reaction is noticed causing fear	→	The fear triggers the fight or flight response
		The increased fear produces a stronger fight or flight response	→ ←	↓ The increased reaction in the body produces more fear

The above anxiety/panic cycle is the next step and key component of panic disorder. An example of how this cycle works occurred when Brian walked up a flight of stairs shortly after the initial episode of frightening symptoms. Brian's increased internalization caused him to notice his increased heart beat and increased rate of breathing. Instead of recognizing these as normal reactions to walking up stairs, his first thought was, "Oh my gosh, here they (the frightening symptoms) come again!" This triggered the fight or flight response and increased the physical reactions he was noticing. This in turn increased his fear, producing an even stronger triggering of the fight or flight response. Within seconds Brian had talked himself into a *self-generated panic attack.*

Brian began experiencing these self-generated panic attacks regularly and was now suffering from panic disorder. As Brian began to associate more situations with the panic attacks, he developed agoraphobia and often avoided situations where he feared a panic attack might occur. As Brian's world grew smaller, his tendency to use rigid thinking, need for control, and need for approval became more exaggerated. He was caught in a series of vicious cycles.

This entire process can be diagrammed as follows:

High anxiety → Frightening physical ← The frightening physical
personality traits symptoms symptoms can be caused by any
↑ ↓ one or combination of the
Childhood Misinterpretation of the following:
background symptoms
↓ 1. Genetic factors that result in
Fear of any similar symptoms, a highly reactive body
negative anticipation, & 2. Physical exhaustion due to
internalization (body scanning) highly stressful life event(s)
↓ 3. The tendency to
Anxiety/Panic Cycle hyperventilate (this may or
↓ may not be due to a genetic
Panic Disorder with or without factor or medical condition)
Agoraphobia 4. Medical condition
↓ 5. Drug reaction
Development and/or
exaggeration of high anxiety
traits

The Inherited Biological Factor

For people with panic disorder, like Brian, the first part of the road back to a normal life begins with an understanding of what caused the initial symptoms and what maintains them. For many people, the initial symptoms were the result of an interaction between the HAP traits and an inborn biological factor. This biological factor is not well understood at present. However, a person with this factor seems to have a more reactive body than the average person. As a result, a person like this responds more intensely to environmental stimuli such as noise, odors, medications, and temperature variations.

A simple way to understand the biological factor is to imagine a house where the electrical wiring is not adequate. The electrical system works fine as long as it is not overburdened. However, when too many electrical appliances operate at the same time, the electrical system is overloaded and circuit breakers begin to trip. In a similar manner, the biological factor produces an exaggerated fight or flight response when a person who has it is overburdened with mental, physical, or emotional stress.

When a person with both the biological factor and many of the HAP traits encounters a stressful event (such as a death in the family, the birth of a child, illness, marital problems, a new job, or moving to a new home), the HAP traits cause this person to exaggerate the stress that normally accompanies these types of events. The HAP traits also tend to cause the physical needs of the body to be ignored. The combination of the weakened body and excessive mental stress now interacts with the inherited biological factor and produces an exaggerated stress reaction. In Brian's case, he had recently received a promotion that placed him in a high stress position and his wife had recently given birth to their first child. Once Brian's panic disorder developed, the prolonged anxiety further weakened his body exaggerating the impact of the biological factor.

Hyperventilation

Hyperventilation (breathing more rapidly or deeply than is necessary), can produce many of the symptoms characteristic of anxiety and offers a second possible explanation for the initial symptoms that trigger panic disorder. The first major panic attack for many people was actually a hyperventilation episode. For others, like Brian, hyperventilation accompanies most panic attacks and accounts for many of the distressing symptoms experienced. It is quite probable that many people have both the biological factor and the tendency to hyperventilate. In some people the tendency to hyperventilate may itself have a genetic component. A more detailed description of the actual mechanics of hyperventilation is given in Lesson 2.

Medical Conditions and Adverse Drug Reactions

A third possible cause of the initial symptoms that triggers panic disorder is a misunderstood or unknown medical condition or adverse drug reaction. As was mentioned earlier in the lesson, there are numerous medical conditions and drugs that can produce one or more of the symptoms commonly associated with anxiety. Andrea is a good example of this. She had a condition called mitral valve prolapse or MVP. This is a minor defect in heart valve, that has been associated with panic disorder and agoraphobia. MVP is found in 5-15% of the population. Normally, no medical treatment is required and 50% of the people with this condition experience no symptoms. Of the 50% who do notice symptoms, the main one is palpitations either in the form of premature contractions of the heart or rapid heartbeat. Other symptoms are breathlessness and vague chest pains. Andrea would experience occasional rapid heartbeat and discomfort in her chest. She had all of the HAP traits and soon found herself constantly aware of her heart and breathing and becoming alarmed whenever her heart "did something funny." Fear of the symptoms, which were harmless but misunderstood, soon led to the development of the anxiety/panic cycle and panic disorder.

Illnesses that are life threatening or that produce unpleasant symptoms can also cause the development of the anxiety/panic cycle. For example, one source reports that about 14% of cardiac patients suffer from panic disorder. A cardiac patient who has most or all of the HAP traits can, like the person with MVP, develop the internalization and negative anticipation which lead to the development of the anxiety/panic cycle.

In a similar manner to the above, medications can also cause symptoms characteristic of a panic attack. Kumar illustrates this. He had hypothyroidism, a condition where the thyroid does not produce sufficient thyroid hormones. During Kumar's initial treatment his prescription of replacement synthetic thyroxin was higher than needed causing many anxiety symptoms. Being an extreme perfectionist with very black and white thinking, Kumar found this very disturbing. These drug induced symptoms soon triggered internalizing and negative anticipation which led to the development of the anxiety/panic cycle.

From the above you can see that any medical condition, illness, or drug reaction that produces symptoms similar to those experienced in a panic attack can interact with the HAP traits to produce the anxiety/panic cycle. The likelihood of this occurring increases if the tendency to hyperventilate and/or the biological factor are present. The rate at which the anxiety/panic cycle develops seems to depend upon what is causing the initial unpleasant symptoms, the intensity of the symptoms, how many of the high anxiety personality traits a person has, and how exaggerated the traits are. Like many others, Brian, Andrea, and Kumar, can remember vividly their first major panic attack and developed panic disorder shortly after it occurred. For others, the anxiety/panic cycle develops over months or years. Sometimes it seems to come and go.

Gradual development of the anxiety/panic cycle usually occurs in the following manner. Mavis was a successful business woman with a very reactive body. She had many anxiety symptoms during a period of high stress at work. The symptoms worried her and she restricted her activities for a while. While Mavis didn't realize it, restricting her activities gave her body a rest. As a result, her body ceased to overreact to normal stimuli. Since the disturbing symptoms were no longer present, she gradually resumed normal activities. Eventually, she again encountered a period of high stress at work. The biological factor then triggered anxiety symptoms that were more severe than the first time. This lead to the development of the anxiety/panic cycle and panic disorder.

The True Cause of Panic Disorder

Many people experience the triggering events described above. While some develop panic disorder and agoraphobia, others do not. What separates those who do develop the anxiety/panic cycle from those who do not seems to be the HAP traits. People with most or all of these traits are more likely to exaggerate the meaning of the initial symptoms, begin to watch their body carefully, and worry about what the symptoms mean and what might happen if they cannot be controlled. In essence, anxiety becomes a sort of "boogie man" that follows them around. They flee from any indication that this boogie man is coming. Unfortunately, most of the symptoms they flee from are normal. They just don't understand this important point.

It is not so much that a person has a very reactive body, a tendency to hyperventilate, a medical condition, or adverse drug reaction that produces symptoms of anxiety or panic. Instead, it is what a person thinks and believes about what has happened that is the key to the development of the anxiety/panic cycle.

[1]   Estimates prepared by the Office of Scientific Information, National Institute of Mental Health and released in March 1990 NIMH. Data comes from the Epidemiologic Catchment Area (ECA) Program. Rates are based on estimates of the U.S. 1987 population—for adults, 180 million persons ages 18 and over; for children, 63 million persons aged 17 and under.

[2]   Studies by G. R. Norton and associates as reported in *Behavior Therapy*, 17, 239-252 and *Journal of Abnormal Psychology*, 94, 216-221.

[3]   Since 1980 the main classification system of mental health-related problems used by psychotherapists in the United States has been the third edition of the Diagnostic and Statistical Manual of Mental Disorders (DSM-III). In 1987 the producers of this manual, the American Psychiatric Association, released a revised version of this manual, the DSM-III-R. The revised edition saw a change in the following categories:

300.01 Panic Disorder (DSM-III) became Panic Disorder without Agoraphobia (DSM-III-R).

300.21 Agoraphobia with Panic Attacks (DSM-III) became Panic Disorder with Agoraphobia (DSM-III-R).

300.22 Agoraphobia without Panic Attacks (DSM-III) became Agoraphobia (DSM-III-R). These changes reflect an increased understanding of the fact that most agoraphobia is simply a result of a person's reaction to panic disorder. In fact, agoraphobia without a history of panic disorder (DSM-III-R: 300.22) seems to be fairly rare. Many professionals and lay people working with anxiety disorders still use the older and simpler DSM-III terminology. This book will use the current terms.

Recommended Activities for Lesson 1

How to Get the Most Out of This Section

Each lesson is accompanied by a set of recommended activities. Each activity is something many people found valuable in overcoming anxiety-related problems. You may find that some of the activities are already a part of your normal behavior and feel very natural to you. Others may seem awkward, uncomfortable, or difficult. This is to be expected since this program is designed to meet the needs of many people and you are unique with your own personal needs and abilities. Spend less time with activities you find easy and more time with those that seem difficult.

The easy activities probably involve skills you have already practiced. The difficult activities probably involve skills you have never practiced and are more important for you. If a particular activity causes undue stress or anxiety, it means you are not ready for it. Skip it and work on it again after a few weeks.

You do not have to apply every idea in this book nor do every activity immediately. The point of this program is to learn how to live a comfortable and enjoyable life and do things in a manner that is right for you. People who are successful with this program frequently do not do everything suggested. However, they usually find they have done most of the recommended activities, even though many are not done until long after the last lesson has been read. That is fine. Do things at your own rate.

People who are working through this program will often stop doing the exercises as soon as they start to feel better. This is a mistake. Continue working through the program until you feel that you have mastered all of the areas it covers. This will insure that you will have mastered all of the skills needed to prevent the redevelopment of the anxiety/panic cycle.

No one can say exactly how long it will take for you to overcome your anxiety-related problems. It depends on how severe your problems are, how long you have experienced them, and how hard you work on the program. If you have a strong commitment to use the program as it is designed, do the reading, and apply as many of the suggestions to your life as is possible (even though you may think they are "silly" or may not understand why they are suggested), it is very likely you will succeed.

Rule Out Possible Medical Problems

The first step in overcoming anxiety-related problems is to rule out all possible organic causes. If you have not had a complete physical examination and discussed your symptoms with a physician recently, make an appointment this week to do so. Be sure to provide your physician with a complete medical history and discuss your diet as well as any medications you are taking. If you find it difficult to talk to a physician, write down the information you believe is important along with the questions you want to have answered. Then either mail the note before your appointment or hand it to the physician in person.

Complete the Pre-Evaluation

The pre-evaluation provides you with a permanent record of where you are as you begin these lessons. Complete it as soon as possible. When you reach Lesson 15, you will use the pre-evaluation to measure your progress.

Create A Simple Explanation

After you have read the chapter two or three times, create a two to four sentence summary of what caused your anxiety-related problem. Write this simplified explanation on a card and read it once a day until you have it memorized. Here is the card Brian made, along with a card made by Norma, a person with Obsessive-Compulsive Disorder:

Brian's Card

A Simple Explanation of Panic Disorder

I experienced unpleasant body sensations due to my sensitive body and all of the stress that I was experiencing. Because I didn't understand what happened, I created a "boogie man." I began watching my body and whenever I noticed any sensation that resembled the frightening ones I told myself lies and ran from the boogie man.

Norma's Card

A Simple Explanation of OCD

My obsessions and compulsions are due to a genetic problem that I was born with. My brain simply gets stuck sometimes. Because I did not understand this in the past, I developed beliefs about myself and thinking patterns that cause me to exaggerate the anxiety that is caused by my neurological quirk.

If you have a Simple Phobia, Post-Traumatic Stress Disorder, or Social Phobia, read Lesson 2 before you make your summary card. A more detailed explanation of these anxiety-related problems is given there. Here are three samples of cards made by the people described in Lesson 2.

Gordon's Card

A Simple Explanation of Simple Phobias

I had fearful experiences with dogs when I was young. I developed a simple conditioned response that triggered anxiety whenever I was near or thought of dogs. I maintained this reaction by repeating statements that exaggerated the danger.

Juliene's Card

> **A Simple Explanation of PTSD Due to an Accident**
>
> I had a terrifying accident. My mind could not handle the entire picture all at once. So, it took little "snapshots" of it in order to deal with it. I also developed a simple conditioned response that triggered anxiety whenever I approached an intersection or saw a car coming in my direction. I maintained this reaction by repeating statements that exaggerated the danger, telling myself I'm crazy and beating myself up whenever I notice some anxiety symptoms. These symptoms are NORMAL and will become less as time goes by.

Martin's Card

> **A Simple Explanation of Social Phobia**
>
> Because I was very shy as a child, I never learned the social skills that most people learn while growing up. I also have had a poor self image and often put myself and my abilities down. This combination of a poor self-image, negative self-talk, conditioned response anxiety, and lack of social skills cause me to become anxious when I'm around people.

Consider Using Supplemental Materials

These lessons can be used by themselves. However, you may find supplemental materials helpful. This is especially true if you find it difficult to understand the material or stick with written lessons. Helpful materials are described in detail at the end of the book.

Developing a Relaxation Response

The triggering of deep muscle relaxation through a set method is called a relaxation response. This week practice developing a relaxation response at least once a day. If you already know how to use meditation, self-hypnosis, biofeedback, or some other method of developing a state of deep relaxation, use it. If not, use one of the methods described in Appendix 1. It usually takes several weeks of daily practice to become skilled at producing a relaxation response; so be patient. It is well worth your time and effort. Many people find that professionally produced audiocassette tapes such as those described at the back of the book very useful when learning how to develop a relaxation response.

Consider Psychotherapy

While many people have used the program in this book to overcome anxiety-related problems without the help of a psychotherapist, others have found it best to use it in conjunction with professional psychotherapy. If you are experiencing extreme difficulty coping with life, find a therapist experienced in working with anxiety-related problems. Guidelines on how to select a therapist are given in Appendix 2.

Be Good to Yourself and Reduce Unnecessary Stress

In the coming weeks you will learn how to relax and calm yourself when you start to become anxious. You will also learn more effective ways to deal with people and situations you encounter. Until you have learned these skills, avoid unnecessary stress. Continue to work and to do what is necessary in your daily routine, but eliminate as many unnecessary activities that produce excessive stress as is possible.

Experiencing severe anxiety over a prolonged period of time is as debilitating as experiencing a severe case of the flu. That is why you are being asked to take a few weeks to allow your body to rebuild its strength and repair itself. Later you will work on problem behaviors, such as avoidance patterns or rituals, you developed as a result of your anxiety. But first things first. Give your body time to heal while you work on mastering the skills in the early lessons.

Find a Study Partner

If possible, find a friend or relative who will be a study partner and read and work through this book with you. This does not need to be a person with anxiety-related problems, but it does need to be someone you are comfortable with and trust. Discussing the lessons with a partner deepens your understanding. This partner will also be able to remind you when you forget to use the skills you are learning.

Consider Joining a Self-Help Group

Many people find that a self-help group is tremendously helpful in overcoming anxiety-related problems. This is true for many people working with a therapist as well as those working on their own. Appendix 3 describes how to find a local self-help group.

> The recommended activities in this lesson
> prepare you for the work in the lessons
> that follow. It is important
> to do them before continuing
> on to the next lesson.

Pre-Evaluation

List any medications you are taking and the usual dosage per day.

Medication: Dosage:

Use the following scale to indicate how much control of your life you feel now (circle one):

(no control) 1 2 3 4 5 6 7 8 9 10 (complete control)

Read the following items. Then choose a number from each of the three scales to indicate how frequently you experienced this problem during the past month, how much discomfort it caused, and how much it interfered with your life. Rate each item with respect to how it affected you during the past month. If you have *not* experienced a particular symptom during the past month, simply check n/a (not applicable). Use an additional sheet of paper if you need to.

Frequency of Occurrence (Freq)	Level of Discomfort (Disc)	Degree to which it interferes with your life (Inter)
1-Never occurs 2-Seldom occurs: once a month or less 3-Sometimes occurs: 2-6 times a month or once per week 4-Often occurs: 2 or more times per week but not daily 5-Always occurs: one or more times daily	1-Comfortable 2-Slightly uncomfortable 3-Uncomfortable 4-Very Uncomfortable 5-Panicky	1-No interference 2-Slight interference 3-Moderate interference 4-Considerable interference 5-Severe interference

A. Physical Symptoms

	n/a	Freq	Disc	Inter
Shortness of breath (dysnea or smothering sensations)				
Choking				
Palpitations or accelerated heart rate (tachycardia)				
Chest pain or discomfort				
Sweating				
Dizziness, unsteady feelings, or faintness				
Nausea or abdominal distress				
Feelings of unreality (depersonalization or derealization)				

	n/a	Freq	Disc	Inter
Numbness or tingling sensations (paresthesia) usually in the fingers, toes, or lips				
Flushes (hot flashes) or chills				
Others:				
Others:				
Others:				

B. Fears Associated With Anxiety

People with anxiety-related problems often think about one or more of the fears listed below. Use the preceding scales to rate each one that applies to you. If you have not thought about a particular fear during the last month, simply check n/a. Use the spaces provided to list specific examples of what you fear. For example, if you fear losing control, exactly what is it you fear you might do?

	n/a	Freq	Disc	Inter
Fear of becoming seriously ill or dying				
Fear of going crazy				
Fear of losing control and doing something that might harm or embarrass myself or others				
Others:				
Others:				
Others:				

C. Panic Attacks

Panic attacks are episodes of intense apprehension, fear, or terror characterized by four or more of the physical sensations or fears listed in items A and B (for example, shortness of breath, accelerated heart rate, dizziness, and the fear you are dying). If you have experienced panic attacks during the past month, use the preceding scales to rate their frequency, discomfort, and degree of interference. If you have not experienced panic attacks check n/a.

n/a _____   Frequency of Occurrence _____

    Level of Discomfort _____   Degree of Interference _____

D. *Episodes of Severe Anxiety*

If you have experienced episodes of high anxiety other than panic attacks during the past month (three or fewer sensations or fears listed in items A and B). Use the preceding scales to rate them. If you have not, check n/a.

n/a _____   Frequency of Occurrence _____

Level of Discomfort _____   Degree of Interference _____

E. *Triggering Events/Situations*

List any events or situations that have been associated with anxiety or which triggered recurring anxiety during the past month. Then use the preceding scales to rate each one on frequency, discomfort, and degree of interference. Since situations like these are often avoided, also rate each one on how often you avoided it during the past month using the following Avoidance Scale (Avoid).

1-Never avoid

2-Seldom avoid: 0 - 1/4 of the time

3-Sometimes avoid: 1/4 - 1/2 of the time

4-Often avoid: 1/2 - 3/4 of the time

5-Always avoid: 3/4 - all of the time

If you have always avoided a particular situation during the past month (5), rate the level of discomfort in terms of how much discomfort you think you would experience in this situation and the degree of interference in terms of how much the avoidance of this situation interferes with your life. Rate the frequency for situations you always avoid at 1 unless it is something you had to face in spite of your best efforts to avoid it.

Situation	Avoid	Freq	Disc	Inter

F. *Compulsions*

People with anxiety-related problems sometimes develop compulsions. These are actions which are ritualistically repeated in order to neutralize or prevent some dreaded event or situation. However, the compulsive behavior is either unconnected in a realistic way with what it is designed to neutralize or prevent, or it is clearly excessive. Repeated hand-washing in response to a fear of contaminating oneself or others is an example of a common compulsion. Other common compulsions include counting, checking, and repeated touching. List below any compulsions you have along with the average number of times you performed the compulsive act EACH DAY during the past WEEK. Then rate it with respect to the degree of interference it has on your life using the same scale you used in the previous sections. If you do not have compulsions, skip this section.

Compulsion	Average No of times/day	Interference

Reducing the Symptoms of Anxiety

Lesson 2

The four skills for reducing the symptoms of anxiety described in this lesson take time to develop. Plan for only modest results at first. However, once these skills are mastered and you combine them with the ideas and skills presented in the following lessons, they become a mighty force for managing stress and anxiety.

☐ *Four Common Roadblocks*

You probably already use some, if not all of the skills described in this lesson. However, it is likely that you have also found they do not always work well. The four main roadblocks that prevent people from using these skills effectively are described below along with suggestions for overcoming them.

Inappropriate use

Skills for reducing anxiety often fail because they are used inappropriately. This roadblock can be overcome by studying the explanations provided in this lesson for how and why each skill works and following the suggestions which are made.

Over-reliance on one or two skills

If you only have one or two methods for reducing the symptoms of stress and of anxiety, inevitably there comes a time when these methods do not work very well.

Overcoming this roadblock requires the use of several different skills to cope with stress and anxiety. Each skill reinforces the others and becomes more effective.

Failure to use at the first signs of distress

If you treat a wound as soon as it occurs, it usually heals without any problems. If you do not attend to it and allow it to become infected, it causes much discomfort and requires more extensive treatment to heal. The same principle applies to the skills described in this lesson. They work best when used at the first signs of stress and anxiety. When you ignore your body, behavior, and thoughts until you are experiencing severe stress or anxiety, the approaches work poorly. The key to overcoming this roadblock is to use these skills as soon as you notice yourself becoming anxious.

Over-reliance on just reducing the symptoms of anxiety

It is not enough to work only at relieving the symptoms of anxiety. You also need to learn how to eliminate the mistaken beliefs and habitual thinking patterns that cause them. The skills presented in this part of the program are, in a sense, a kind of Band-Aid designed to help you feel more comfortable and regain some control over your body. They are much like medications to relieve the pain of a broken leg. While this is important, it is also essential to repair the damage and learn how to avoid injury in the future. This is not meant to minimize the importance of the skills you are developing this week. They are an essential part of overcoming severe anxiety. In fact, as you progress through the program and become better able to minimize the sources of stress and anxiety you have control over, the skills described in this lesson become even more powerful.

☐ *Four Basic Skills for Reducing the Symptoms of Anxiety*

Take your time as you develop the four skills presented in this section. Plan to return to this lesson and work with these skills many times before they are mastered.

Cue-Controlled Relaxation

At the turn of the century, a Russian scientist named I. P. Pavlov conducted a classic experiment. He presented a neutral stimulus to hungry dogs, such as ringing a bell, then followed it by giving the animal food. The food caused the dog to salivate. With repetition, the neutral stimulus (the bell) eventually would trigger salivation. When a response is triggered by a stimulus as a result of this type of conditioning, it is called a *conditioned response*.

Many human reactions and behaviors are a type of *conditioned response learning*. Consider the saying, "Mom's cooking tastes best." Mom could be a terrible cook and this would still be true because her children would have been conditioned to her cooking. This is why food in foreign countries often tastes "funny." The same is true with clothing fashions. Pictures of clothes worn ten years ago look funny because we have been slowly reconditioning ourselves to the fashions of today.

When a person experiences high anxiety, the various sensations and events present during the time that the person is anxious tend to become a conditioned response stimuli. For example, if a person has panic attacks while driving, simply being in a car may trigger mild anxiety symptoms. Anxiety generated by this form of conditioned response learning plays a very subtle but important role in maintaining panic disorder. Even though a person may consciously understand the dynamics that caused the original symptoms and is confident that there is no danger, he or she will still continue to experience anxiety generated by conditioned response learning. This type of conditioned response learning can be reversed through a process called *desensitization* explained in detail later in the program or by using *cue-controlled relaxation.*

Cue-controlled relaxation refers to relaxation triggered by a cue in a conditioned response manner just as Pavlov's dogs were conditioned to salivate to a bell. The actual cue can be anything. Commonly used cues include a word such as "relax," an imaginary scene, or a simple physical cue such as putting your thumb and finger together.

The first step in developing cue-controlled relaxation is to learn a method that enables you to produce a relaxation response like those described in Appendix 2. The second step is to decide on a cue and begin associating it with the relaxation response you are practicing. For example, you might place your thumb and two fingers together while practicing your relaxation response exercise. With time, the act of placing your thumb and fingers together would act as a cue or trigger for the relaxation response. Sometimes this type of cue is called a *relaxation response anchor* because the response is anchored to it.

At first, the anxiety triggered by conditioned response learning will be much stronger than the relaxation generated by your relaxation response training. This is to be expected since you have been unconsciously reinforcing the conditioned response anxiety for a long time. Even with practice, your cue-controlled relaxation will, by itself, probably not eliminate anxiety but only reduce it. However, when used in combination with the other skills in this lesson, cue-controlled relaxation becomes a powerful tool for reducing anxiety. With time and practice, you can desensitize yourself and eliminate the conditioned response anxiety.

Diaphragmatic Breathing

Hyper (too much) *ventilation* (air movement) is simply overbreathing. It occurs when a person breathes more rapidly, more deeply, or a combination of both than is needed to meet the body's demands for oxygen and removal of carbon dioxide. Breathing in this fashion causes the level of carbon dioxide to drop in the bloodstream. Forceful hyperventilation can reduce the carbon dioxide level in the blood by 50% in as little as 30 seconds. Most people would think this is good since they were taught in school that carbon dioxide is a "waste" product. However, carbon dioxide is very important in maintaining a proper acid-base or pH level in the blood and is the chemical used by the body to regulate breathing.

Hyperventilation raises the pH level in the nerve cells making them more excitable, and it also tends to activate the fight or flight response. This sets off a chain reaction of activity in the body that can produce any of the following symptoms:

- Heart palpitations, tachycardia (racing heart), heartburn or chest pain.
- Numbness or tingling of the mouth, hands, or feet.
- Dizziness, faintness, lightheadedness, poor concentration, blurred vision, or a sense of separateness from the body (depersonalization).
- Shortness of breath, "asthma," or choking sensation.
- Difficulty swallowing, lump in the throat, stomach pain, or nausea.
- Tension, muscle pains, shaking, or muscle spasms.
- Sweating, anxiety, fatigue, weakness, poor sleep, or nightmares.

Most of the above symptoms will develop in under a minute. While they can be uncomfortable, none of the symptoms causes lasting harm. Most people who hyperventilate do not realize they are hyperventilating. Instead of reporting a problem with hyperventilation, they complain of various specific or vague symptoms from the above list. Hyperventilation can occur with any of the following:

- When at rest, you breathe with your upper chest instead of with your diaphragm.
- When you breathe through your mouth because of either habit or because of physical or medical problems.
- When you sigh or yawn because you have been holding your breath.

Let's look at each of the above individually.

Humans have two basic breathing patterns. In thoracic or *upper-chest breathing* the chest lifts upward and outward and breathing tends to be shallow and rapid. In *diaphragmatic breathing* the inhalation tends to be deeper and slower. When the lower lungs fill with air, they push down on the diaphragm and cause the abdominal region to protrude, making the stomach appear to be expanding and contracting with each breath.

Upper-chest and diaphragmatic breathing have their own purposes and functions in everyday life. During strenuous exercise, your body uses upper-chest breathing to provide the large amounts of oxygen needed. In contrast, relaxed diaphragmatic breathing is your body's normal breathing pattern when physical activity and the corresponding need for oxygen is low. A healthy breathing pattern during moderate, everyday activities usually involves movement in both the upper chest and diaphragm.

Many people with anxiety-related problems use upper-chest breathing as their primary breathing pattern. Many others find they quickly convert to upper-chest breathing whenever they become anxious. The reason for this is unknown. However, it is known that upper-chest breathing is a normal but usually brief response to any threatening or anxiety-provoking situation. It is triggered by the fight or flight response and is your body's way of preparing for the strenuous activity of fighting or running away from danger. One possible explanation for habitual upper-chest breathing is that a person who continually feels threatened by normal, everyday situations is simply triggering this breathing pattern via the activation of the fight or flight response.

Another explanation involves our culture's obsession with thin bodies and flat stomachs. During adolescence, when there is much concern about one's appearance, many people develop an unconscious habit of constantly tensing their abdominal muscles in order to meet this ideal image. Since it is impossible to use diaphragmatic breathing when the abdominal muscles are tensed, the body begins to use upper-chest breathing as its primary breathing pattern. Wearing tight-fitting clothes which restricts the movement of the diaphragm can also contribute to upper-chest breathing.

Another common form of hyperventilation is due to mouth breathing. People with allergies, asthma, or obstructions are often forced to breathe in this manner because it is difficult to breathe through their nose. When excited, stressed, or doing mild exercise, these people will sometimes experience mild hyperventilation symptoms.

Hyperventilation associated with *breath-holding* is yet another common form of hyperventilation. People who tend to hold their breath when anxious often find themselves yawning or sighing. Any deep yawn or sigh will cause the carbon dioxide level to drop markedly. This in itself can produce subtle symptoms of hyperventilation. If this habit is present along with a tendency to use upper-chest breathing as a primary breathing pattern, it can trigger more severe hyperventilation. This is especially true if the initial vague symptoms are noticed and cause alarm. That is why the tendency to constantly internalize (described in the first lesson) plays such an important role in many forms of severe anxiety.

The three forms of hyperventilation described above offers a simple explanation for how a panic or anxiety attack can seem to strike "out of the blue" with no apparent reason. It only takes minor degrees of hyperventilation to trigger the effects of increased heart rate, constriction of blood vessels, and a rise in the blood's pH level. The symptoms these reactions produce are noticed and trigger the anxiety/panic cycle, which then results in the "mysterious" panic or anxiety attack.

It may seem that all of the unpleasant symptoms associated with severe anxiety are due to hyperventilation. For many people this is true. However, for many others (for example, people with a definite physical condition such as mitral valve prolapse), it is the unpleasant "skipped" beat of the heart or some other non-hyperventilation symptom that is noticed and triggers a panic attack. The type of internalization associated with the anxiety/panic cycle makes a person very sensitive to any internal sensation considered unusual or a sign that the dreaded anxiety or panic attack is about to occur. The following three tests can provide a good indication of whether or not hyperventilation is a problem for you.

First, become aware of your normal breathing pattern. Place one hand on your chest and one hand on your stomach. Take a slightly deeper breath than you normally do and see which hand moves the most. If most of the motion is in the hand on your chest, you are an upper-chest breather and the chances are very good that hyperventilation is a major contributor to your symptoms. If most of the motion is in the hand on your stomach, you are using diaphragmatic breathing. While this is very good, it does not rule out the possibility that some form of hyperventilation plays a role in your anxiety symptoms.

Second, count your breathing rate. You can do this yourself or have someone else do it when you are unaware it is being counted. A normal breathing rate at rest is eight to sixteen breaths per minute. One study of people with panic disorder found an average resting breathing rate of twenty eight breaths per minute.

Third, deliberately hyperventilate in order to experience the effects. Breathe sixty times a minute (once every second) for three minutes. Everyone who attempts this test will notice feelings of dry mouth and throat, and many people will report some lightheadedness, slight changes in vision, numbness and tingling. If you begin to experience feelings you associate with anxiety or panic, hyperventilation probably plays a role in your anxiety symptoms. If at any point during the test the feelings you experience make you very anxious or panicky, stop the test. This test is perfectly safe for the vast majority of people reading this book; however, there are some medical conditions such as angina (heart pain) and seizures (epilepsy) that can be made worse by hyperventilation. If you are in doubt about whether this third test is safe for you, consult your doctor.

The recommended activities for this lesson include an exercise on diaphragmatic breathing. Many people find the ability to use diaphragmatic breathing is one of their most effective skills for controlling the symptoms of severe anxiety.

Coping Self-Statements

The various situations in which you find yourself usually resemble past ones in one or more important ways. The feelings and thoughts triggered by a particular situation are the result of both your conscious and unconscious interpretation of the situation. This interpretation process is usually based upon automatic, habitual thinking patterns. The key to changing this type of learned habit pattern lies in the fact that thoughts are really silent sentences you say to yourself. Since your emotions are partly controlled by your conscious interpretation of the situation, statements that calm and tranquilize you when you feel afraid or anxious also help you reinterpret the situation so it is not as frightening. These types of statements are called coping self-statements because you say them to yourself and they help you cope with a given situation effectively.

Consider the last situation you were in that produced anxiety. Recall what you said to yourself. If you think about it for a moment, you will probably find the thoughts or statements you repeated to yourself are the same ones you say to yourself in similar situations. Furthermore, they are probably statements that increase your level of anxiety. It is as if a little tape recorder automatically plays your particular set of negative statements over and over inside of your head. Common examples of this type of negative self-talk include the following:

"This is terrible."
"I can't breathe."
"I'm dying."
"I shouldn't be feeling/acting this way." (Usually a symptom associated with
      anxiety such as difficulty in breathing or a racing heart.)
"I can't handle this."

"Why is this happening?"
"This is all wrong."
"I can't stand this."
"This is so stupid. Why can't I handle even this simple thing?"
"I'm not doing this right."
"I'm never going to get better."
"I can't do this."

Each of the above statements is either false or expresses an irrational fear. Remember, your symptoms began when you experienced unpleasant symptoms and told yourself lies about what they meant. They are maintained by a combination of conditioned response anxiety, internalization (constantly watching your body for signs of the "boogie man" anxiety), negative anticipation, and the negative habit pattern of telling yourself lies about what the body sensations you notice mean.

Decreasing the amount and intensity of this type of negative self-talk is one of the keys to reducing anxiety. One way to do this is to repeat coping self-statements whenever you become tense or anxious. At first, this may have only a small effect; however, with practice, you create a set of positive messages or "tapes" that replace the old negative messages. As you repeat these messages you gain confidence that they are true. Use coping self-statements like the examples that follow to challenge fears, help you stay focused on the task at hand, remind you to use your anxiety reducing skills, and concentrate on problem-solving rather than on your symptoms or inadequacies.

"Anxiety is NOT dangerous—just uncomfortable. I've survived feelings like this and worse before."
"I can be anxious and still function effectively; stay focused on the task at hand."
"Trigger your relaxation response, take three or four *relaxed* diaphragmatic breaths then distract yourself."
"Remember that the scary things you have thought about your symptoms are lies—anxiety is just a nuisance and no more."
"Look at your list of coping skills and use them."
"There is no need to fight what I am feeling. Even though it's uncomfortable, it's just adrenaline and will pass."
"Check your breathing. Now focus on and describe what is going on around you. Externalize and distract."
"My current symptoms are just a type of conditioned response. They will become less as I desensitize myself."
"These feelings are just a reminder to use my coping skills." (a response to symptoms of anxiety)
"The symptoms are now occurring because I'm just like Pavlov's dogs—instead of salivating, I get anxious when certain "bells" ring. This conditioned response is normal and will fade with time."
"What I'm feeling is just an unpleasant body sensation. It is NOT dangerous. I don't have to let it stop me. I can continue to function even though I don't like what I'm feeling."

"These feelings of anxiety are just old habit patterns. I have practiced them for so many years there is no reason to be surprised when they occasionally recur. They will eventually disappear. Now, take a couple of relaxed, diaphragmatic breaths and focus on what you need to do here and now."

"This is not a test; it is only an opportunity to practice using my skills."

"I can do this; I am doing it now."

"I can be a little anxious and still function well."

"I don't have to do this perfectly. Ease up a little and allow yourself to be human."

"My body may be reacting strongly right now but it doesn't really matter. It's just an old habit pattern that will pass with time."

"This is not an emergency or test. Just take things one step at a time. There's no need to rush."

"This will be over soon. Keep focused on the present and externalize. Now, what is it I need to do?"

"I always have options. I'm free to come and go according to my comfort."

"No negative self-talk. Stay focused on positive, rational, and realistic thoughts. Now take a few relaxed, diaphragmatic breaths and continue."

"This will only take a short time. Soon it will be over and I will be very pleased with myself."

"It doesn't matter what others think. Just stay focused on what you have to do."

"Relax and go slowly. There is no need to push right now."

Because your thinking is so automatic when you're anxious, it is often difficult to think of effective coping self-statements. The best way to overcome this problem is to prepare several statements and write them on a card or piece of paper. If you like the examples listed above, use four or five of them exactly as written. If the examples do not fit your personality or life situation, change the wording or create new ones that do apply to you. It is important that your statements have power and meaning for you.

After you have developed your list, practice reciting it until you can recall the statements from memory without much effort. Then, when you are in one of the above situations, use a small part of your mind to repeat the coping self-statements while most of your mind stays focused on what you are doing. It helps to revise your statements periodically so they don't become stale. Eventually, you will find yourself using coping self-statements spontaneously.

Distraction (Redirection)

Distraction is the process of shifting or diverting your attention from one activity to another and is sometimes called *redirection*. Distraction uses an important principle: shifting your attention *toward* something neutral or positive is always easier than shifting it *away* from something negative. Trying to reduce anxiety by thinking or saying phrases such as, "Don't be anxious," or "I must not be anxious," rarely works. The process of telling yourself not to be anxious focuses your attention and energy on your anxiety and usually causes it to increase. The five forms of distraction described in this section provide a more effective way to reduce anxiety by redirecting your attention away from anxiety towards a neutral or positive activity.

One important feature of most forms of distraction is *externalization*. Externalization is the act of focusing your attention on sensations originating outside your body. It is the opposite of internalization, the focusing of your attention on sensations originating inside your body described in Lesson 1. Distracting your attention away from your body and focusing externally prevents the initial alarm reaction that triggers the anxiety/panic cycle. Using distraction after the cycle has been triggered helps calm you by interrupting negative self-talk and breaking the cycle of escalating fear over self-generated symptoms.

The following forms of distraction are listed from simpler to more complex forms. The simpler forms are fairly easy to learn and use but only work moderately well when anxiety is high. They also are most effective when used to cope with an anxiety-producing situation which only lasts a short time, such as crossing a bridge, waiting in line, or using an elevator. The complex forms take longer to master, but are more effective since the more interesting or demanding an activity is, the more distracting it is.

Simple externalization

Simple externalization is the use of one or more of your senses to focus on some external sensation. Five common types of simple externalization are listed below. They work best when done systematically. For example, if you are using the design on a wall to distract yourself, don't just look at it, but identify where the design repeats itself and all of the variations it contains.

Observing carefully: Read signs; examine the design of a nearby wall, clothing, or carpet; observe the intricate activities of people around you; or observe surrounding scenery.

Listening attentively: Listen to random conversation or background noises such as a ticking clock or a passing plane.

Feeling textures: Feel the texture of clothing, paper, a gum wrapper, or the steering wheel of the car you are driving.

Tasting or smelling: Taste and smell gum or candy you carry with you, note the various odors surrounding you.

Doing repetitive activities: Count floor tiles, lights, or cracks; tap a finger rhythmically; fold a piece of paper in a systematic manner.

Changing our surrounding or activities: If you're inside, go outside; if you're sitting, go for a walk; if you're in the living room, go into the kitchen.

Simple tasks that require concentration

Simple mental activities that require concentration such as recalling the words to a song, determining how much a total purchase will cost, balancing a checkbook, timing an event such as a trip to a friend's house, or recalling an event that arouses positive emotions such as happiness, satisfaction or joy. These are often difficult to do when you are very anxious. However, with practice they become effective distractors.

Conversation

Conversation is an effective form of distraction that can be used almost anywhere. Talking over the telephone can be just as effective as talking with someone in person. Even a stranger such as a person standing in line next to you can offer distraction. Conversation works best as a distractor when you are an active speaker rather than as a passive listener. It is also best if the topic of conversation is unrelated to your anxiety symptoms or to the situation generating the anxiety.

Work

Many people use work as a form of distraction without even knowing it. Work can be mental or physical and can involve household chores or work related to a job outside the home. Work is most distracting when it is interesting, pleasurable, or involves competition. Activities that have become automatic because you have done them often do not work as well as ones which demand more attention. One way to increase the distracting quality of routine work is to do it in a somewhat different manner. For example, you can change the order in which you do the various steps of a given chore.

Play

Play includes anything that is both interesting and pleasurable. Working crossword puzzles, playing video games, dancing, and working at hobbies are examples of play that can be used to distract yourself. Activities requiring physical activity are usually more distracting than games where you are passive. Also, the more pleasure you derive from an activity the more distracting it is. The key element is that the activity holds your interest.

Play can often be combined with other forms of distraction. For example, you can make a game out of simple externalization by trying to connect the dots on acoustical tile to form faces or make up stories about people around you. You can create simple games which require concentration such as guessing the number of telephone poles on a stretch of road. At first, it may be difficult to be playful and find humor in anxiety-producing situations. However, with practice it becomes easier.

Medication

Three main groups of drugs are used to treat anxiety-related problems. They include the following:

- *Tricyclic antidepressants* such as imipramine (Tofranil), desipramine (Norpramine), nortriptyline (Pamelor), and amitriptyline (Elavil).

- *Monoamine oxidase inhibitors (the MAOI's are another class of antidepressants)* such as phenelzine (Nardil), isocarboxizid (Marplan), and tranylcypromine (Parnate).
- *Benzodiazepines* such as alprazolam (Xanax), clonazepam (Klonopin), lorazepan (Ativan), and diazepam (Valium).

Other classes of drugs that are sometimes used include the beta-blockers such as propranolol (Inderal) and non-benzodiazepine tranquilizers such as Buspirone (Buspar). The Anxiety Disorders Association of America has a very good pamphlet by Dr. Dennis J. Munjack called *A Consumer's Guide to Medication for Panic Disorder* that describes the various types of medications used with anxiety-related problems along with how they are used.

While none of these medications will prevent panic attacks, they do reduce the overall level of anxiety a person is experiencing. For many, this helps to reduce the number and intensity of panic attacks. The antidepressants are also very effective in reducing depression. This can often be helpful when a person has not yet developed effective skills to deal with anxiety and is facing stressful life events. On the "negative" side, medications often require much trial and error to find the right medication and correct dosage for a particular person. There are sometimes problems with side effects and withdrawal problems. In addition, relapse rates for people who are only receiving medication are very high.

On the "positive" side, medications can be especially helpful when a person has, what is often called, endogenous depression. This is depression that is due to an as yet poorly understood metabolic mechanism. Medications such as fluoxetine (Prozac) and clorimipramine (Anafranil) that increase the level of the neurotransmitter called seritonin also seem to be very useful with obsessive-compulsive disorder.

In short, medications have a definite role in treating anxiety. However, they are not for everyone. The primary goal of this program is to present skills and methods for changing the way you think and act which will allow you to overcome anxiety-related problems and live a normal life—without the need for medication. Many people find that using medication in the early stages of a program like this is helpful. Others find it is not. If you are currently taking medication to relieve your anxiety symptoms, the chances are excellent there will come a time when you will no longer feel the need for it. Many people who relied on medication to relieve their anxiety symptoms have found the approach used in these lessons did just that.

There are some general guidelines you need to know if you are currently using medication or are considering using it:

- Make sure the medication is prescribed by a professional experienced with anxiety-related problems who has conducted a careful assessment of your individual needs.
- Some medications take time before results are seen. Discuss this with the physician prescribing the medication.
- Medications often have the potential for side effects. Talk to your physician about this so you will understand what to expect.

- Make sure the physician who prescribes the medication monitors you to ensure its safe and effective use.
- If the medication is producing side effects that are more troublesome than the anxiety symptoms it is meant to relieve, consult with your physician immediately.

One word of caution is needed concerning the discontinuation of medications. After being taken daily, many medications can produce undesirable and even dangerous results if stopped abruptly. So when you do wish to discontinue or lower the dosage, it is imperative that you discuss it with the professional who prescribed the medication and has been monitoring its use. In addition, there are some medications, depending upon the length of use and dosage, that can produce some anxiety symptoms as they are discontinued. These withdrawal symptoms can usually be avoided if the medications are discontinued gradually. However, if you do happen to experience symptoms while discontinuing a medication, use coping self-statements to remind yourself that it is just the medication.

☐ *Causes for Several Types of Anxiety Problems*

Simple phobias are often the result of conditioned response training that is maintained by negative self-talk, internalization, and negative anticipation. Gordon, who had a fear of dogs, is a good example of this. When Gordon was young, he was timid and became startled one day when a big, but friendly dog who wanted to play jumped on him. The next time Gordon saw a dog, the previous negative experience triggered anxiety. Soon, Gordon developed the belief that he could not be around dogs. Whenever he saw a dog he would tell himself, "I can't stand being around dogs. They terrify me." Whenever he was near a dog he would notice the conditioned response and repeat his negative self talk. This would escalate his anxiety as described in the description of the anxiety/panic cycle in Lesson 1. Even thinking about dogs would lead Gordon into the anxiety/panic cycle.

Conditioned response learning plays an even clearer role in Post-Traumatic Stress Disorder or PTSD. Juliene was in a severe automobile accident where she was broadsided at an intersection and suffered severe injuries. During the early part of her recovery, she experienced frequent "flashbacks" where images of the accident would suddenly intrude into her thoughts without warning. Flashbacks like these are common when a person experiences trauma. It is as if the mind is unable to absorb all of the events of the trauma at once so it takes little "snapshots" of the incident until it has been completely digested.

Shortly after her recovery, Juliene was in a car and experienced one of these flashbacks that was accompanied by simple conditioned response anxiety as she approached an intersection and saw a car waiting at the cross street. Because she did not understand that this was a normal reaction, she began telling herself that something must be wrong with her. This triggered increased anxiety. Because the symptoms were so severe, Juliene dreaded coming to the next intersection on her trip. Her worry about anxiety reinforced the conditioned response anxiety and set up an anxiety/panic cycle that was soon triggered by many different driving-related situations and thoughts.

Conditioned response learning can play a similar role in Social Phobia. Martin was very shy as a child. This trait was reinforced by his family who labeled him as "shy" and had very low expectations of him. In addition, his older brother would often tease him and make Martin the object of hurtful pranks. For example, his brother might throw water on Martin's pants and tell his friends that Martin had wet his pants. Martin's embarrassment, lack of assertiveness, and poor self image caused him to withdraw from situations like this and made him an easy target for the teasing common during childhood. Because Martin rarely engaged in the normal social activities of childhood and adolescence, he never gained the social skills acquired by most people through the normal growing up process. Martin eventually developed conditioned response anxiety that was triggered by any social situation. He reinforced this anxiety with his negative self-talk and beliefs about himself.

Each of these three people eventually overcame their anxiety-related problems. Gordon found that he mainly needed to learn how to manage his anxiety with the skills in this lesson and then go through the desensitization process as described in Lesson 9. Juliene found it necessary to go through Lessons 4, 5, and 6 before starting the desensitization process described in Lesson 9. Because Social Phobia is a more complex problem and has many different factors that maintain it, Martin found it necessary to go through the entire program in a step-by-step manner.

Recommended Activities for Lesson 2

Begin Developing Cue-Controlled Relaxation

Continue practicing a relaxation response exercise at least once a day. Have more than one practice session a day if it is practical. If you have not yet tried all of the approaches described in Appendix 1, decide now when and where you will try each one. Also, if you have not yet tried taping the scripts, select one and tape it this week. Then use it as directed.

As you practice your relaxation response, begin using a cue that will become associated with the response. Three common types of cues are listed below. Decide which type you like best and begin using it. However, be sure to use *same* cue each time you practice.

- *Word Cues:* Any word repeated over and over as you relax will work. Common word cues include "relax," "peace," "calm and controlled," and "one".
- *Imaginary Cues:* Imagine any scene or image you find relaxing such as a mountain meadow, the beach, or a forest.
- *Physical Cues:* Physical cues work best if they involve an action that is out of the ordinary. At the same time, it needs to be inconspicuous so you can use it in public. Three common physical cues include touching the thumb and first two fingers of either hand, touching an elbow, or touching the back of a wrist.

It may take several weeks for you to develop the ability to produce a state of deep relaxation through a set method. It may take a little longer for the association between your cue and the relaxation to become firmly established. However, once you are able to trigger a relaxation response, you will find it a valuable skill.

Develop Relaxed Diaphragmatic Breathing

This lesson discussed in detail the importance of learning relaxed diaphragmatic breathing for people with anxiety-related problems. Some people master this skill in one or two days. A few take several weeks. If upper-chest breathing is your normal breathing pattern, continue practicing the exercise until diaphragmatic breathing becomes your normal method of breathing. If diaphragmatic breathing is already your normal method of breathing, practice this exercise for at least one week.

Exercise

Do this exercise twice a day, once at night before you go to bed and once in the morning right after you awaken. At these times you are wearing loose fitting clothes and can easily lie down. This is especially important if diaphragmatic breathing is difficult for you.

Lie down and place one hand on your abdomen over your navel and breathe in such a way that it moves up and down in a relaxed manner. Your chest may move a little while you do this; however, most of the movement needs to be in the abdominal region. If you are unable to tell what your chest is doing, place your other hand on it so you can feel how much it is moving in relation to your abdomen.

Most people are able to breathe in this manner fairly easily. If you have difficulty, try sucking in the abdominal region as you exhale (breathe out). Then simply relax and do nothing as you inhale (breathe in). Your abdominal region will naturally expand outward on its own.

Each practice session only needs to last about a minute, just long enough to take four or five relaxed and comfortable diaphragmatic breaths. DO NOT make this hard work. It is also important to avoid over-breathing. If you breathe too deeply or too rapidly instead of taking slow, gentle breaths, you might produce a sense of lightheadedness or one of the other symptoms characteristic of hyperventilation. If this occurs, it means you are working too hard at the exercise. Take smaller and more relaxed breaths.

Your goals are 1) to be able to tell when you are breathing with your diaphragm without the need to place a hand on your abdomen, 2) know what a comfortable, *relaxed* diaphragmatic breath feels like, and 3) breathe in a gentle, relaxed manner with your diaphragm whenever you want to without effort.

After you can breathe with your diaphragm while lying down, practice two or three times a day while standing. An easy way to remember to practice is to take three or four relaxed diaphragmatic breaths just before you sit down for your regular meals. After you have practiced diaphragmatic breathing while standing and are able to breathe in this manner without effort, begin practicing while sitting. People who are upper-chest breathers usually find sitting is the most difficult position in which to breathe with the diaphragm. This is especially true for very heavy people. However, with practice, most people find diaphragmatic breathing eventually becomes easy even while sitting. If you have difficulty, wear loose-fitting clothing.

From now on, whenever you begin to feel anxious or panicky, check your breathing. Taking three or four slow, relaxed diaphragmatic breaths helps quiet the fight or flight response.

Severe hyperventilators are frequently told to carry a paper bag and breathe into it whenever they experience the symptoms of severe hyperventilation. This technique is based upon the fact that the level of carbon dioxide in the blood is the means by which your body regulates its breathing. As the oxygen in the bag is used up and replaced with carbon dioxide, you breathe in more carbon dioxide and this slows your breathing.

The paper bag technique works. However, many people find it embarrassing to use it in public. Others find that by the time they use the paper bag, they are already experiencing severe symptoms. Furthermore, this technique only removes the symptoms, it does not deal directly with the cause of the symptoms, the tendency to hyperventilate.

Becoming skilled at relaxed diaphragmatic breathing enables a person to stop hyperventilation symptoms before they become serious. Taking several relaxed diaphragmatic breaths whenever you are in an anxiety-producing situation is also a good way to prevent hyperventilation symptoms from the beginning. This is especially true for people who are upper-chest breathers or breath holders.

List Coping Self-Statements on a Card and Memorize Them

Review the examples of coping self-statements in the lesson and list the ones you have created on a card. Cards created by Brian, Andrea, Mavis, and Gordon who were mentioned in Lesson 1 are shown below to provide you with further samples. These were the statements they used when first learning these skills.

BRIAN'S CARD

1. Anxiety is not dangerous—just uncomfortable.
2. I can be anxious and still function effectively.
3. Trigger your relaxation response, take three or four *relaxed* diaphragmatic breaths then distract yourself.
4. Remember that the scary things you have thought about your symptoms are lies—anxiety is just a nuisance and no more.
5. The symptoms are now occurring because I'm just like Pavlov's dogs—instead of salivating, I get anxious when certain "bells" ring. This conditioned response learning will fade with time.

ANDREA'S CARD

1. My heart is fine. The symptoms are simply due to a NORMAL variation and are NOT harmful.
2. Trigger the relaxation response anchor and take three relaxed diaphragmatic breaths.
3. I will be fine in a few moments. Just take things slowly and get involved in something—DISTRACT YOURSELF.

MAVIS' CARD

1. Anxiety is not dangerous, just uncomfortable.
2. The original symptoms were caused by too much medication. I told myself lies about what they meant. The symptoms continued because I began to watch my body and repeated the old lies to myself.
3. My current symptoms are just a type of conditioned response. They will become less as I desensitize myself.
4. Stay focused on the truth, use diaphragmatic breathing and relaxation response anchor then distract yourself.

GORDON'S CARD

1. Anxiety is not dangerous, just uncomfortable.
2. My anxiety is just a conditioned response reaction—a learned habit pattern—it will become less as I desensitize myself.
3. Stay focused on the truth, use diaphragmatic breathing and relaxation response anchor then distract yourself.

Basic Skills Checklist for Anxiety Producing Situations

Many people forget to use these skills when in the middle of an anxiety-producing situation. This tendency can be overcome by carrying a card that lists these skills similar to the sample shown below. Sometimes a support person can help by reminding you to look at your card and use the above skills.

1. Use the cue that triggers your relaxation response.
2. Take three or four *RELAXED* diaphragmatic breaths.
3. Use coping self-statements to minimize negative self-talk and redirect your energy into productive activities.
4. Distract yourself with one or more of the following:
   a. Simple Externalization
   b. Simple Tasks Which Require Concentration
   c. Conversation
   d. Work
   e. Play

These skills work best at the first signs of anxiety. If you wait until you are experiencing severe symptoms, your skills will be less effective.

Eliminate Caffeine

People with anxiety-related problems tend to be more sensitive to both man-made and natural chemicals. Because of this, caffeine, a stimulant and the world's most widely used mood-altering drug, can be a major source of anxiety. In fact, as little as four cups of coffee can produce panic attacks in some people with panic disorder. Even people who are not naturally hypersensitive to chemicals find the extra stress produced by anxiety-related problems can make them more sensitive to stimulants like caffeine.

When you are having a problem with anxiety, it does not make sense to put anything into your body that can increase anxiety. While you are working through these lessons, eliminate caffeine from your diet by drinking decaffeinated coffee, herbal tea, and caffeine free soft drinks. Read the labels of over-the-counter medications and be aware of any hidden caffeine they may contain.

Some people who have overcome anxiety-related problems find they can resume drinking moderate amounts of caffeinated drinks without experiencing any negative side effects. Many others find they are caffeine-sensitive and that it is best to continue to avoid caffeine. By the time you overcome your anxiety-related problems, you will know which approach is best for you.

Continue to Eliminate Unnecessary Stress

People with anxiety-related problems often use large amounts of energy in self-defeating behaviors such as negative self-talk. Additional energy is lost through increased body tension. This leaves less energy for dealing with the everyday stresses of life. The result is that a daily routine which seemed easy to deal with before the anxiety-related problem developed often becomes difficult.

Lesson 1 asked you to be good to yourself and reduce as many sources of unnecessary stress as possible. Your body needs time to begin healing itself from the ravages of the stress it has been under and replenish its supply of energy. This does not mean you are to avoid life; it does mean you need to apply the concept of the body as a machine with a limited supply of energy to your current condition. Continue to do this for the next few weeks as you learn your basic anxiety reduction skills.

For Those Who Are Having Difficulty Sleeping

Sleep is essential for good mental and physical health. If you are having sleep problems, read *Appendix 4: Getting a Good Night's Sleep*. Developing skills that help you sleep well helps to reduce anxiety. It also makes it much easier to understand the ideas in these lessons and apply them to your life.

If you have not already begun doing the
exercises in the recommended activities,
begin now. Also, be sure to re-read
the lesson so you understand it fully.

Understanding and Reducing Stress

3
Lesson

People with anxiety-related problems tend to be poor at managing stress. The overview of stress and stress management in this lesson provides a firm foundation for the skills presented in the lessons that follow. Be patient as you study.

☐ *What Is Stress?*

Stress is anything that triggers your fight or flight response. The effects of stress can be positive or negative. One example of positive stress is the excitement an experienced musician feels just before a performance. In this case, the fight or flight response helps to improve the performance. Another example is the excitement of being in love.

Negative stress can be short-term (such as the fear, pressure, and need for quick decisions produced when a car suddenly swerves into your path) or long-term (such as the stress you might feel in a complex, high pressure job). Too much stress, especially over a long period of time can drain energy, cause undue wear and tear on the body, and make you vulnerable to illness, and premature aging. Pictures of presidents before and after four years of one of the most stressful jobs there is provides a vivid example of this fact.

Stress can be divided into two major types: *physical stress* and *psychological stress*. Physical stress is created by physical demands on the body such as those caused by accidents, illness, chemical toxins, a demanding work schedule, or prolonged psychological stress. Psychological stress is created by mental or emotional demands on the body. Psychological stress can simply be the result of physical stress. However psychological stress is more often caused by mental or emotional demands from your personal beliefs, family, work, or friends.

This lesson focuses on psychological stress. The four basic types of psychological stress are defined as follows:

Pressure: An internal or external demand either to complete a task or activity within a limited time or in a specific manner.

Frustration: The blocking of needs or wants.

Conflict: The need to make a choice between two or more competing alternatives.

Anxiety/Fear: One of two basic emotional responses to a perceived threat (the other is anger).

There are three important points about stress which need to be understood in order to develop a complete approach to stress management. First, distress involves the triggering of the fight or flight response and the release of energy which is not actually needed to cope with an external situation. As explained in Lesson 1, this is what generates the symptoms of anxiety.

Second, your body responds to any thought as though the thought concerns an event occurring in the present. It does not matter whether the thought is about the past, present, or future. This is why a vivid thought accompanied by strong emotion about a past negative experience or a possible future problem triggers the fight or flight response.

Third, people who experience the prolonged stress of severe anxiety usually have beliefs, attitudes, and habitual thinking patterns which tend to perpetuate the stress. This important point is dealt with in detail later in the program.

The process of reducing daily stress is usually referred to as *stress management.* The word "management" is of particular importance. Your goal is not to eliminate stress. This is impossible if you are to live a normal, healthy life. Your goal is to manage stress so it does not prevent you from living the life you want.

☐ *Basic Stress Management Principles*

People with anxiety-related problems usually understand the three basic stress management principles discussed in this section. Unfortunately, they usually do not *apply* them to their daily life. Embracing these ideas and making them the basis of your daily life is one of the keys to overcoming anxiety.

Accept Your Body as a Machine with a Limited Supply of Energy

The first step in stress management is to treat your *body as a machine* which needs regular rest, maintenance, and care in order to work properly. When you wake up each morning you begin your day with a *limited supply of energy*. It is as if your body starts with a charged battery and tank full of fuel. The exact amount of energy you have each day varies and is different from what other people have. Once this supply of energy is used up, it can only be replaced by taking time to rest and nourish yourself. If you fail to do this, your body starts to break down.

While almost everyone with anxiety-related problems has an intellectual understanding of the concept of the body as a machine with a limited supply of energy, few actually apply it to their lives. Sometimes, childhood training leads to the belief that the body is unimportant. An excessive need for approval, rigid thinking, high expectations of self, or a tendency to suppress some or all negative feelings can also cause people to ignore the needs of their bodies.

Learn to Recognize the Early Signs of Stress and What They Mean

In order to apply the concept of the body as a machine, you need to know when stress is beginning to have a negative effect on you. Learning to recognize and pay attention to these early warning signs allows you to know when you are running low on energy and apply the ideas that are discussed in the next section. The Stress Symptom Inventory that follows is designed to help you identify your own unique set of warning signs. Complete it before going on with this lesson.

Stress Symptom Inventory

Think of several times when you have experienced excessive stress and check any of the symptoms you experienced during those times of high stress.

Physical Symptoms

- ❏ Appetite change
- ❏ Colds/flu
- ❏ Digestive upsets
- ❏ Fatigue
- ❏ Finger-drumming, foot-tapping, etc.
- ❏ Frequent sighing, yawning
- ❏ Headaches

- ❏ Increase of accidents
- ❏ Increased alcohol, drug, tobacco use
- ❏ Insomnia
- ❏ Irregular breathing, hyperventilation
- ❏ Muscle aches
- ❏ Pounding heart

- ❏ Rash
- ❏ Restlessness
- ❏ Teeth grinding
- ❏ Tension
- ❏ Weight change
- ❏ Others:
- ❏ _____
- ❏ _____

Mental

- ❏ Boredom
- ❏ Confusion
- ❏ Difficulty in thinking clearly
- ❏ Dull senses
- ❏ Forgetfulness

- ❏ Lethargy
- ❏ Low Productivity
- ❏ Negative attitude
- ❏ Poor memory
- ❏ Reduced ability to concentrate

- ❏ "Weird" or morbid thoughts
- ❏ Whirling mind
- ❏ Others:
- ❏ _____
- ❏ _____

Emotional

- ❑ Anxiety
- ❑ Bad dreams or nightmares
- ❑ Crying spells
- ❑ Depression
- ❑ Discouragement
- ❑ Frustration

- ❑ Increased use of profanity, put-downs, or sarcasm
- ❑ Increased emotionalism
- ❑ Irritability
- ❑ Little joy

- ❑ Mood swings
- ❑ Nervous laugh
- ❑ Short temper
- ❑ The "blues"
- ❑ Others:
- ❑ _____
- ❑ _____

Spiritual

- ❑ Apathy
- ❑ Cynicism
- ❑ Doubt
- ❑ Emptiness
- ❑ Inability to forgive
- ❑ Loss of direction

- ❑ Loss of faith
- ❑ Loss of meaning
- ❑ Martyrdom
- ❑ Need to "prove" self
- ❑ "No one cares" attitude
- ❑ Pessimism

- ❑ Sense of helplessness
- ❑ Sense of hopelessness
- ❑ Others:
- ❑ _____
- ❑ _____

Relational

- ❑ Avoidance of people
- ❑ Blaming
- ❑ Distrust
- ❑ Fewer contacts with friends

- ❑ Increased arguing/ disagreements
- ❑ Intolerance
- ❑ Lack of intimacy
- ❑ Lashing out
- ❑ Less loving and trusting

- ❑ Lowered sex drive
- ❑ Nagging
- ❑ Resentment
- ❑ Others:
- ❑ _____
- ❑ _____

You probably noticed that many of the items in this inventory applied to you. This is even true for people who do not suffer from anxiety-related problems. However, if you go back through the items you checked, you will find several that would be especially important warning signs. Put a star beside three to six symptoms you feel would be the most important indicators that stress is beginning to affect you in a negative way. Do not be surprised if your key indicators change from time to time. The way stress affects you varies depending on its source and your current physical condition. For example, those symptoms associated with distress due to a heavy workload may vary from those due to the emotional distress of marital problems.

One of the great lessons you need to learn is to assign new meaning to the physical symptoms of anxiety. These symptoms simply mean you have not taken care of yourself in one or more important areas of your life. The result is that your body reacts to the excessive stress it experiences by producing anxiety symptoms. To prevent this, you need to develop skill in both recognizing the early signs of distress and taking appropriate action at that time. By doing this you prevent your body from becoming stressed to the point where you experience excessive anxiety.

When people suffering from anxiety-related problems are introduced to the ideas in this section, they often wonder why they experience anxiety symptoms when stressed while others do not react in this manner. The answer is simple. All bodies are not created equally. People with anxiety-related problems often have highly reactive bodies. For many, this highly reactive body is due to inherited genetic traits. For others it is the result of their bodies reaching the breaking point due to excessive stress from physical illness, injury, relationship or work-related problems, or an unhealthy lifestyle.

A highly reactive body is yours for life. This does *not* mean you are doomed to experience severe anxiety for the rest of your life; it simply means you must learn how to adjust to the fact that your body reacts more strongly than the average body when it is over stressed.

The first step in learning how to live with a highly reactive body is to understand that symptoms of anxiety are simply messages that you have not taken care of some important need. This need may be physical, mental, emotional, spiritual, or relational in nature. Understanding and accepting this idea helps you avoid exaggerating the importance of anxiety symptoms when they occur. The next step is to identify what that need is and decide on the best way to take care of it. This is a problem that we will return to many times in the lessons to come.

Build Stress Tolerance With a Balanced Diet and Exercise

A strong, healthy body tolerates stress much more effectively than an unhealthy one. This is especially true for a person with a highly reactive body. To increase your body's physical ability to tolerate stress you need a well-balanced diet and regular exercise.

A well-balanced diet builds stress tolerance in three ways: it increases physical endurance, increases resistance to disease, and promotes increased emotional stability. Unfortunately, the first thing to suffer during a period of high stress or anxiety is usually one's diet. Stress and anxiety tend to interfere with the digestive system through the fight or flight response. In addition, "junk foods" with a low nutritional value but a high emotional value, such as chocolate and sweets, are commonly used as a coping device. This loss of a balanced diet runs the body down and exaggerates the effects of stress and anxiety even more. The ingestion of excessive sugar can also produce mood swings.

It is not necessary to become a food fanatic to prevent these negative effects. Food by itself will not make you stress-free and eliminate your anxiety. However, food is very important to your health and moods. Keep in mind the concept of the body as a machine that needs proper fuel to run efficiently. If you are not sure what a balanced diet is, there are many excellent books on nutrition available at your local bookstore.

Within any reasonable diet there is plenty of room for "fun" foods. However, your ability to tolerate foods with a low nutritional value is greatly reduced during times when you are experiencing severe anxiety or stress. During times of high stress and anxiety, pay extra attention to what you eat. In addition, when you know you will be facing an activity that is stressful, pay extra attention to your diet the day before as well as the day of the activity. This prepares your body to cope more effectively with the additional stress.

Regular exercise increases stress tolerance by increasing physical endurance, releasing tension, and providing a post-exercise relaxation that can help reduce the symptoms of anxiety. Aerobic exercise done a minimum of three times a week for at least twenty minutes also helps give you a more positive outlook. If you do not already exercise on a regular basis, it is important to check with your physician before starting or drastically changing your exercise routine.

☐ *Three Guidelines for Periods of High Stress*

Everyone faces periodic times of high stress. The excessive stress during a time like this may be due to an unusual event such as a major illness in a loved one or losing one's job. The stress may also be due to many normal events that all happen at one time. For example, Brian who was introduced in Lesson 1 had his first panic attack shortly after he received a promotion that required him to move to a new town. At the same time, his wife gave birth to their first child. All of these are normal events. However, the accumulation of leaving his support network, moving, facing a new stressful job and adjusting to a new baby all added up to produce a simple stress reaction that he did not understand.

The following guidelines are based on the basic stress management principles outlined above. Following them during times of high stress enables you to reduce the effect of the stressors you are facing and function more effectively in all areas of your life. This is especially important if you have a sensitive body.

Set priorities and reduce your overall activity.

Whenever you are facing more stress than usual, reduce your activities. This is not a time to try to beat old performance records and do extra things. It is a time to do less by setting priorities, establishing realistic short-term goals, and delegating more responsibility to others. This does not mean you avoid all activity. Instead, it means you apply the concept of the body as a machine with a limited supply of energy to your current situation. Since stress drains your energy, you have less energy during times of high stress than during times of low stress. Setting priorities and reducing your overall activity is one way to use the limited amount of energy you have wisely.

This is often difficult because stress affects the way you think. Small things that don't have much importance when you are feeling good often take on exaggerated importance. In order to combat this tendency, you may have to stop periodically and ask yourself, "What really needs to be done now? What can I let go of until some other time?"

Spend extra time with decisions.

It cannot be said too many times: stress interferes with your ability to think. The greater the stress, the more likely it is that you will make poor decisions. Whenever possible, avoid making major decisions during times of high stress. Wait until you are feeling less stressed. When a major decision must be made during a time of high stress do two things. First, take more time to make the decision. Slowing down the decision making process helps you use your reduced ability to think more effectively. Second, consult with people you trust and who are objective. They may see problems or options you didn't think of because of your reduced ability to think logically.

Plan ahead and take action during times when stress is low.

Often, you know ahead of time when a period of high stress is coming. This may be a job where there is a large increase of work at regular times. It may also be a one time event such as a wedding or family reunion. When you know that a stressful event is coming, plan ahead, make decisions, and take action in advance while you are feeling good. This reduces the amount of thinking and action you must take during time of high stress. For example, if an important function at work is coming, plan to do routine things in advance. Also plan to let go of little things during the high stress time. Having a plan like this helps you concentrate on what is important and let go of things that are less important.

Many people take action or make decisions only when pushed into a corner or prodded by discomfort, then wonder why they make so many poor decisions and act ineffectively. Developing the habit of planning ahead and taking time when you are unstressed to face important issues and take action results in better decisions and more effective behavior.

☐ *Develop a Life Style Based on Stress Management Principles*

Earlier in this lesson, it was pointed out that anxiety is just a message that some important need is not being satisfied. Unfortunately, it is often difficult in our fast paced, modern world to develop a life style that balances your various physical, mental, emotional, relational, and spiritual needs. People in our modern society tend to live in a manner where important needs are ignored. People with anxiety-related problems usually have life styles that are not balanced.

The seven areas discussed in this section describe activities and attitudes that are most commonly missing in the lives of people with anxiety-related problems. When you first read through this section you may feel overwhelmed at the thought of applying all of these ideas to your life. This is a normal reaction since it usually takes many weeks or months to make all of them a part of your life. During the time you are working with this lesson, select two or three areas that are not currently part of your life style. Put most of your time and energy into these. Do not be concerned if you are only able to work on these two or three areas at this time. As you proceed through this program there will be many opportunities to return to this lesson and work with those approaches you skip at this time.

Relaxation

Taking time to relax is not only important, it is essential for physical and mental health. Develop the habit of scheduling regular time for relaxation. While you are developing this habit, remind yourself of the concept of the body as a machine with a limited supply of energy. Scheduling regular times for relaxation is the same for your body as performing regular maintenance on a car.

There are many different ways to relax. Some are passive while others are active. The activities you choose are not important as long as you feel more at ease and refreshed when you have finished them. Here are some commonly used forms of relaxation.

Passive Forms of Relaxation	Active Forms of Relaxation
Biofeedback	Avocational classes such as photography or cooking
Diaphragmatic Breathing	
Hot tubs, showers and baths	Dancing
Massage and body-work	Hobbies and crafts such as art, fishing, gardening, or woodworking
Meditation and prayer	
Movies and theater	Individual sports such as tennis or golf
Music (both as background and just sitting and listening)	Informal afternoons or evenings with friends
Reading	Jogging, swimming, and other forms of exercise
Relaxation response exercises	
Self-hypnosis	Road trips and vacations
Sleep	Shopping
Television	Team sports such as baseball or basketball
Yoga	
	Video games
	Walks

Since an activity that relaxes one person might cause anxiety or distress in another, you need to select activities that match your personality and current abilities. Use the above lists as a starting point and identify several activities you find relaxing. During this and coming weeks, find ways to make the activities you identify a regular part of both your daily and weekly routine.

Decompression Routines

People with the high anxiety personality traits tend to plunge from one stressful activity into another. Time is not allowed for the mind and body to recover in between. Taking time to develop and use decompression routines is one way to overcome this tendency. It is especially important if you are working at a job or are involved in daily activities that are very stressful.

A decompression routine is any sort of ritual or routine used to unwind after a stressful event or day. In a sense, it is a specialized form of relaxation. Many people find solitary activities such as reading, working at a relaxing hobby, or just sitting work best. Others prefer activities involving children, spouses, or friends. Many of the activities suggested in the previous section can be used as part of a decompression routine.

Avoid using chemicals such as alcohol or marijuana as part of your decompression routine. Using the so-called "recreational drugs" to self-medicate in an attempt to relieve stress and anxiety is very risky. Many people suffering from alcoholism and other forms of chemical dependency began by using chemicals to relieve the symptoms of anxiety.

Play

Play is essential for good mental and physical health. Unfortunately, many people feel it is "childish" and therefore undignified to "play." However, your ability to play and relax correlates directly with your productivity and ability to minimize the effects of daily stress. Playing also reduces physical tension, increases stress tolerance, and revitalizes your sense of humor.

Play can include a broad range of activities such as romping with the kids, talking with a friend, playing cards, shopping, or having lunch with someone you enjoy. Many of the activities mentioned under the heading of "Relaxation" can be a type of play. In fact, play and relaxation often go together. Even when play is tiring, it produces a form of mental and physical release that allows for increased relaxation afterwards. The essential point is to do something that is both entertaining and fun on a regular basis.

Humor

A good sense of humor is one of your greatest allies in overcoming the effects of stress and anxiety. People with anxiety-related problems tend to take themselves and everything else too seriously. Small and insignificant events are often magnified into major anxiety-producing issues. Maintaining your sense of humor helps to keep things in perspective. Humor helps you see your limitations as simply an aspect of your humanness instead of as a sign of inadequacy.

From now on, whenever you notice that you are taking yourself, your skills, your progress, your limitations, or your flaws too seriously, find something to laugh about. This does not mean ridiculing or putting yourself down, but enjoying the comical aspect of life in a good-natured way.

Emotional Support

People are social beings who need emotional support in order to maintain mental and physical health. Loneliness and isolation are two of the most destructive forms of stress. Unfortunately, because people suffering from severe anxiety often have an exaggerated need for approval and are busy trying to be supportive of others, they frequently fail to allow others to support them. They may even feel guilty whenever they become aware of their need for emotional support. Receiving from others is just as important as giving. In fact, a person cannot truly give unless he or she knows how to receive.

The recommended activities for Lesson 1 suggested finding a study partner to provide emotional support as you go through the process of overcoming anxiety-related problems. Other sources of emotional support include family, friends, co-workers, church membership, specialized support or self-help groups, clubs, service organizations, professional therapy, and pets.

Emotional support can be conditional or unconditional. Conditional support means it is given as long as you behave in a certain way. Frequently, this is the type of support given by friends and co-workers. It may or may not be the type of support you receive from your family. There is nothing wrong with this type of support. However, it is useful to have at least one source of unconditional support. This refers to support that is available regardless of how you are feeling or what you have done. Pets are a common source of unconditional love and support. This is why they are so treasured by their owners. Sometimes, unconditional support can also be found in clubs and organizations.

If you are unable to find people who can provide emotional support, you may need to find it with a good therapist. A skilled therapist can offer many types of help. However, one of the most valuable aspects of therapy is often the unconditional emotional support it provides. Many people find therapy is the one place where they can really be themselves and have someone listen to what they say. The healing quality of this aspect of therapy is often as valuable as any of the therapeutic approaches used. Having one person to talk with honestly and openly removes the burden of carrying your "secrets" alone. It also helps you feel better about yourself and be more honest and open in all of your other relationships. If you decide to seek the help of a therapist, refer to the guidelines for selecting a therapist in Appendix 2.

Spiritual Support

Spiritual support refers to having something in your life that helps you make sense out of the world in which you live. It helps you give a positive meaning to events within the context of a universe much larger than yourself or your immediate surroundings. Clarifying your spiritual or philosophical beliefs may also provide the key to accepting uncertainty and finding peace when you make mistakes or fail to meet your goals.

There are many ways in which you can fulfill the spiritual side of yourself that is so often neglected in our modern world. Traditional religions are the most commonly used form of spiritual support. Philosophy, taking time for private meditation, or reading inspirational books are other common sources. If you already have a strong source of spiritual support, you are deeply aware of the strength and serenity it provides. If you have a strong source which has helped to strengthen you in the past but which you have neglected to use at this point in your life, renew your relationship with it. If you do not have a strong source of spiritual support, begin to consider how you might fulfill your need to see events in a larger context and feed your inner need for personal meaning.

Traditions and Routines

The ability to use the various approaches described in this lesson does not just happen by itself. It requires structure. One important way to create this structure is to develop traditions and routines which make the above approaches part of your everyday life. If you do not create structures in the form of traditions and routines, they probably will not be used.

Take time this week to schedule activities that are fun and regenerating. Continue to do this on a regular basis. For example, do something fun with your partner or significant other at least twice a month (preferably once a week) such as a special dinner, a visit with good friends, a movie at a theater or a movie on home video. If you have children, have special time with each child daily if possible but at least once a week. Special time is one-on-one time where you do something together you both enjoy for at least fifteen minutes. Other traditions might include engaging in a relaxing activity at a particular time or the scheduling of time for a daily decompression routine after work.

Developing traditions and routines that reinforce the use of the various concepts presented in this lesson play a key role in the process of overcoming anxiety-related problems. Traditions and routines also help to ensure that the problems do not recur in the future.

Recommended Activities for Lesson 3

Continue Developing Cue-Controlled Relaxation

Continue practicing your relaxation response exercise once a day. Be sure to continue associating the same cue you selected last week with the deep relaxation you are practicing. If you have not yet begun this activity, do so this week. Appendix 1 describes four different methods for producing a relaxation response. Try each one several times and decide which one works best for you. Your goal is to master at least one technique that produces physical relaxation. The Recommended Activities in Lesson 2 describes how to associate a conditioned response cue with the relaxation in order to develop a cue-controlled relaxation response.

Continue Practicing Diaphragmatic Breathing

Continue practicing diaphragmatic breathing until you have accomplished the following:

- You can tell how you are breathing without the need to place a hand on your lower abdomen; you have developed the ability to use your internal sensors to "feel" when you are using diaphragmatic breathing.
- You can take a *relaxed* diaphragmatic breath whenever you want without effort.
- When you are relaxed, your normal method of breathing is diaphragmatic breathing.
- You usually continue to use diaphragmatic breathing (as opposed to upper-chest breathing) in anxiety-producing situations.

While some people reach the above goals very quickly, others take three or four weeks, occasionally longer. It all depends upon what type of breathing pattern you used when you began practicing and how consistent you are while practicing.

One word of caution concerning the use of diaphragmatic breathing during times when you are anxious: do not become overly concerned about how you are breathing. Watching how you breathe tends to interfere with the natural process and may make you more anxious. To avoid this, simply take three or four relaxed breaths and move your attention to your coping self-statements and distractors. Your breathing will then readjust on its own.

Examine Your Diet

This lesson pointed out the importance of eating a well-balanced diet. It also provided general guidelines to follow. This week examine what you have been eating. If you are not sure what constitutes a well-balanced diet, you may find it useful to read a book on nutrition. Your physician may know of one he or she can recommend. If you have any medical problems or questions, it is best to consult your physician before making any major changes in your diet.

There is one important guideline to follow concerning your diet. Stay away from books or nutritional counselors recommending unusual or fad diets. Your goal is to develop the habit of eating a well-balanced diet based on sound nutritional principles.

Consider Exercise

If you do not currently engage in regular exercise, plan to make exercise a part of your weekly routine. Any aerobic exercise done at least three times a week for at least twenty minutes each time can help increase your ability to tolerate stress and reduce anxiety. You do not have to become an exercise fanatic or purchase expensive equipment. There are many good, common-sense books available on exercise. There are also many good exercise programs on television. Some people find joining a health spa helps them keep their commitment to exercise regularly. Whatever you decide on, consistency and moderation are the keys to success.

Before starting a new exercise program or drastically changing your current one, it is best to check with your doctor. This is especially true if you have any physical condition that an inappropriate exercise program could adversely affect.

Begin Applying Stress Management Principles to Your Life

Decide when and how you will apply the stress management principles outlined in this lesson to your life. Be sure to review this lesson periodically to see if there are any additional ways in which you can apply these principles to your life.

Helping Others

One common tendency among people with a strong need for approval is the need to "help" others with their personal problems. If this is true for you, refrain from this while working on this program. At this time you simply do not have the time or energy to spare. Devote your time and energy to the work of learning new ways of thinking and acting. After the old anxiety-related patterns have been overcome, you will have the extra time and energy needed to help others. You will also have a whole new set of skills and insights that will make you a more effective resource.

Spend at least one week with this lesson.
It takes time to absorb new ideas
and apply them to your life.

Identifying and Reducing the Sources of Anxiety

4

Lesson

Most of your anxiety is generated not by events, but by the meaning you give to events. Since the way in which you think is simply a learned habit pattern, this is something you can learn to control. This lesson helps you understand how emotions are generated and provides you with a powerful method for reducing the most common source of anxiety—"should/must" thinking.

☐ *Needs and Beliefs*

You have many psychological needs. Five of the most important needs are: the need to give and receive love, the need to belong and feel significant, the need to feel secure, the need to explore and learn, and the need to create. As a child, you learned to satisfy these needs by imitating the behaviors of adults, by being taught directly through the way you were disciplined and trained, and by experiencing the consequences of your actions through a process of trial and error.

As you learned to satisfy your needs, you developed a set of core beliefs. The many ideas which make up your set of core beliefs can be divided into the following three areas.

Beliefs About Yourself: These beliefs, sometimes referred to collectively as your self-concept or self-image, include beliefs about your personal value or worth, your talents and limitations, and your place in the world.

Beliefs About Others: These beliefs include all your beliefs about human relationships such as how others should be treated, what relationships between men and women are like, and what type of behaviors can be expected from the various people you meet.

Beliefs About The World: These beliefs include beliefs about the meaning and importance of everyday events, as well as beliefs about abstract concepts such as God, patriotism, and morality.

Many of the basic elements of your core beliefs were established by the age of seven. Because young children lack many adult reasoning skills, have very little life experience, and tend to accept what adults say without much questioning, many of these beliefs are irrational and unrealistic. While it is possible to examine these beliefs as an adult and replace irrational ideas with rational ones, most people fail to do so. They either do not understand the importance of these beliefs or are so busy with other activities they never take time to examine them in a systematic manner. The tragic result is that most people go through their entire life basing their actions on a set of core beliefs developed when they were children. When you think of human behavior in these terms, it is easy to understand why there is so much pain and suffering in the world. You also glimpse the source of much anxiety.

☐ *How Emotions Are Generated*

Most of your emotions are the result of the interpretations you make of events taking place around you. The only exceptions are emotions that result from interference with the normal functioning of the brain or central nervous systems, such as injury, illness, mood-altering drugs, and, in some cases, diet. This process can be diagrammed as follows:

Event　　→　　Interpretation　　→　　Emotion　　→　　Action

You are usually unaware of the role interpretation plays in the generation of emotions because it takes place very rapidly and usually unconsciously. This is essential to your survival. You could not function effectively if you had to evaluate and assign meaning to everything going on around you in a slow, deliberate manner.

An example of the mind's ability to interpret and assign meaning to events quickly and automatically is the seemingly simple act of driving a car. This is actually an extremely complicated process which requires you to judge distances, decide what the actions of pedestrians and other drivers mean, and make many other interpretations every second. The mind does all of this so quickly you are usually unaware of the fact that this process is even occurring. Instead, you listen to the radio, talk to a passenger in the car, or do something else unrelated to driving.

The mind's ability to interpret events quickly and automatically has led to the widespread misconception that people and events generate emotions. Most people don't realize that it is the meaning they assign to people and events that actually generates emotions. Commonly used statements such as, "He made me mad," "She made me sad," or "That really made me happy," not only reflect this mistaken belief but actually reinforce it.

If this mistaken idea were true, a specific event would generate the same emotion in everyone experiencing it. For example, consider how different people react to a rainstorm. Some feel depressed by the lack of sunshine or become angry as they think about the inconvenience caused by the rain. Others feel happy as they look forward to being inside a warm, cozy house or glad because the rain brings needed water. Even though these people are all experiencing the same event, their emotions are different because each one interprets it differently.

□ *Why Do We Have Emotions?*

The exact way in which the biological mechanisms of emotions work is only poorly understood by scientists at this time. However, it is clear that emotions are part of an intricate inherited biological mechanism designed to help you survive.

While emotions can be modified by learning and maturation, they show a remarkable consistency both within and across species. Emotional expressions are the same in both sighted people and those who have been blind since birth. Many emotional expressions are present in a very similar manner across different cultures and races. The expression of emotion in infants and adults is very similar even though this expression in infants is prior to the time when they could have learned how to do this. Furthermore, several basic emotions and emotional expressions emerge in an infant at fairly consistent times.

In animals emotions have two primary functions. They prepare the animal for action and serve as a form of communication from one member of a species to another. For example, fear both prepares an animal for immediate action and communicates danger to other animals causing a similar response in them.

Emotions also serve these two functions in humans. Since babies do not have verbal language, parents rely on emotional expressions to guide their interaction and gauge the needs of a child. Likewise, emotional expression in adults is usually a more powerful form of communication than verbal expression.

While humans and animals seem to share the same genetic aspect of emotions, there is an important difference between animals and humans. Emotions in animals are controlled by instinct or a combination of instinct and simple types of learning. In humans there are no true instincts. Babies are born with an innate startle response and fear of falling. Other fears emerge at predictable times such as "separation distress" at 4 months and "stranger distress" at 7-9 months. However, by the time a person becomes an adult, their entire emotional mechanism is controlled by a complex set of beliefs and learned response patterns. It is similar to the biological mechanisms which operate voluntary muscles in your arms and legs. These systems are also complex biological systems that, when functioning normally, are ultimately controlled by thoughts and learned response patterns.

In simplistic terms, emotions work in the following manner. A part of your mind constantly evaluates events in terms of your needs and wants. This process of assigning meaning to events is usually done automatically and unconsciously. If a need or want is or may be satisfied, you experience the various positive emotions such as joy, excitement, or satisfaction. If a threat is present you experience anger (ranging from irritation to rage) or fear (ranging from apprehension to panic). If you encounter a loss you experience sadness, grief, or depression depending on the nature of the loss. Of course, events are often complex. They can satisfy some needs and frustrate others. This is why we often experience mixed emotions. This process of interpreting needs and wants can be diagrammed as follows:

		A need or want is or may be satisfied	→	Various positive emotions such as joy, excitement, or satisfaction
Event → Interpretation →	↗ ↘	A need or want is or may be threatened	→	Anger or Fear
		A loss of some sort has been or may be experienced	→	Sadness, grief, or depression

When emotions motivate you to take actions that help you respond effectively to opportunity, loss, and danger and achieve your life goals, they are *self-fulfilling emotions*. Unfortunately, emotions often do not work in this manner. Sometimes we experience *self-defeating emotions* that interfere with our ability to be effective in relationships, work, and play and which prevent us from reaching our life goals. Emotions can become self-defeating if they occur when there is no apparent reason for them to occur, if they occur at an exaggerated level of intensity, or if they last for an extended period of time. Examples include becoming anxious when no threat exists, becoming enraged over a minor incident, and remaining depressed for days over a minor loss or disappointment.

If the function of emotions is to help protect you and satisfy your needs, why then do you experience self-defeating emotions? The answer is simple. Every person has at least some, and in most cases many, beliefs and habitual thinking patterns that are irrational or unrealistic. This causes the automatic evaluation process to interpret events in an irrational or unrealistic manner and trigger self-defeating emotions.

This automatic aspect of your mind is like a computer. It has the ability to examine vast amounts of information coming in through your senses and make split-second decisions about whether or not an event satisfies or threatens your needs and wants. In the computer field there is a saying, "garbage in, garbage out." This saying refers to the fact that a computer fed inaccurate information or given a faulty program makes faulty calculations.

☐ *Habitual Thinking Patterns*

One of the wonders of the human mind is its ability to learn an action so well it becomes automatic. Some actions that took years to learn—such as dressing yourself—are now so automatic you don't think about them. The way in which you think, the words you use, and the events you choose to remember and focus on are all automatic habit patterns and differ little from all of the other automatic behaviors you learned while growing up. In fact, you spend most of your day on "automatic pilot". Unfortunately, just as you developed many irrational beliefs, you also developed many irrational ways of processing information that are now part of this automatic thought process which contributes to your anxiety.

A constant dialogue goes on inside of yourself. This silent internal conversation is called *self-talk*. Most self-talk takes the form of sentences repeated over and over. The other part of this internal automatic thinking process concerns the memories you choose to recall and the events on which you choose to focus.

While you have a wide variety of memories from which to choose, you usually recall those that reinforce your current state of mind. When you are sad, you recall sad memories. When you are happy, you recall pleasant ones. You also have a set of memorized stories and explanations you recall for specific events and situations. For example, when you are asked to say something about yourself, your work, or your childhood, you probably recall a set of stories and explanations that are similar each time you are asked. In the same way, you have a selective point of view and notice only certain aspects of daily life. You may only be aware of flaws and errors, or you may be aware of opportunities and the positive aspects of the situations in which you find yourself.

Your automatic self-talk, selective remembering, prepared stories and explanations, and selective points of view make up your *habitual thinking patterns*. The interpretation process that generates your emotions is, for the most part, based upon a combination of these automatic, habitual thinking patterns and your beliefs. By changing them, you can change the way you interpret events and dramatically and positively alter your experience of life.

□ *The Cognitive Approach*

The ideas you are studying this week come from an approach to psychology called *Cognitive Therapy*. The word "cognitive" refers to how you think. Therefore, a cognitive approach involves learning how to change the way you feel and act by changing the way you think. The process of changing the way you think is called *cognitive restructuring*.

The primary skill used by the cognitive approach is *rational self-talk*. This skill can help you 1) change the way you feel and act by changing the way you interpret events, 2) perceive the world more rationally and realistically, 3) increase your sense of personal power, and 4) take advantage of opportunities and choices you were unaware of in the past. The seven different types of rational self-talk commonly used to accomplish these goals are listed below. The coping self-statements described in Lesson 2 use ego strengtheners, questioning, and redirecting statements.

Ego strengtheners: Statements that offer self-encouragement or remind you of specific positive abilities you possess.

Substitution: The substitution of words or phrases that characterize rational thinking for ones characteristic of irrational thinking.

Questioning: The use of questions to direct your attention to key issues or to emphasize the irrational nature of a particular form of self-defeating thinking. Questioning is usually followed by a rational challenge, objective evaluation, cost-benefit analysis, or redirecting statement.

Rational challenge: The use of memorized statements or rational arguments to correct faulty assumptions that underlie specific types of irrational thinking or self-defeating behaviors.

Objective evaluation: The objective analysis of your current situation, thoughts or behavior. The goal is to stop unconscious thoughts and actions by using your ability to discriminate and reason in a more deliberate manner. This helps you replace automatic thoughts and behaviors that are self-defeating with self-enhancing thoughts and behaviors.

Cost/benefit analysis: The listing and evaluation of advantages or disadvantages for a particular belief or behavior. This is often part of an objective evaluation and helps you become more realistic when irrational thinking has caused you to view the world in an unrealistic and self-defeating manner. It also helps correct irrational beliefs that support an unrealistic view of the world.

Redirecting statements: Statements that redirect your attention and energy into more rational and productive activities. Redirecting statements usually follow one of the above approaches.

The above terms will be used throughout the rest of the program. People with a strong analytical bent often find it useful to memorize the above terms; others do not. These terms will be listed in parentheses in the examples of rational self-talk that are given in this and following lessons. If you find it useful to label the different types of rational self-talk, refer back to this section. If you find labeling confusing, disregard this section.

☐ *Should/Must Thinking*

Should/must thinking refers to the transformation of *personal choices*, wants, or preferences into *universal absolutes*. This is usually done by thinking in words and phrases such as "should," "must," "ought," and "have to." When you use should/must thinking three things tend to occur. First, you focus your attention on the undesirable aspects of a problems and the discomfort you are experiencing rather than on finding possible solutions. Second, you tend to waste time and energy criticizing and condemning the person or thing that is breaking the should/must rule. Third, you lose some contact with reality as you enter the fantasy world of how things "should" be.

One evening, Donna had an experience that illustrates these three aspects of should/must thinking. While going to a friend's house for a casual dinner party, she was caught in a traffic jam. Because Donna had the rule, "I must always be on time," she reacted with the following self-talk: "Oh no! I'm not going to make it on time. I can't be late. This is terrible! I must be on time." Donna's should/must rule created the false belief that there was only one possibility in this situation. Donna had to be on time. Nothing else was acceptable. This kept her mind focused on the undesirable aspects of an event she had no power to predict or prevent. She was unable to adopt a *problem-solving* approach and consider practical and positive ways of dealing with the problem of the traffic jam.

Soon, Donna found herself condemning the person who broke the should/must rule—in this case herself. "Boy have you blown it. You can't even get to a simple dinner party on time. You should have known better than to leave when you did." She also spent time condemning people and events that contributed to the problem: "Stupid drivers. Why can't people drive like they're supposed to? And why can't they do something about this road anyway?" Because most should/must rules like this come from childhood, Donna, like many people, found her self-talk sounding like an internal critical parent.

When you say something should or must exist and it actually does not exist, to some extent, you lose contact with reality and enter a fantasy world. Donna's fantasy held that there was no substitute for being on time. In the real world, she is occasionally going to be late. As reality intruded upon Donna's fantasy, she experienced tremendous anxiety along with resentment toward anyone or anything that delayed her further. She even found herself driving recklessly—risking her life, her automobile, and the lives of other drivers. As she arrived late, Donna punished herself with self-condemnation for breaking her should/must rule.

From the above it would be easy to assume that all should/must thinking is undesirable. However, should/must thinking is often essential for survival when living in harsh circumstances with limited choices. For example, if you live in a totalitarian society where the secret police might imprison you for "incorrect" words or actions, you need rigid rules about what you say and do. Likewise, it is also valuable for a child growing up in a dysfunctional household to develop rigid rules about how to act around a parent who is drunk or has a volatile temper.

The key to challenging should/must thinking is training yourself to accept reality and focusing on the choices that are available to you in a given situation. The following types of rational self-talk can be used to do this.

Substitution

Whenever you catch yourself saying or thinking "I should," "I must," or "I have to," change it into "I like," "I want," "I choose," "I have decided," or "I prefer." This helps you become more aware of the fact that life is a series of choices. There is nothing you *have* to do in life. You choose to do things that bring something desirable or help you avoid something undesirable.

If you say or think:	"I have to be on time."
Restate or rethink it as one of these:	"I like to be on time." "I want to be on time." "I prefer to be on time."

If you say or think:	"The lawn should/must be cut every Saturday."
Restate or rethink it as one of these:	"I like to cut the lawn every Saturday." "I choose to cut the lawn every Saturday." "I have decided to cut the lawn every Saturday."

Whenever you catch yourself saying or thinking: "He (she, they, or it) should/must/has to," change it into "I would like," "I want," "I would prefer," or "It would be nice." For example:

If you say or think:	"He should be polite."
Restate or rethink it as one of these:	"I would like it if he were polite." "I would prefer it if he were polite." "It would be nice if he were polite."

If you say or think:	"They should be fair."
Restate or rethink it as one of these:	"I would like them to be fair." "I want them to be fair." "It would be nice if they were fair."

Questioning

Ask yourself, "Who says I should/must...?," "Why should/must I...?," or "Where is it written that I should/must...?" This exposes the arbitrary nature of should/must rules and the fact that they are actually personal values and preferences rather than universal absolutes. Follow this type of questioning with one or more of the following approaches.

Objective Evaluation

List the choices that are available and choose the one that seems best for you. Your goal is to choose thoughts and actions that are appropriate for the situation you are facing instead of blindly following an arbitrary set of should/must rules that probably do not reflect reality. For example, Donna can acknowledge that she is going to be late and decide what her choices are. She can find a telephone and call ahead to let someone know she is going to be late. She can just arrive late and make the best of the situation. She can also decide whether or not she needs to leave earlier next time in order to arrive at the time she wants to arrive.

Cost/Benefit Analysis

Some should/must rules concern behaviors or values that are valuable and which you may want to keep. In order to determine this, make a list of the advantages and disadvantages of acting in this way or having this value. This can either be a mental list or something you do on paper. If you decide a particular rule is useful, be sure to rephrase it using the language described in the first approach in this section titled, "Substitution."

Rational Challenge

When you identify a should/must rule you want to eliminate, challenge the rule with logical arguments whenever you notice yourself thinking or using automatic behavior that reflects it. These arguments can include reasons why the should/must rule is undesirable along with a clear statement of a more desirable rule or value. These types of self-defeating rules are often something a teacher, or relative frequently said when you were young. When this is the case you can also remind yourself that you are no longer a child but an adult who is fully able to take responsibility for making your own rules and decisions.

After learning the above rational cognitive skills, Donna again found herself in a traffic jam. This time it occurred while she was driving to work. As is often the case, her first reaction was to react with her old pattern of should/must thinking. However, she now recognized what she was doing and used the following rational self-talk to challenge the old patterns.

"Wait a minute. Here I am getting upset about being late again when there's nothing I can do about it. I like to be on time (substitution). However, there is no way this is going to happen today. My boss understands the problems with traffic in the city and doesn't really mind my occasionally being a little late. In fact, he often complains about this same stretch of road. It looks like I'll only be about ten minutes late and it's the only time I've been late this year. When I get to work I'll just explain what happened (objective evaluation). Now let's just relax and listen to the radio and get to work as soon as I can (redirecting statement).

When reading the various examples of rational self-talk in this and following chapters, remember that there is no one correct form of rational self-talk for a given situation. The various cognitive approaches can blend together in many different ways. Different people use different forms of rational self-talk for the same situation. As you gain experience, finding the right combination of approaches that fits both your personality and the specific should/must rule you are challenging becomes automatic. Here is another example of rational self-talk applied to a different situation:

Example: Jim has just finished dinner and catches himself thinking, "I should do these dishes now that dinner is over."

Jim's rational self-talk: He notices what he is thinking and has the following internal dialogue: "Who says I should do these dishes now? Where is it written that they have to be done immediately after dinner (questioning)? I guess mom always told me to do them as soon as I got up from dinner. Well, I'm an adult now and can make my own rules and decisions (rational challenge). Let's see, I can do them now, stack them and do them later, or soak them and do them tomorrow. I guess I really don't want to leave them until tomorrow. I also want to just sit and relax for a while (objective evaluation). I think I'll choose to leave them for now and do them later (substitution)."

Circular Questioning

Circular questioning is a common form of should/must thinking where you ask yourself over and over questions that are either irrelevant or have an answer you already know but are unwilling to accept. Common examples include "Why am I like this?" "Why can't I change?" "How could he/she do that?" and "How could that happen?" Circular questioning like this usually occurs when a should/must rule has been violated. Your mind becomes "stuck" because you refuse to accept some aspect of reality and slip into the fantasy world of your should/must rules.

"Why am I like this?" usually means "I should be different and can't stand the way I am." "Why can't I change?" usually means "I have to change." or "I can't change and it's awful." "How could he/she do that?" usually means "He/she shouldn't have done that and it's terrible that they did." "How could that happen?" usually means "That shouldn't have happened."

The first step in challenging circular questioning is to identify the should/must rule that has been violated. This can usually be done by simply changing the question into a should/must or can't statement. Occasionally there is an additional should/must rule implied by your statement that also needs to be challenged. "Life should be fair" is a common should/must rule that can generate circular questioning like the above examples. This and other common underlying irrational beliefs will be explored in later lessons.

Once you have identified the should/must rule that is generating your circular questioning, challenge it with the rational self-talk approaches described in the preceding section.

Example: Jeff lives with Mark, who is often inconsiderate. When his friend acts thoughtlessly, Jeff usually begins thinking "Why is Mark like this? How could he be so inconsiderate?" over and over as he becomes anxious and upset.

Jeff's rational self-talk: "Wait a minute. Here I go with the 'hows' and 'whys' again. Actually, I'm saying Mark should be different and it's appalling that he isn't (change the questions into a statement). While I would like Mark to be different, it is a fact that he is who and what he is. He is frequently very inconsiderate and I need to decide how I am going to respond when this happens (objective evaluation). Now, what are my choices (redirecting statement)?"

Can't Thinking

The use of the word "can't" to describe a need, want, decision, or choice is another common form of should/must thinking. For example, saying "I can't go to the store," when you actually mean "I don't want to go to the store," or "I shouldn't go to the store."

As long as you either "must" or "can't" do something, you create the illusion that you have no responsibility or control over that area of your life. This causes you to also lose your ability to change and exert power in that area of your life. You are failing to recognize that life is a series of choices. You choose to do or not do something because it brings you pleasure or helps you avoid discomfort. As soon as you begin to realize that you are choosing to do or not do things, you begin to take back the power you need to change the way you live and create the life you want.

Changing the words you use is an easy way to begin taking back the power you need to change your life. Whenever you catch yourself saying or thinking "I can't," change it into, "I won't," "I don't want to," "I choose not to," "I don't like," or "I don't feel like." For example:

If you say or think:	"I can't go to the store."
Restate or rethink it as one of these:	"I won't go to the store."
	"I don't want to go to the store."
	"I don't feel like going to the store."
If you say or think:	"I can't drive."
Restate or rethink it as one of these:	"I won't drive."
	"I choose not to drive."
	"I don't like to drive."

People frequently avoid situations associated with anxiety or panic. If this is true for you, it is important to keep in mind that you have not really lost any of your former abilities. You still can do anything you have done before. You could probably do even more if there were sufficient reason. Consider a situation in which someone you love was seriously ill or dying and you were the only person who could help. You would be able to go wherever you needed to go and do whatever needed to be done to save this person's life. You might have an anxiety or panic attack after it was all over, but you would have done it.

Right now you may be choosing to avoid some situations and activities because you do not want to experience the anxiety they produce. This is something everyone does and is perfectly all right. As you continue to work through these lessons as instructed, you will eventually change enough of your attitudes and master enough of the skills to overcome your current avoidance patterns. Until then, you are choosing to avoid some situations because you do not want to experience the discomfort associated with them. Do not condemn yourself for doing this. Techniques for overcoming avoidance patterns are presented later in the lessons. Your task right now is to work at changing the way you think so you will be ready to apply those skills.

The Locus of Control

All of the forms of should/must thinking described in this lesson place the locus (or center) of control outside of you. When you use them you tend to act and feel like a child who has a critical parent watching over you waiting to punish you if you break one of the rules. When you start to use the rational self-talk described in this and following lessons, you bring the locus of control inside of yourself.

Eliminating should/must thinking does not mean you do not have rules. It is good to have guidelines for your life. Donna, the person described earlier, still has the rule that she likes to be on time. This is a useful rule in her situation. When being on time was a rigid should/must rule it ruled her like a tyrant and often caused much unnecessary distress. After learning about should/must thinking, Donna is now in control of the rule rather than it being in control of her.

Recommended Activities for Lesson 4

Continue Developing Cue-Controlled Relaxation

Continue practicing your relaxation response at least once a day. When you experience more stress then usual, schedule an extra session. Also, be sure to continue to associate the same cue you selected while doing Lesson 2 with the deep relaxation you are practicing.

After three weeks of daily practice, some people still find it difficult to produce a state of deep relaxation. If this is true for you, reread the instructions in Appendix 1 carefully. If you have not been practicing daily, decide now when and where you will practice and make a firm commitment to do this important activity. If you have only tried one approach, use each of the other methods described in Appendix 1. Be sure to have at least five practice sessions with each method. If you have not yet tried taping the scripts, do so and use them as instructed.

If you have done everything suggested above and are still finding it difficult to produce a relaxation response, consider buying a professionally produced relaxation tape. The basic set of cassettes that accompanies this book are designed to help people with anxiety-related problems develop cue-controlled relaxation. They work well with people having difficulty developing deep relaxation. A full description and order form is at the back of this book. Relaxation or stress reduction cassettes are also available in book and record stores. You may find it necessary to try more than one to find one that suits you. When you find one that works well for you, begin associating a cue with it as explained in Lesson 2.

Begin Making a Record of Your Self-Talk During Times when You Are Anxious or Upset

As described in this lesson, self-talk plays an important role in the interpretation process that generates your emotions. Record your thoughts in a notebook or binder. Spend five minutes every other day recalling times when you were anxious, angry, hurt, or depressed. Take a moment to mentally place yourself back into the event and recall what you were thinking or saying to yourself. Record your thoughts in the notebook.

The first step in changing how you think is to identify precisely how you think. This record of your thoughts will be an initial "snapshot" of your thought process that will be analyzed in the following lessons.

Re-Evaluate Your Should/Must Rules

Make a list of your personal should/must rules. Take several days to list things you catch yourself thinking or saying that contain the word or idea of should, must, or have to. Don't forget circular questioning and can't thinking are simply disguised forms of should/must thinking. Here are some examples:

"I should be calm when I go out."
"The house has to be cleaned by 11:00 a.m."

"Why can't I get to places on time?" = "I should always be on time."
"How could that person say such a rude thing?" = "People shouldn't say rude things."

After a few days, go through your list and evaluate the advantages and disadvantages of each should/must rule. Make a conscious decision about whether you want to keep, change, or eliminate any of the rules you have been following. Whenever you find yourself saying, thinking, or basing your actions on a rule you want to eliminate, use the various rational self-talk skills to challenge it. Practice using accurate and positive language when thinking or speaking about rules you decide to keep.

Be Patient

Remember that you progress at your own rate. You are currently at the beginning of this program and have much to learn. Whether or not you overcome the behaviors and symptoms associated with anxiety at the end of the fifteen lessons depends on many things.

- How severe your symptoms were when you began.
- How long you have experienced your symptoms.
- Your own individual personality.
- The strength of your commitment to change and overcome your old patterns.
- How much time and effort you put into the reading.
- How carefully you follow the instructions in the recommended reading.
- How much time and energy you put into practicing the activities you are asked to do.
- Whether or not there are any complicating factors such as a poor marriage or physical disability.

The above combination of factors is different for every person using this program. Some people overcome all the symptoms associated with anxiety in a few months. Others need to work on these skills for a year or more. Some people simply have more work to do to unlearn old patterns and develop new ones to replace them. How long it takes is not important. What is important is that you spend the time and energy required to reach your goal and use the lessons as they are intended to be used. If you are doing this, you will overcome the old patterns that generate and maintain your anxiety.

One common error many people with anxiety-related problems make is to have the goal of eliminating all anxiety. This is impossible. The only people who never experience anxiety are psychotic, brain damaged, drugged, or dead. Anxiety is a natural part of living and is often the most appropriate response to a real threat.

You are working towards two different goals: minimizing the overall amount of anxiety you experience, and managing the anxiety you do experience more effectively so it does not limit or interfere with your ability to enjoy life. Because this requires learning new skills as well as changing old thinking patterns and old attitudes, it is a gradual process. You are not in competition with anyone; just move along at your own rate, one that is just right for you.

Reward Your Successes

You will progress more rapidly if you develop the habit of rewarding yourself whenever you experience success with the skills you're developing. This does not mean you wait for your skills to work perfectly. Learn to congratulate yourself whenever a skill works, even it if is only a partial success. The easiest way to do this is with statements such as the following:

"I did it!"
"The skills I'm learning worked. I was able to do it!"
"Even though there was some anxiety, I didn't let it stop me."
"Wait until I tell my friend/spouse about this!"
"It wasn't as bad as I expected. It was actually much easier."
"I did well."
"It's getting better each time I use my skills."
"I'm really pleased with the progress I'm making."
"When I used my skills, it was easier than I thought it would be."
"I've just taken another step forward."

Saying complimentary statements like the above is often difficult for people with many of the high anxiety personality traits. If this is true for you, make a deliberate effort to learn how to compliment yourself. Another way of rewarding yourself after successes is to treat yourself to a special food or activity.

Negative Friends

At one time or another, everyone has known a negative person. This is someone who is always noticing flaws and dwelling on problems, illnesses, or unpleasant symptoms. Keep the following points in mind when you are around a negative person.

- When you are anxious or tense, you are more susceptible to the negativity of others.
- You are working on changing your habitual ways of thinking and acting. People with a negative outlook will slow you down and may even sabotage your work.
- Negative people are very energy draining. At this time you need to devote all of your energy to the task of overcoming your anxiety-related problems. You don't have energy to spare.

While working with these lessons, you may find it important to "let go" of negative friends and spend as little time with them as possible. The easiest way to "let go" of a negative friend is through "creative neglect." Simply be busy or unavailable whenever the negative friend wants to talk or spend time together. After overcoming your anxiety-related problems, you may resume these friendships.

Sometimes the negative person in your life is a relative, co-worker, or someone else you need to deal with on a regular basis. Here are three guidelines for dealing with negative people who are difficult to avoid.

Keep time spent with this person to a minimum.

Maintain as much emotional and physical distance as possible. If this person is a parent this is especially important since the parent-child relationship can be a very strong force and pull you back into old patterns very quickly. When you visit a negative parent, go for just an hour or at most a day. Two short visits are often easier to handle than one long visit. It is also useful to plan some neutral event as the focus of the visit such as a dinner, a game, or an outing to some event. You can then redirect the flow of conversation away from "hot" topics to the neutral event.

Use decompression routines.

After you have been in contact with a negative person, do an activity that helps to neutralize this person's negative influence. Do this as soon as possible after leaving the negative person. Examples of neutralizing activities are: spending time alone, reading the lesson on which you are currently working, doing a relaxation response exercise, or talking with someone who is positive and uplifting. This last suggestion is especially useful when you are dealing with a negative parent or parent figure. A short conversation or meeting with a positive support person is often enough to counteract the negative impact of time spent with a negative parent. In extreme cases a visit to a therapist is needed to undo the impact of a strong negative experience.

Develop defense mechanisms for dealing with negativity.

One approach that is useful when dealing with negative people is to be "unconscious." The best example of being unconscious is the reaction many children have towards their parents when the parents are nagging or scolding them. Just as a child can become "parent deaf," you can learn to be deaf and unconscious to the negativity of others. This becomes easier as the weeks go by and your skills in other areas increase.

Another approach is to use your imagination. Create an imaginary fence around yourself. Then imagine the negative thoughts and actions coming from the negative person bouncing off this imaginary shield. You can use this simple method to protect yourself whenever you are around a negative person. You can also imagine a trusted support person or religious figure standing next to you. You can even imagine how a person you respect would deal with the situation and pretend that you are this person.

As you work your way through this program you may discover other ways to reduce the influence negative people exert on you. When you do, be sure to write them down so you can refer to them when you are not thinking clearly and are going to be around a negative person. You may also find that as you change, the way you are treated by negative people may also change.

Spend at least one week on this lesson and
read it at least three times. If you feel
the urge to move ahead before a week is
over, use the time to review and practice
the skills presented in the previous lessons.

Eight Common Forms of Distorted Thinking

5 Lesson

With this lesson you have reached an important milestone in your quest to conquer anxiety. As you combine the knowledge and skills in this lesson with what you have already learned, you will begin to see your rate of progress increase more rapidly.

☐ *The Eight Common Forms of Distorted Thinking*

The following forms of thinking are called distorted thinking because they cause an irrational or unrealistic interpretation of events. This creates a distorted view of the world, yourself, and your place in the world which often causes self-defeating behaviors. From time to time you use most, if not all, of these forms of distorted thinking. This is especially true whenever you experience excessive stress, hunger, fatigue, or illness. Mark those forms which are most typical of the way you think and speak. Spend most of your time and energy with the ones you mark as you reread and study this lesson.

Each of the following descriptions includes an explanation of how rational self-talk can be used to challenge that particular form of distorted thinking. In the examples for this and following lessons, the specific types of rational self-talk used are labeled in parenthesis. If the different types of rational self-talk are confusing, make frequent reviews of their description in the section titled, The Cognitive Approach, in Lesson 4

Should/Must Thinking

Lesson 4 defined should/must thinking as the transformation of *personal* choices, wants, or preferences into *universal* absolutes. This is usually done by thinking in words and phrases such as "should," "must," "ought," and "have to." Lesson 4 also discussed two common variations of should/must thinking called circular questioning and can't thinking. There is one other common form of should/must thinking called *all-or-nothing thinking.*

All-or-nothing thinking—sometimes called dichotomous thinking—is the evaluation of personal qualities and events in terms of black-and-white categories. The words that are most frequently associated with this type of thinking are "right," "wrong", "good," and "bad." All-or-nothing thinking is always based on rigid should/must rules that forces experience into absolute "good" and "bad" categories. This creates a distorted view of the world that generates increased anxiety and depression. Events are rarely completely "good" or "bad."

All-or-nothing thinking plays a major role in perfectionism because it magnifies the importance of mistakes and imperfections. It also lowers self-esteem since any personal flaw or error causes you to view yourself as inadequate and worthless. All-or-nothing thinking also causes your experience of the world to be negative since events are rarely good enough to be considered positive.

The most effective rational self-talk approach to use when correcting all-or-nothing thinking is a rational challenge, followed by redirecting statements. Concentrate on finding examples that contradict the black-and-white categories you have created. Challenge any should/must or can't rules you identify as part of the all-or-nothing thinking and remind yourself that this is a perfectionistic form of thinking.

Example: Choy was in the process of overcoming social phobia and experienced a moderate amount of anxiety during part of a social event. She reacted by thinking: "I'm really blowing this. I wish I could do things right."

Choy's rational self-talk: "Wait a minute. What do I mean 'I'm really blowing this?' And what do I mean by 'doing things right?' (challenging questions). I'm really not doing that bad even though I'm somewhat uncomfortable. In fact, I have actually enjoyed part of this event (objective evaluation). There is no one "right" way to act. There are many ways to act and feel at an event like this. The way I am acting is just fine even though I may not like the way I feel. This anxiety only means I still sometimes become anxious in this type of situation (rational challenge). Now, let's practice using my skills (redirecting statement)."

Overgeneralization

Overgeneralization is the changing of a single negative event into a never-ending pattern of defeat or misfortune. This is usually done by using words like "never," "always," and "every."

The best way to reverse an overgeneralization is to remind yourself that a single negative event is just that—a single negative event and nothing more. Recalling at least one event that contradicts the negative overgeneralization also helps. Some people find their rational self-talk is strengthened if they begin with a question that emphasizes the extreme nature of the overgeneralization such as "Is it really true that I ALWAYS...?"

Example: Andy was planning an outing but woke up to bad weather and began thinking: "Why does it always rain when I plan something? I guess I can't do anything right."

Andy's rational self-talk: "Does it *always* rain when I plan something? And do I *never* do anything well (emphasizing the overgeneralization with a question)? I guess this is an overgeneralization. Actually, this is the first time this year I've planned an outing and it rained. I also have to admit that the last outing I planned went very well (objective evaluation)."

Labeling is a common form of overgeneralization in which you define yourself or your behavior in terms of a simplistic and usually negative label. Labeling is usually the result of internalizing labels that were used by parents or other adults to describe you when you were a child. As you matured, you internalized these labels and they became a habitual, automatic response that now occurs when flaws are noticed or when a mistake is made. Often, this is done because you have failed to distinguish between your actions and your personal worth as a human being. Here are some common negative labels. Check any you frequently use for yourself.

aggressive	illogical	selfish
bitchy	immature	sensitive
born loser	impolite	shrill
bossy	incapable	silly
castrating	insensitive	sissy
chauvinist	irrational	slow
childish	irresponsible	softy
cold	klutz	stubborn
competitive	lazy	stuck-up
compulsive	mean	stupid
conceited	nagging	superman/woman
crazy	nit-picking	thoughtless
critical	nosy	too sensitive
demanding	overactive	too idealistic
disgusting	overly emotional	troublemaker
dull	parental	ugly
dumb	passive	unassertive
egotistical	petty	ungrateful
emotional	pig	unimportant
failure	push	uninteresting
frigid	repulsive	weak
harsh	rotten	willful
hostile	self-pitying	wimpy
hysterical	self-centered	wrong

Sometimes seemingly positive labels can be as bad as negative ones. For example, a "nice guy" might allow himself to be taken advantage of rather than risk losing his positive self-image. Other examples of labels that seem positive but can create similar problems are gracious, good parent, good person, and in charge.

Labeling like the above is totally nonproductive. It is also inaccurate because one mistake or even a series of mistakes does not mean you are unable to change or be successful. Furthermore, since these types of labels are usually emotionally loaded, they generate strong negative feelings that often paralyze you or trigger self-defeating behavior.

Several types of rational self-talk can be used to combat labeling. Start with substitution. Dismiss the label for what it is—an inaccurate overgeneralization—and substitute more accurate, opposite, and positive words to describe the event or actions. The use of ego strengtheners is a good idea if you've been very hard on yourself. Finally, make an objective evaluation of the event or situation. If your labeling is in response to a mistake that you have made, use redirecting statements to remind yourself of the only two logical alternatives you have: a) do something practical to correct your error, and b) decide how you can reduce the chance of this event or error from recurring in the future. If your labeling is in response to a personal flaw or shortcoming you have noticed, use a rational challenge and remind yourself to separate your actions from your worth as a person.

Example: Pat is a shipping clerk who has sent a shipment to the wrong location. She catches herself dwelling on how she is worthless and always makes a mess of things.

Pat's rational self-talk: "Wait a minute. I am not a worthless screw-up! I am simply a human being who has made a mistake (substitution). People do this all the time. Actually, I'm a very good worker who is just as accurate and productive as the other clerks (ego strengtheners). Now, exactly what went wrong? It seems I punched the wrong code into the computer when I coded the address labels (objective evaluation). I guess the first thing I need to do is make sure that shipment gets re-routed. Then I can figure out how it got mixed up (redirecting statements)."

Magnification/Minimization

Magnification refers to two different types of exaggeration. The first, called *catastrophizing,* is the act of turning small personal flaws, minor negative experiences, or errors into major catastrophes. The second type of magnification is the exaggeration of someone else's achievements or abilities.

One common type of catastrophic self-talk involves phrases such as, "I can't stand this," or "I can't take it." These are inaccurate phrases. You may be unhappy, uncomfortable, and may even be responding ineffectively; however, since you are not dead or comatose, you are "standing it." Another common type of catastrophic self-talk is the labeling of events as terrible, awful, or horrible when they are actually only inconvenient. Words like these rarely describe everyday events or personal limitations accurately. When these types of catastrophic exaggerations become habitual reactions to everyday inconveniences, they trigger exaggerated emotional responses and unnecessary anxiety. More importantly, they paralyze you and prevent you from solving your problems and improving the situation.

One effective type of rational self-talk to use with catastrophizing is the substitution of more accurate language for the catastrophic descriptions. Sometimes a direct rational challenge or objective evaluation is also helpful. Remind yourself that you can stand events. An event may be inconvenient or a disappointment and may even involve negative consequences; however, it is only a tragedy when you define it as such, exaggerate its meaning, and magnify your limitations.

Example: Fred is having difficulty with an algebra homework assignment when he thinks: "This is awful. I can't stand not knowing how to do this."

Fred's rational self-talk: "What am I saying? It is true this is difficult and I am finding it frustrating. However, it is certainly not 'awful' (substitution). Saying I can't stand not knowing how to do this is also untrue. Even if I never figure this out, I'm not going to die (rational challenge). I always have the choice of quitting if I decide this frustration is more than I choose to endure. But now that I think about it, it's really not that bad. In fact, it's relatively minor compared with events that are truly awful. I am willing to experience some frustration in order to pass this class and receive my degree (objective evaluation)."

Exaggerating the achievements or abilities of others creates the illusion that your own achievements or abilities are of little value. It can also cause you to give up working toward developing a skill or ability since magnifying similar abilities or achievements in others makes them appear unattainable. All of this lowers self-esteem and can produce anxiety, depression, and self-condemnation.

When you catch yourself magnifying the abilities or achievements of others, evaluate their abilities objectively and use ego-strengtheners to remind yourself of your strengths and abilities. Redirecting statements can also be used to channel your energy into a different and more positive activity. Sometimes it helps to use a rational challenge. Remind yourself that anyone free from brain damage and physical disabilities can learn any skill if an effective method is used and enough time and energy are devoted to it. This does not guarantee you will become an expert, but you can at least achieve an average level of skill. In most human activities, from job skills to interpersonal skills, this is all you need to be successful.

Example: As Fred works on his assignment, he thinks: "Bob and Kay both seem to pick this stuff right up. In fact, everyone in the class seems to do better than me (this last statement is both a magnification and an overgeneralization)."

Fred's rational self-talk: "Hold on. Here I go again. I know I may never be as good at algebra as Bob and Kay. They are the best students in the class. However, I can do well enough to pass the class and that is all I need for my purposes (objective evaluation). Come to think of it, I received B's on my first two quizzes. That was better than many of the other people in class. So, I guess I can do just fine (ego strengtheners). Now let's take another look at this problem and come up with the best way to solve it. If I can't figure it out on my own, I'll ask Bob for help (redirecting statements)."

Minimization is the depreciation of personal strengths, abilities, and achievements as well as the mistakes and imperfections of others. Minimization and magnification usually occur together. For example, when you magnify another person's positive qualities and achievements, you also tend to minimize this person's negative qualities and failures. Likewise, when you magnify your own faults and errors, you usually minimize your strengths and successes.

When you catch yourself minimizing your own positive qualities and achievements, combat it with an objective evaluation and ego strengtheners. Identify specific personal strengths and achievements and affirm their importance and value. When you find yourself making others perfect by minimizing their mistakes and shortcomings, make an objective evaluation of their skills and accomplishments and identify specific shortcomings and flaws. At the same time, identify areas where you have skills and talent.

Example: While at a company dinner Margaret, a successful manager, found herself thinking: "Mary is such an excellent office manager. Her unit always runs so smoothly. I wish I had one-tenth of her ability."

Margaret's rational self-talk: "There I go putting myself down again. All my evaluations have very high ratings and I've been told many times how productive my unit is. I guess I really am a pretty good manager (objective evaluation/ego strengtheners). I also know that while Mary can do some things better than me, there are others at which I am the best. Her unit has its occasional problems and glitches just like mine. Last week's foul-up with the Mondale account is a good example (objective evaluation). So I guess we're both good, each in our own way (ego strengthener)."

Minimization is often called *discounting* and sometimes becomes so extreme that neutral and even positive experiences are interpreted as negative ones. When a person with this tendency cannot twist a positive event into a negative one, the person reduces it in importance by saying something such as, "This doesn't really count since it was just a fluke and wouldn't happen again in a million years." This type of discounting plays a major role in maintaining a negative belief system about oneself and is commonly associated with both depression and anxiety. With time the basic rational self-talk approach of pairing an objective evaluation with ego strengtheners will successfully overcome this type of minimization.

Example: Fred receives a compliment after helping out a friend at work and thinks: "Jim is probably just being nice and doesn't really mean it. He probably wouldn't even say that if he really knew how I was feeling today."

Fred's rational self-talk: "Wow! There I go discounting a perfectly wonderful compliment. If Jim had done the same for me, I would be genuinely grateful. So, why shouldn't Jim respond in the same manner? I guess he really is sincere (objective evaluation). While it feels funny, it's nice to be complimented like this. I deserve it (ego strengtheners)."

Personalization

Personalization, assuming responsibility for a negative event when there is no basis for doing so, is a major source of guilt. The key flaw in personalization is the confusion of *influence* with *control*. While you may exert much influence in some situations, your ability to control people and events usually exists only in your mind. Personalization usually leads to self-blame and negative self-labeling and is characteristic of people who experience life as helpless victims.

Personalization can be successfully challenged as follows. List the factors that could have caused the negative event for which you are assuming responsibility and assess the amount of influence you have over each factor. After you have evaluated all the factors you can think of, rate the degree of control you feel you have over the event. If you have difficulty with this process, ask someone you trust to help you. With practice you will be able to list many factors for a given event and evaluate them objectively on your own.

Example: Jean offers a mild constructive criticism to a friend, Jim, who becomes angry even though the criticism is valid and worded positively. Jean responds by thinking: "Now there I go again hurting someone. When will I learn to just keep my big mouth shut. It's all my fault that Jim is so upset and will not enjoy the rest of this event."

Jean's rational self-talk: "It looks like I'm falling into the personalization trap. Now, what are some factors that could have caused Jim's anger? What I said is certainly one factor. Jim has been under a lot of pressure from work lately and he also tends to be overly sensitive at times. I also know that people are always interpreting what events mean and sometimes interpret them incorrectly. So how much influence do I really have over these factors? I have complete control over how I say things; however, I have no influence over Jim's work or the way he interprets events. I also know the way I stated the criticism was positive and would have been received well by most people I know. I guess Jim is reacting badly for reasons over which I have no influence (objective evaluation). I guess my next decision is to decide whether I want to do something about what happened or just forget about it (redirecting statement)."

Mind Reading

Whenever you assume what other people are thinking or feeling with little or no evidence to support the assumption and no attempt to confirm or deny the assumption, you are mind reading. This type of distorted thinking is a major source of discord in relationships and helps maintain a host of irrational beliefs.

When you catch yourself mind-reading, ask the question, "What evidence do I have to support my assumption?" If there is little or no evidence, decide how evidence could be obtained. During an objective evaluation of someone's behavior it often helps to ask yourself, "Would this mean the same thing if I did it?"

Example: Barbara walks by a friend who is reading a book and says, "Good morning." The friend, Jack, does not say anything and Barbara begins thinking: "I guess Jack is angry with me. I wonder what I did?"

Barbara's rational self-talk: "Stop right there. What evidence do I have to support my assumption that Jack is angry with me? All that happened was I saw him reading, said, 'Good morning,' and he did not respond. When I don't respond to someone, does it always mean I am angry? Sometimes, but not always. Jack was reading a book. I guess sometimes I get so involved in what I am doing I don't hear what people are saying (objective evaluation). I guess I could just ask Jack if he heard me. If he did, I could ask why he didn't respond (redirecting statements).

Fortune Telling

When you make a negative prediction and then convince yourself it is an established fact, you are fortune telling. Essentially, fortune telling is the confusion of a *possibility* with a *probability*. This type of negative prediction often becomes a self-fulfilling prophecy.

When you notice yourself making a negative prediction, stop and evaluate the prediction objectively. Ask yourself: a) "What is the probability (or possibility) of this occurring?" and b) "What facts do I have to support the estimate I have just made?" If this type of evaluation is difficult for you, ask someone you trust to help. It also helps to remind yourself that there is no way for you to know what will happen since you are not omniscient. A prediction is merely a guess about what might happen. The fewer facts you have, the poorer your guess.

Example: Gary is considering taking a new job. He has no experience in this field and begins to think: "I've never really done that type of work before. I bet it will be hard to learn. What if I can't catch on to what I am supposed to do? I don't think I can do this job. What am I going to do?"

Gary's rational self-talk: "It seems I am acting as if I knew what was going to happen when I'm just guessing. What is the probability of my not being successful at this job (question "a")? Right now I would guess it is fairly high. What facts do I have to support the guess I have just made (question "b")? Actually, very few. The closest job I've ever had to this one was my last job. I was pretty good at it. I also know I learn things fairly quickly even though I am somewhat of a perfectionist and often don't give myself credit for what I have accomplished. I guess the chances of my succeeding are really very good. The probability of my being unable to do the work is low (objective evaluation)."

Accepting Questionable Sources as Authoritative

This refers to the acceptance of a person's opinion or advice as reliable and authoritative even though it is colored by vested interest, ignorance, lack of experience, or prejudice. If you frequently accept questionable sources as authoritative, develop the habit of making an objective evaluation of the opinions and advice you receive. Do this by asking yourself: a) "What experience or training makes this person an expert in this area?" and b) "Does this person have any biases or interests that might influence the opinion or advice being offered?" After evaluating the source, you are ready to make an objective evaluation of the opinion or advice given.

Example: Sharon was planning to take dance lessons. Her friend Ann told her she would not do well because she had poor timing and lacked coordination. Sharon began thinking: "I guess I'll have to give up my plans to take dance lessons."

Sharon's rational self-talk: "Wait. What makes Ann an expert (question "a")? Does she dance well? No. Has she ever taken dance lessons herself? No, not to my knowledge. Does Ann have any biases or interests which influenced this advice (question "b")? Yes. She is very negative and always tells people they won't succeed (evaluation of the source). Now, let's look at what Ann actually said. I really don't need excellent timing and coordination for the kind of dancing I want to learn. All I want to do is have some fun and be able to hold my own on a dance floor. I don't think you need to have more than average ability to do that. I don't think Ann's opinion is at all valid (objective evaluation of the opinion)."

Emotional Reasoning

Emotional reasoning is using emotions as objective evidence of a truth or to validate a belief or thought. Decisions or evaluations are based solely on your emotional reaction without an objective evaluation of the facts involved. For example, you feel awkward in a situation and use this as the sole basis for deciding you do not belong there and should leave. Emotional reasoning is sometimes called analogical reasoning because the analogy between one's emotions and objective reality is taken as fact even though it may not be true.

Lesson 4 described how emotions only reflect your interpretation of an event. Emotions provide important information because they are triggered by needs and wants being met, frustrated, or threatened. However, needs and events can be easily distorted by irrational beliefs and faulty habitual thinking patterns. Emotions generated by distorted thinking feel just as strong and seem just as valid as emotions generated by rational thinking. This is why it is self-defeating to follow emotions blindly as is characteristic of emotional reasoning. The information provided by emotions is important but needs to be evaluated objectively for an accurate understanding of what it means.

From the above it might seem that all decisions should be made on the basis of pure logic. This is not true. In fact, people who actively suppress their emotions and try to rely on strict logic often experience just as many inappropriate emotions and self-defeating behaviors as emotional reasoners. The reason for this is simple. Because emotions signal when a need or want is either being satisfied, frustrated, or threatened, suppression of emotions tends to block awareness of when needs are not being met.

When an important need is not met, it eventually generates one or more of the following: 1) a physical reaction due to the constant triggering of your fight or flight response; 2) an inappropriate emotional response—the three most common ones being anger, anxiety, or depression that is either too intense for a given situation or occurring for no apparent reason; or 3) self-defeating behaviors.

Popular self-help books often state that it is important to be "in touch" with your emotions. Unfortunately, this often means that it is important to be more emotional or use emotional reasoning. The healthy management of your emotions involves the following three steps:

- Accurately identifying the emotion you are experiencing.
- Accurately identifying the need or want that is generating the emotion.
- Developing a plan that meets the need or want in an appropriate and realistic way.

Because effective decisions are usually based on both emotion and reason, the most effective rational self-talk approach to use with emotional reasoning is an objective evaluation that involves the above three steps. Whenever you experience strong emotions, first label the emotion. Then identify the need or want that is generating the emotion. Only then can you objectively consider the situation and decide on the best course of action. Sometimes emotional reasoning takes the form of a recurring pattern involving a certain type of emotion in a certain type of situation. When this is the case, it can also be helpful to recall past situations in which you experienced similar emotions and decide whether the emotions were the result of rational or irrational thinking.

Emotional reasoning is often accompanied by other types of distorted thinking. Identify the types and use rational self-talk to correct them. Take a few minutes to calm down before doing this. As you examine your thoughts, relabel magnified emotions more accurately.

Example: Charles has a high-stress job. One day he begins to feel very anxious and somewhat confused and thinks: "I feel like I'm going crazy! Why can't I even handle simple things? I'm really beginning to crack up!"

Charles's rational self-talk: "Wait a minute. I think I'm using emotional reasoning. Let's calm down and use those three steps I read about. The emotion I'm feeling is anxiety (identify the emotion). That means some need or want is threatened in some way. That's easy to identify. I want to do well and I'm afraid I might do poorly. I'm also afraid that this might cause people to think poorly of me and laugh at me. This is just my old excessive need for approval "button" getting pushed again (identify the need or want). Now, let's come up with a plan to deal with these fears. I do feel somewhat disoriented but that is really not being 'crazy.' I'm just over stressed right now and exaggerating the importance of what I'm feeling. I've handled many situations far more difficult than this and am really doing fairly well at this one. Because I'm tired and overworked, I'm just not doing as well as I usually do. I am not going to lose my job. As far as people laughing at me or thinking poorly about me, most of the people in this office are reacting the same way and are sympathetic. In fact, some have said I'm doing very well (objective evaluation/relabeling). As I think about it, this is something I have often done in the past. Whenever I get over stressed I begin to think there is something wrong with me emotionally when I'm really just tired (recalling a past event and identifying the pattern). I need to cut back on my outside activities and get some rest. Then I'll feel like my old self again (redirecting statements)."

☐ *Changing the Way You Think*

Changing behavior is essentially a three step process. First, you identify precisely those behaviors you want to eliminate. Second, you identify precisely those behaviors you do want. Third, you practice substituting behaviors you want for those you wish to eliminate. A good example of this process would be Cyrus who has been using incorrect fingers while typing but who now wants to improve his speed. First, he needs to identify which keys he has been hitting with the correct fingers and which keys he has been hitting with incorrect fingers. Then he identifies the correct fingers he needs to practice. Finally, he practices exercises that emphasize the correct usage of the fingers he has been using improperly. With time and practice the new patterns replace the old ones.

Changing the way you think is a similar process. First, you need to identify precisely when and how you think irrationally. Next, you develop rational self-talk that challenges the specific forms of distorted thinking you use. Finally, you practice the rational self-talk until it becomes automatic. At first, this practice usually is done after an incident has occurred. However, with time, the use of rational self-talk becomes more spontaneous. The recommended activities for this lesson describes exercises that accomplish each of these steps in detail.

As a first step in this process, take a moment to examine the summary of the eight forms of distorted thinking described in Lessons 4 and 5 listed below. Everyone uses all of them some of the time. However, a person usually has some that are used more than the others. Put a check by those you use most frequently.

☐ *Should/Must Thinking:* The transformation of *personal* choices, wants, or preferences into *universal* absolutes. This is usually done by thinking in words and phrases such as "should," "must," "ought," and "have to." Should/must thinking can also be expressed indirectly through:

> *Circular questioning:* The repeated asking of questions that are irrelevant or have an answer you already know but are unwilling to accept. Common examples include "Why am I like this?" "Why can't I change?" "How could he/she do that?" and "How could that happen?"

> *Can't thinking:* The use of the word "can't" to describe a need, want, decision, or choice.

All-Or-Nothing Thinking: The tendency to evaluate personal qualities and events in extreme, black-and-white categories. This is often expressed with the words "right," "wrong," "good," and "bad."

❑ *Overgeneralization:* The transformation of a single negative event into a never-ending pattern of defeat or misfortune. Often this is done by using words like "never," "always," and "every." A common variation is:

Labeling: The use of simplistic and usually negative labels to define yourself or your behavior that exaggerates the importance of shortcomings or mistakes.

❑ *Magnification/Minimization:* Magnification includes two types of exaggerations: catastrophizing, which is the exaggeration of personal flaws, small negative experiences, and mistakes; and the exaggeration of the abilities of others. Minimization, sometimes called discounting, also comes in two forms: the depreciation of personal strengths, abilities, or achievements; and the depreciation of mistakes and imperfections in others.

❑ *Personalization:* The act of assuming responsibility for a negative event when there is no basis for doing so.

❑ *Mind Reading:* Assuming what other people are thinking or feeling with little or no evidence to support the assumption and no attempt to confirm or deny the assumption.

❑ *Fortune Telling:* Making a prediction and then convincing yourself it is an already established fact.

❑ *Accepting Questionable Sources as Authoritative:* Accepting as reliable an opinion or advice colored by vested interest, ignorance, lack of experience, or prejudice.

❑ *Emotional Reasoning:* The use of emotions as the primary or only means for evaluating a situation, event, or belief.

Recommended Activities for Lesson 5

Continue Developing Your Relaxation Response

Continue practicing your relaxation response at least once a day. Also, continue to associate the cue you selected while doing Lesson 2 with the deep relaxation you are practicing. Continue this daily practice for the rest of the program.

Take Your Time with this Lesson

It is easy to feel overwhelmed when you first read this lesson. There is a lot of information in it. Applying it all to your life usually takes many weeks or months. Fortunately, you do not have to do everything during the week you are working on this lesson. Future lessons refer back to the various types of distorted thinking described in this one and provide you with additional opportunities to work on them. Do as much as you can during the week you work with the lesson. If you are very busy consider spending two weeks with this lesson.

Learn the Words Used to Identify Distorted Thinking

The lesson stated that the first step in changing behavior was to identify precisely those behaviors you want to eliminate. Before you can do this, you need to learn the words used to identify distorted thinking.

Practice Identifying Distorted Thinking in Vignettes

A series of vignettes are located at the end of this lesson. These are simply samples of negative self-talk that various people recorded during times when they were upset. Identifying the forms of distorted thinking used in each vignette.

Practice Identifying Distorted Thinking in Others

While you talk with others, watch television, listen to people talking on the radio, or listen to people talking around you, identify the various types of distorted thinking they use. It helps if you make a game out of it. Do not tell others what you are doing as you do this exercise. Many people become either defensive or offended when their distorted thinking is pointed out.

This is a powerful and important exercise for two reasons. First, it's an excellent way to become skilled at identifying distorted thinking. If you are like most people, it is easier to see distorted thinking in others rather than yourself. Second, you soon come to realize that humans are terribly irrational. We pride ourselves on our ability to reason, and much of the time we do think in a fairly logical manner. However, whenever we are feeling strong emotions, we tend to use many, if not all, of the forms of distorted thinking described in this lesson. Seeing this distorted thinking in others enables you to see it as normal and avoid labeling yourself as "crazy" or "weird" because you often used distorted thinking. This, in turn, makes it easier to both accept and identify your own distorted thinking.

The Block Method

The way you think is a learned habit pattern. The Block Method applies the steps for changing behavior described in the lesson to the task of changing the way you think. The three steps are as follows:

Record samples of self-talk during times when you are upset.

Lesson 4 asked you to obtain a notebook or binder you can use to record your thoughts. If you have not done this, do so this week. Spend five minutes every other day recalling times when you were anxious or upset or doing a self-defeating behavior. Take a moment to mentally place yourself back into the event and recall what you were thinking or saying to yourself. Then list as many of the thoughts you had at that time as you can recall. When possible, record your thoughts while you are in the middle of an upset or self-defeating behavior. When recording your thoughts in the middle of an upset or self-defeating behavior, simply take a moment to monitor your self-talk and list your thoughts at the top of a piece of paper.

Identify the forms of distorted thinking that are present and develop rational self-talk that challenges the distortions.

After you have listed as much of your self-talk as you can recall, reread what you have written and identify any forms of distorted thinking that are present. When you identify a sentence or phrase that represents distorted thinking, rewrite the statement a little lower on the page. Label the statement by writing the name for the type of distorted thinking the statement represents after it. Then, just below the statement, write out a rational self-talk response.

Rehearse the rational self-talk you have developed.

After you have analyzed your self-talk and completed your rational responses, spend a few minutes rehearsing the rational responses you developed. Mentally place yourself in the situation and practice saying the responses. Rehearsing the rational self-talk responses you develop in this manner is the quickest way to make this new way of thinking a part of your automatic behavior. In time it will replace the irrational, automatic self-talk that generates much of your anxiety.

Here is an example of how Elliot applied the Block Method to a situation where he became anxious while waiting to meet his friend, Bob. The following sample of self-talk is condensed from a paragraph Elliot wrote while he was waiting.

Record samples of self-talk during times when you are upset.

"Where is Bob? I can't stand it when this happens. Bob is going to forget and I'll be left standing here forever. Why do I do this to myself?"

Identify the forms of distorted thinking that are present and develop rational self-talk that challenges the distortions.

(Note: The negative self-talk and corresponding rational responses are labeled to make the example easy to follow. You do not need to label everything you write when using this method)

Self-Talk: "Where is Bob?" (rational thought)

Rational response: This is a normal and rational thought. I was uncomfortable not knowing where Bob was and wondering if something had happened to him.

Self-talk: "I can't stand this." (magnification)

Rational response: "I can stand this. I may be anxious, but I am functioning well."

Self-talk: "Bob is going to forget and I'll be left standing here forever." (fortune telling and magnification)

Rational response: "It's possible that Bob may forget. However, he is very reliable and usually remembers appointments. As far as standing here forever goes, it was only a few minutes. I know I can always wait fifteen minutes, leave a note and go. Fifteen minutes is really not that long."

Self-talk: "Why do I do this to myself?" (should/must thinking in the form of circular questioning and magnification)

Rational response: "I'm actually saying I shouldn't be this way and it's terrible that I am. While I want to change and don't like some of the things I do, given my background I am exactly who and what I "should" be. Furthermore, I am in the process of learning how to think and act in new and more effective ways. This is a process that takes time. As for this being terrible, it is really only inconvenient."

Rehearse the rational self-talk you have developed.

Elliot rehearsed his rational responses several times then laid his work aside. Elliot experienced more incidents like this over the next few weeks. For each one, he recorded his self-talk, analyzed and developed rational responses, then rehearsed the rational responses. Eventually, he found himself challenging his distorted thinking almost as fast as it occurred. As this began to take place, he found himself using less distorted thinking.

One of the recommended activities in Lesson 4 asked you to begin monitoring your self-talk and record thoughts and phrases you noticed yourself repeating during times when you were anxious or upset. Use the Block Method to analyze what you wrote and develop rational responses. If rational self-talk is difficult for you, select appropriate examples from this lesson and copy them exactly as they appear. Then see if you can change the examples to fit both your personality and the situation more closely.

Continue recording your thoughts during times when you are anxious or upset and using the Block Method to challenge them for the rest of this program.

The Good Day Rule

The good day rule is simple: *work hardest at developing the skills presented in this program when you are feeling your best—on your good days.* People tend to work hardest when they are feeling their worst. Pain can provide strong motivation to take the actions required to change behavior. When you're feeling good, it's easy to discount the need to continue working. Since you do not complete the work needed to change the thinking and behavior patterns that generate anxiety, you set yourself up for a relapse into old patterns when you again encounter the right stressors.

Remind yourself periodically of this tendency to put off work when things are going well. Then commit yourself to the task of working with this program hardest when you are feeling good. When you do, you find that ideas and skills that seemed very difficult when you were having a bad day, are easy to master on your good days. Following the "good day rule" is the fastest way to progress.

Indications Your Body Is Sick, Hungry, Tired or Overstressed

Irrational thinking, self-defeating behaviors, and unpleasant physical symptoms increase whenever you are sick, hungry, tired, or overstressed. This is normal. Everyone experiences this to some degree. As pointed out in Lesson 3, the best way to minimize these reactions is to become skilled at identifying the early signs of stress and fatigue. Here are several common symptoms:

- Irritability.
- Tension or pain (common places are the head, neck, shoulders, stomach, arms, or legs).
- A change in the way you use language (often the increased use of profanity, put-downs, sarcasm, or other negative language you normally do not use).
- Increased emotionality (you become upset or excited more easily than normal).
- Inability to concentrate or think straight.
- Memory deficiency (you cannot remember things as well as you usually do and may forget important things).
- Unusual behavior or thoughts ("weird" or morbid thoughts).

Your specific signs may be one or more of the above or they may be something not on the list. Review the symptoms you listed in Lesson 3 on the Stress Symptom Inventory. Identify three to five specific symptoms you can use this week which indicate your body has used its limited supply of energy and needs time to rest and rebuild itself. Whenever you notice one of these symptoms, reduce your activities and take care of your body's physical needs.

Two or Three Steps Forward, One Step Backward

Progress is rarely continuous. Often, you go two or three steps forward then one step backward. There will be times when you slip into old patterns or need to stop briefly to practice what you have learned. Unfortunately, people with anxiety-related problems often attach great significance to lapses into old behaviors or resting periods. The result is usually self-talk similar to the following.

"This experience proves that nothing works (all-or-nothing thinking)."

"I will never get over this (fortune telling)."

"This experience is awful (magnification) and has undone all of the work I have done (overgeneralization/fortune telling)."

"If I return to past behavior this one time it means I will always return to it (overgeneralization). I will never change or overcome this condition (fortune telling)."

"This is a major setback (magnification/labeling). I guess I haven't really changed anything (minimization)."

Whenever you have a lapse into old behaviors or are in a resting period, challenge this type of negative self-talk with rational self-talk. Remind yourself that it is normal to slip into old behavior patterns periodically. It is not a failure. Eliminate the term "setback" from your vocabulary and start referring to these experiences as "lapses," "learning experiences," or "resting periods." Then examine the experience objectively by answering the following questions.

Trouble-Shooting Checklist

- Was I tired, sick, or hungry? (this will be the primary cause of most lapses)
- Did I use the skills I have been learning?
- If so, how did I use them?
- Did I forget to use one or more important skills? (refer to the summary at the end of this set of recommended activities)
- How can I handle this type of situation more effectively in the future? (answer this question in detail)

Using the above checklist turns lapses into old behaviors into valuable lessons and creates a firm foundation for future growth. As you begin to accept these negative experiences as a natural part of the relearning process, you no longer view them with alarm. With time your lapses into old patterns become fewer and farther apart.

Summary of Skills for Reducing Anxiety

The following is a summary of the skills for managing stress and reducing anxiety that have been presented so far in the program. Page references for each skill can be found in the index at the back of the book.

Methods for Reducing the Symptoms of Anxiety

1. Understand what causes and maintains severe anxiety
   - You experienced frightening physical symptoms and told yourself lies about what the symptoms meant.

- Because the symptoms frightened you, you worried about them and became aware of any body sensation that resembled the frightening symptoms in any way.
- Whenever you noticed a physical sensation that resembled the frightening symptoms in any way, you repeated the lies you had been telling yourself about the symptoms. This caused the symptoms to increase and you fell into the anxiety/panic cycle.
2. Use cue-controlled relaxation or, if practical, a relaxation response exercise.
3. Check your breathing and use relaxed diaphragmatic breathing to correct any tendency to hyperventilate that is present. (Do not spend too much time focusing on your breathing.)
4. Use coping self-statements to tell yourself the truth about your physical symptoms and remind yourself of your various coping skills.
5. Distract yourself with one or more of the following:
   - Simple externalization: observing carefully, listening attentively, feeling textures, tasting or smelling, doing repetitive activities.
   - Simple tasks which require concentration.
   - Conversation.
   - Work.
   - Play.
6. Other things to do when experiencing severe anxiety:
   - Eliminate caffeine intake.
   - Be patient.
   - Reduce contact with negative friends.
   - Wait to help others until after you have overcome your condition.
   - Work hardest at developing the skills presented in this program when you are feeling your best.
   - Reward yourself when you have successes, even small ones.
   - Turn negative experiences into valuable learning experiences by reviewing them in an objective, trouble-shooting fashion to determine what you could do differently next time.

Make effective stress management a part of your daily life.

1. Basic stress management principles:
   - Treat your body with respect by understanding and using the concept of your body as a machine with a limited supply of energy.
   - Learn to recognize the early signs of stress and what they mean.
   - Build stress tolerance with a balanced diet and exercise.
2. Guidelines for periods of high stress:
   - Set priorities and reduce your overall activities.
   - Spend extra time with decisions. For major decisions, consult with people you trust who are objective.
   - Plan ahead for high stress periods and take action during times when stress is low.

3. Develop a life style based on stress management principles
   - Eat a balanced diet.
   - Exercise regularly.
   - Make relaxation a regular part of your life.
   - Develop a decompression routine if working at a high stress job.
   - Take time to play.
   - Develop a good sense of humor.
   - Build a strong emotional support system.
   - Develop a strong source of spiritual support.
   - Create traditions and routines that support the above.

Reduce a major internal source of anxiety by using the Block Method to identify and challenge distorted thinking you are using.

Vignettes

Use the following series of vignettes to increase your ability to identify distorted thinking. As you read each vignette, circle the answer or answers that describes a form of distorted thinking present in the vignette.

Sample: Shirley has had a disappointing day. As she goes outside, she finds a large bird dropping in the middle of her car's front windshield. She thinks: "Look at that! A million cars and birds always seem to find mine. I can't stand it. It seems like things always go from bad to worse. I guess Bob was right when he said I'd never make it in this business. I feel like such a failure. I guess I'm pretty worthless."

a. Overgeneralization
b. Magnification/Minimization
c. Accepting questionable sources as authoritative
d. Emotional reasoning

Answer: If you circled any of the above answers you were right. Here is a detailed breakdown: "A million cars and birds always seem to find mine (overgeneralization). I can't stand it (magnification). It seems like things always go from bad to worse (overgeneralization/magnification). I guess Bob was right when he said I'd never make it in this business (accepting questionable sources as authoritative). I feel like such a failure. I guess I am pretty worthless (emotional reasoning and overgeneralization in the form of labeling)."

The answers for the rest of the vignettes are at the end of the quiz. Remember that the labels for the distorted thinking are arbitrary. A given thought may reflect two or more different types of distorted thinking.

1. A friend calls Mike to cancel a luncheon date because of illness. Mike is very disappointed and thinks: "It looks like Mr. Nobody strikes out again. I guess I don't even make a good luncheon companion. I wonder what I did to foul things up this time."

a. Mind reading
b. Fortune telling
c. Overgeneralization
d. Magnification/Minimization
e. Personalization

2. Lorna has a four-year-old son. Lorna's friend has no children but suggests that Lorna should be teaching her son how to read. Lorna reacts by thinking: "I guess Sue is right. I should be doing more. She always seems to know so much more than I do."

    a. Overgeneralization
    b. Accepting questionable sources as authoritative.
    c. Fortune telling
    d. Should/must thinking
    e. Magnification/Minimization

3. Ralph has just learned that one of his employees has been caught stealing. He thinks: "Why does this type of stuff always happen to me. I feel so foolish for not knowing that something was going on. I guess I am responsible for letting this happen.

    a. Should/must thinking
    b. Overgeneralization
    c. Emotional reasoning
    d. Personalization
    e. Mind reading

4. Yuriko meets a close friend who seems somewhat quiet and aloof and thinks: "Mary seems angry with me. I wonder what I've done? I know it's going to be impossible to find out what it is."

    a. Should/must thinking
    b. Mind reading
    c. Emotional reasoning
    d. Personalization
    e. Fortune telling

5. Alex has just completed refinishing a chair. A friend is commenting on how nice it looks when Alex notices a small spot that was not done very well. Alex thinks: "Look at that spot on the leg. It ruins everything. Why didn't I see it before? I bet Bob sees it but is just being polite by saying how nice the chair looks."

    a. Overgeneralization
    b. Emotional reasoning
    c. Should/must thinking
    d. Mind reading
    e. Magnification/Minimization

6. Maria has completed this book and made much progress in overcoming her anxiety-related problems. During a three day period she falls back into several of her old, self-defeating patterns and begins to think: "This is terrible. The last few weeks must have just been a fluke. I guess this stuff is no good after all. I'm never going to get better."

   a. Magnification/Minimization
   b. Accepting questionable sources as authoritative
   c. Should/must thinking
   d. Fortune telling
   e. Mind reading

7. Larry's roommate, Ted, is very sloppy and does not help much with cleaning. When Larry asked Ted for more help, Ted became angry and Larry began to think: "I guess Ted is right, I do expect a lot from him. He really does try to help and is really not that sloppy. I feel bad that I upset him."

   a. Accepting questionable sources as authoritative
   b. All-or-nothing
   c. Magnification/Minimization
   d. Emotional reasoning
   e. Personalization

8. Jane has been putting off working on a report for work. As the deadline for its completion approaches she thinks: "I'm so lazy. I'll never get this report done. I'm just not able to do these types of things."

   a. Should/must thinking
   b. Labeling
   c. Fortune telling
   d. Magnification/Minimization
   e. Overgeneralization

Answers

1. C, D. E: "It looks like Mr. Nobody strikes out again (overgeneralization in the form of labeling). I guess I don't even make a good luncheon companion (minimization and overgeneralization in the form of labeling). I wonder what I did to foul things up this time (personalization)."

2. B, D, E: "I guess Sue is right (accepting questionable sources as authoritative). I should be doing more (should/must thinking). She always seems to know so much more than I do (magnification)."

3. A, B, C, D: "Why does this type of stuff always happen to me (overgeneralization & should/must thinking in the form of circular questioning: this shouldn't happen)? I feel so foolish for not knowing that something was going on. I guess I am responsible for letting this happen (emotional reasoning/personalization)."

4. B, D, E: "Mary seems angry with me (mind reading). I wonder what I've done (personalization)? I know it's going to be impossible to find out what it is (fortune telling)."

5. A, C, D, E: "Look at that spot on the leg. It ruins everything (Overgenralization and should/must thinking in the form of all-or-nothing thinking: I should do things with no mistakes). Why didn't I see it before (should/must thinking in the form of circular why questioning—I should have seen it)? I bet Bob sees it but is just being polite by saying how nice the chair looks (mind reading and minimization)."

6. A, C, D: "This is terrible (magnification). The last few weeks must have just been a fluke. I guess this stuff is no good after all (minimization and should/must thinking in the form of all-or-nothing thinking: this program should work perfectly with no relapses into old patterns). I'm never going to get better (fortune telling)."

7. A, C, E: "I guess Ted is right. I do expect a lot from him (accepting questionable sources as authoritative). He really does try to help (magnification) and is really not that sloppy (minimization). I feel bad that I upset him (personalization)."

8. A, B, C, D: "I'm so lazy (overgeneralization in the form of labeling). I'll never get this report done (fortune telling). I'm just not able to do these types of things (minimization and should/must thinking in the form of can't thinking (not able = can't): I should be able to do these do reports perfectly with no procrastination)."

> The concepts and skills presented in this
> lesson form the foundation for much of the work
> presented in the following lessons.
> If your time is limited or if you are finding
> it difficult to develop rational self-talk
> skills, spend an extra week with this lesson.

Learning to Enjoy Being Human

This lesson shows you how to use the skills you developed in the earlier lessons to overcome perfectionism. Learning to laugh at mistakes and enjoy being human is one of the keys to conquering anxiety. Take your time and learn this lesson thoroughly.

☐ *The Characteristics of Perfectionism*

Perfectionism has three primary characteristics. The first is the tendency to set unrealistically high personal standards and goals. The second is the tendency to use all-or-nothing thinking when evaluating one's actions and to consider as a failure any achievement not meeting the unrealistically high standards. The third characteristic is a selective point of view that focuses on small flaws and errors rather than on one's overall progress or achievement.

These perfectionistic tendencies can be restricted to one or two areas of a person's life or can dominate one's entire existence. They tend to cause personal achievements to be considered inadequate and often lead to self-condemnation. When this occurs, the result is a lowering of self-esteem and a poor self-image. In addition, these tendencies can also generate a fear of failure which causes a person to avoid taking risks and trying new, unfamiliar activities.

Many people are unaware of their perfectionistic tendencies. However, people with anxiety-related problems usually find that perfectionism plays at least some part in their anxiety-related problem. Common examples of perfectionistic self-talk are listed below in the left column. The form of distorted thinking that each one represents is listed in the right column. Take a moment to read the examples of self-talk in the left-hand column and place a check by any of the phrases you use or that are similar to ones you use. Do not read the descriptions in the right hand column until you have done this. Be sure to record in your notebook any phrases you use frequently that are variations of the examples.

"I should be able to (or have to) do this right."	Should/must thinking.
"I shouldn't have made that mistake."	Should/must thinking.
"Why can't I do this right?"	Should/must thinking in the form of circular questioning: I should always do things correctly.
"Why didn't I see that mistake?"	Should/must thinking in the form of circular questioning: I should never make mistakes.
"How could I let something like that happen?"	Should/must thinking in the form of circular questioning: I should be able to prevent this.
"I can't do that."	Should/must thinking in the form of can't thinking: I don't want to do this or I shouldn't do this.
"This is all wrong."	Should/must thinking in the form of all-or-nothing thinking: I should never make mistakes.
"I just can't seem to find a good answer."	Should/must thinking in the form of all-or-nothing thinking: I should always be able to find the perfect solution to problems.
"Why do I act so stupid?"	Should/must thinking in the form of circular questioning and overgeneralization/labeling: I should always understand things.
"I'm *always* so clumsy (thoughtless, etc.)."	Overgeneralization/labeling with the underlying should/must rule: I should always be graceful, witty, and never make mistakes.
"I *never* seem to get this right."	Overgeneralization with the underlying should/must rule: I should never make mistakes.

"*Every* time I try to make one of these it comes out all wrong."	Overgeneralization with the underlying should/must rule: I should be skilled at everything I do.
"No matter how hard I try I *always* seem to come up short."	Overgeneralizaton with the underlying should/must rule: I should always be skilled at everything I do.
"This is awful (said in response to a small error)."	Magnification with the underlying should/must rule: I should never make mistakes.
"I can't stand not knowing how to do this (or do this right)."	Magnification with the underlying should/must rule: I should never make mistakes.
"Look at this error; it ruins everything I've done."	Magnification with the underlying should must rule: I should be able to do things perfectly.

Now go back through the above list and read the description in the right hand column that identifies the type of distorted thinking that is being used with each phrase you checked.

☐ *Challenge Beliefs that Support Perfectionism*

A complex trait like perfectionism is a combination of many different irrational beliefs and learned habit patterns. Unfortunately, people with this trait often are unaware of their irrational beliefs because they are part of the core beliefs developed during childhood. The reasons for this are discussed in detail in Lesson 4.

Fortunately, most of the irrational beliefs and habitual thinking patterns from childhood are not that hard to identify. All you need to do is examine your current thoughts and behavior carefully. As an old saying states, "If it looks like a duck, walks like a duck, and sounds like a duck, it's probably a duck." In the same way, if you look like you believe an idea, act like you believe an idea, and sound like you believe an idea, that idea is part of your belief system and generating at least some of its behavior.

Whenever you act, think, or talk in ways similar to those described in the preceding section, you are basing your interpretation of events on perfectionistic should/must rules. These rules are themselves generated by one or more of the perfectionistic beliefs described below. Whenever you notice yourself acting or thinking in a perfectionistic manner, take a moment to challenge the irrational belief generating your perfectionistic interpretation with the rational self-talk described in the following.

The Irrational Belief that Perfection is Possible

The first and most basic irrational, perfectionistic belief to challenge is the notion that perfection is possible. Here are several examples of statements that challenge this irrational belief.

- The idea of perfection is an abstract concept that only exists in theory.
- There is always some imperfection, some improvement that can be made in everything you see and do.
- Because we live in an imperfect world a person who strives for perfection is guaranteed failure.

The Irrational Belief that a Person's Worth Is Determined by Achievement

Underlying much of your behavior is a search for belonging and significance. People with perfectionistic tendencies often base their behavior on the irrational belief that worth is determined by achievement. The combination of this mistaken idea and perfectionistic tendencies creates a no-win situation in which you feel worthwhile only when you achieve, yet your achievements always fall short of your perfectionistic standards. The result is a feeling that you never do enough and are always falling short of what is required in any situation.

The irrational, perfectionistic belief that worth is determined by achievement can also generate the need to excel above others in order to feel "important." When this occurs it becomes a major source of anxiety. No matter how talented you are in a given area, there is usually someone more talented. A person who needs to excel above others in order to feel important often feels glad or relieved when others fail or do poorly at an activity in which this person feels competitive. Sometimes a person like this may even resort to sabotage in order to insure that others will do poorly.

Many people have found the following ideas effective challenges for the irrational belief that worth is determined by achievement.

- When older people look back on their lives, they usually find the satisfaction they received from relationships and how they lived were far more important than what they did.
- As far as healthy, satisfying, long-term relationships are concerned, who you are as a person is far more important than what you achieve.
- Your value as a person is entirely separate from the value of the activities you do. Equating worth with achievement is an arbitrary value system for which there is no objective support. Technically you are only a human being who does various activities. You are not those activities. While your activities may or may not be valuable, they do not add or subtract from your value as a person.
- You probably treat others with respect because you believe people have value in and of themselves as a member of the human race. You have this same intrinsic value as others simply because you are human.

- You do not need to be especially talented to be happy and successful in life. Many very happy and successful people have below-average talent and ability.
- People usually achieve more when achievement is the result of enjoying an activity rather than the result of being sought as a source of self-worth and self-esteem.
- Overconcern with achievement creates anxiety that interferes with your ability to achieve.

If you have religious beliefs, you will probably find many additional ideas which are part of your faith that can be substituted or added to the above list. Take time this week to examine your philosophical or religious beliefs and clarify what you believe is important in life. Also, clarify your beliefs about the value of people and life.

The Irrational Belief that All Mistakes Are Terrible

When a perfectionist makes a mistake, it is usually seen as one of the worst things that can happen. This is usually true even when the mistake is a minor one with no real negative consequences. Often, this is due to parents who train a child by constantly pointing out what the child is doing wrong but rarely state what the child is doing well. This is usually not done out of malice. These parents want the child to do well. Unfortunately, it often teaches the child to fear making mistakes and takings risks. It also can generate the tendency to focus on small flaws and errors and magnify the importance of mistakes.

Most mistakes are unimportant. Take a moment to recall all of the mistakes you have made in the past twenty-four hours. Now, consider the effect each will have on your life one day, one week, or one year from now. Unless this is a very unusual day for you, you will probably agree these errors will have no real lasting effect on your life. While mistakes sometimes have unfortunate consequences, most of the mistakes you make in daily life do not seriously effect you and are, at most, minor inconveniences. Most mistakes take on major importance only when magnified by the fear of failure and perfectionistic all-or-nothing thinking.

But mistakes are more than just nuisances having little lasting effect. Mistakes are an indispensable and natural part of the learning process. They offer wonderful opportunities to gain knowledge and develop skills. This process can be diagrammed as follows:

Information $\rightarrow$ Practice applying the information $\rightarrow$ Mistake
or using a skill

                                 $\uparrow$ $\downarrow$

Increased mastery and additional $\leftarrow$ Evaluation of and
knowledge   correction of the
mistake

Every complex skill you have was gained through the above process. This includes everything from walking and talking to reading and cooking. It is also the process you are now using to learn how to think and act in positive new ways. In this sense, mistakes are gifts of wisdom.

□ *Changing Perfectionistic Behavior*

This section describes ten powerful approaches for replacing perfectionistic tendencies with their positive opposites. It usually takes many weeks or months to make all of them a part of your life. During the time you are working with this lesson, put most of your time and energy into the first three. If your situation allows you to work with additional approaches, do so. However, do not be concerned if you are only able to work with the first three. As you proceed through this program there will be many opportunities to return to this lesson and work with those approaches you skip at this time.

Develop and Practice Rational Self-Talk that Challenges Perfectionistic Beliefs

The first step in changing perfectionistic tendencies is to develop rational self-talk you can use to challenge the irrational beliefs that cause you to interpret events in a perfectionistic manner. The following example shows how Steffany challenged her perfectionistic beliefs with ideas from the preceding section.

Example: Steffany was trying a new recipe. She misread the directions causing the dish she was preparing to turn out poorly. Her first thought was, "This is terrible! Why can't I do anything right?"

Steffany's rational self-talk: "Here is that old perfectionistic self talk again. I am really saying I should be able to do this perfectly and never make mistakes (identify the distortion). This is irrational because perfection by definition cannot be achieved. Mistakes are also not that bad (rational challenge). As for my *never* doing anything correctly, I am actually a pretty good cook. Most of what I make turns out well. As for this mistake, it's really no big deal. Besides, I know how to make it come out the way I want next time (objective analysis and substitution). That's great (ego strengthener)."

Develop a Problem-Solving Approach to Mistakes

The previous section pointed out that mistakes are often a major source of anxiety. If you frequently dwell on mistakes, condemn yourself when you make mistakes, or avoid activities because you fear making mistakes, memorize the following three-step approach and begin applying it to every mistake you make.

Identify why the mistake was made.

This is often the most difficult step since perfectionists tend to be sidetracked by self-condemnation and negative self-labeling. When you notice this occurring, remind yourself that you are simply trying to identify the source of the mistake so you can take positive action. Also remind yourself that mistakes are expected—a natural part of the learning process. If it is difficult to remain objective during this step you may need to recall the short phrases you memorized that challenge the three irrational perfectionistic beliefs discussed earlier: perfection is possible, a person's worth is determined by achievement, and mistakes are terrible.

Sometimes, you will not be able to identify the cause of a mistake. When this occurs, go on to the next step.

Identify any action that can be taken to correct the mistake and, if practical, take it.

Your task at this step is to evaluate objectively whether or not an error can be corrected and whether you wish to take the action that would be required. Just as it is not always possible to identify the cause of a mistake, it is not always possible to correct a flaw or error. Other times, the correction of a flaw or error is simply not worth the time, energy, or money required.

Identify actions that can be taken to reduce the likelihood of repeating the mistake in the future and, if practical, take it.

As with the previous steps, this is not always possible. However, it is a step that many people with perfectionistic tendencies never arrive at because they dwell on the awfulness of the mistake or their personal inadequacy. When considering possible actions, remember that rehearsing new behaviors increases the likelihood of your using them in the future. Take time to identify exactly what you would say or do differently if you were in a similar situation again. Then rehearse those words or actions several times in your mind.

When you use this three-step approach, you transform mistakes into gifts of wisdom. With time, this process becomes as automatic as your old patterns.

Focus On Positives

Whenever you change a habit pattern it is not enough to simply stop the old, negative pattern. You must also practice a new, positive pattern that will, with time, replace the old one. One of the main characteristics of perfectionism is the tendency to focus on small flaws and errors. The opposite positive tendency is the habit of focusing on positives. From this day on, make it a habit to take a moment during any activity, no matter how small, to find something positive about it.

Eliminate the "But" Habit

People with perfectionistic tendencies often use the word "but" to cancel positives. Here are three examples of self-talk using "but" in this manner:

"I had a fairly good week, but there was one afternoon when things didn't go very well."

"I did more yesterday than I have ever done, but I felt somewhat nervous the whole time."

"I made the best afghan I have ever made, but one section just isn't right."

Notice how the negative second half of each sentence cancels out the positive first half. One way to eliminate this habit is to begin reversing the order of your thoughts or statements and put the negative part first. This allows the positive to reduce or cancel out the negative part. Doing this with the three examples produces the following:

"There was one afternoon when things didn't go very well, but I had a fairly good week."

"I felt somewhat nervous the whole time, but I did more yesterday than I have ever done."

"This one section isn't right, but I made the best afghan I have ever made."

Another approach that is even better is to simply leave off the second negative half. For example:

Instead of saying: "I had a fairly good week, but there was one afternoon when things didn't go well."

Simply say: "I had a fairly good week."

If you are a hard-core perfectionist, the second approach may be difficult. You may feel as though you are not being completely "honest." However, persist until it does become comfortable. As you learn to focus on positives and leave off the negative details you will find most people will enjoy your company and conversation more. People usually do not want to hear about all the problems you are facing.

Set Realistic Goals

The following suggestions will help you set more realistic goals.

- Consider what you would expect if you were setting the goal for someone else. Most perfectionists are more realistic when setting goals for others.
- Set goals in your normal fashion, then reduce them somewhat. For example, if you believe you "should" produce 100 items an hour at work, set 80 items an hour as your goal.
- Be aware of any should/must thinking that creeps into your goal setting such as, "I have to get an A." When you discover this type of thinking, use the ideas presented in this lesson along with the rational self-talk tools presented in the previous lessons to challenge it.
- Give yourself permission to make errors and re-evaluate your goal. Make the acceptance of some errors and flaws part of your goal.
- Aim to simply "do" or "do well" instead of "doing perfectly."
- Aim to simply better your own performance rather than to be perfect or exceed the performance of others.
- Discuss your goal with an objective person you trust in order to get a "reality check."

Select those ideas from the above list which match your personality, and memorize them. Use them whenever you set a goal for yourself. This includes all your goals, from how much exercise you will do to what type of job you will take.

Give Yourself Permission to Experience Pleasure

Perfectionists rarely give themselves permission to experience pleasure. Often this is because they are too busy seeking the impossible goal of perfection to be bothered with pleasure. People who believe that worth only comes from achievement may also believe that pleasure has no value. In addition, when perfectionism is accompanied by an excessive need for approval and low self-esteem, the perfectionist places the needs of others first and ignores personal needs.

The way to remedy this situation is simple and fun. Every day, do at least one thing for yourself that is fun and pleasurable. This may be an activity you do by yourself or with others; it can be simple or complex, short or long. The point is to choose an activity for the enjoyment it brings to you rather than for the benefits or pleasure it brings to others. Several examples are listed in Lesson 3 in the section on relaxation.

Develop a Process Orientation

Spend more time and energy focusing on the process of doing an activity than on the end product or achievement. One way to do this is to read this section at the beginning of the day and give yourself permission to enjoy the pleasurable aspects of what you do. You may even want to post cue cards that remind you to take time to enjoy what you are doing. Here are a few process-oriented sayings you can put on your cue cards:

Enjoy the "doing."
In life, the journey is far more important than the destination.
Seek enjoyment rather than accomplishment (the two often go together).
How I live is more important than what I do.
Savor the present.
Stop and smell the roses.
Live now!

Another way to develop a process orientation is summarized by a popular joke which asks "How do you eat an elephant?" The answer: "One bite at a time." Because perfectionistic thinking is overly concerned with the end result, large projects often seem overwhelming. This usually generates unnecessary anxiety and a tendency to procrastinate.

Whenever you are faced with a large project, divide it into several small ones. Concentrate only on the part you are doing instead of the whole project. For example, if you are going to clean your house, divide it into many small projects each of which can be done in a short amount of time such as the dishes, floors, dusting, and so on. If you start with the dishes, concentrate only on doing that job. Pretend this is the only thing in the world you need to do. This "elephant" approach helps you become more productive, enjoy what you are doing, and become less concerned with the end results of large projects.

Many of the other approaches in this lesson can be combined with this one. For example, you may want to schedule how much time you want to spend with each task and then stick to your schedule whether you have completed the task or not. Another one that is especially useful is to note and compliment yourself on the positive aspects of each job as you complete it.

Use the "Bottom Line Technique" to Eliminate Fears Underlying Perfectionistic Behavior

Perfectionistic behavior is usually driven by one or more underlying fears. The Bottom Line Technique is a variation of the Block Method described in Lesson 5. It provides a simple method for identifying these underlying fears as well as any forms of distorted thinking that might be involved. Use this approach whenever you are becoming upset because of a mistake or because your performance is not as good as you would like it to be.

Begin by describing the mistake you made or the goal for which you are striving. Next, list the worst possible thing that could happen as a result of this mistake or as a result of your unsatisfactory performance. After you list the negative outcome, ask yourself if there is anything worse than that. Continue until you find yourself unable to come up with any new responses. Here is an example that Maribeth wrote after wrapping a present for a friend:

Situation: I'm doing a terrible job of wrapping this present!

And what would happen if it weren't wrapped well? My friend would think I didn't care.

So what if he thought that? My friend would not like me.

So what if he didn't like you? It would be terrible; I would feel alone and horrible.

So what if that happened? I couldn't stand it.

So what if that happened? I would feel alone and no one would like me.

At this point Maribeth could not think of anything worse and began repeating the previous responses. This indicated the fear of rejection and the mistaken idea that worth is determined by achievement were underlying this behavior. Here are the rational self-talk responses she developed:

Self-talk: I'm doing a terrible job of wrapping this present! (Magnification)

Rational response: I'm exaggerating the minor imperfection in my work. It's not as good as I'd like it to be, but it's O.K.

Self-talk: My friend would think I didn't care. (Fortune Telling & Mind Reading)

Rational response: I'm making a prediction and acting as if it were a fact. I'm also mind-reading since I don't really know what my friend would think. However, it's most likely that she'll like the gift very much.

Self-talk: My friend would not like me. (Fortune Telling)

Rational Response: Now I'm really making a wild guess about what would happen and acting as if it were a fact. It's very unlikely that she'll react in this manner. Besides, what kind of friend would she be if she rejected me just because I'm not an expert at wrapping gifts?

Self-talk: It would be terrible; I would feel alone and horrible. (Magnification)

Rational response: Even if my friend did reject me over such a minor thing, I would survive and find new friends. While it would be unfortunate and I would not like it, it would not really be so "horrible."

Self-talk: I couldn't stand it. (Magnification)

Rational response: I would survive and find new friends. I would be able to "stand it" even though I might not like it.

Self-talk: I would feel alone and no one would like me. (Overgeneralization)

Rational response: No-one would like me? I have many friends and they really don't care how I wrap presents. They like me even though I have imperfections. I now see that along with the fear of rejection, the mistaken idea that I only have worth when I do thing well is underlying this behavior. I know that worth is *not* determined by achievement.

Schedule Activities

Set strict time limits for all of your activities. If you wish to change your schedule, do so only at the beginning of the day. Be sure to quit a given activity at the end of the time you have set aside for it whether you have completed it or not. Then go on to the next activity you have scheduled.

If procrastination is a major problem for you, repeat this activity periodically. It is especially good to repeat it whenever you find yourself becoming too concerned with "getting things done" or faced with a complex or long-term project.

Practice "Response Stopping"

This exercise is only meant for people with minor compulsive behaviors. If compulsive behaviors are a major problem for you, skip this exercise. The use of response stopping with major compulsions is explained in more detail later in the program.

Perfectionistic tendencies are frequently accompanied and reinforced by compulsive tendencies. One of these is the habit of repeated checking to see if an activity has been done such as locking a lock or turning off a light or heater. Another is the tendency to become obsessed with a key or book that has been misplaced and compulsively search for it even though you know it is best to just forget about it and wait for it to show up. Still another is the need to always wear a particular watch or piece of jewelry because you feel undressed without it.

Response stopping is an effective technique for overcoming these types of simple compulsive behaviors. The first step is to identify the specific compulsive behavior you wish to stop. Once this has been done, you simply refuse to do the compulsive habit and allow yourself to experience the anxiety it provokes. Within a short period of time the anxiety subsides and you gain a greater sense of control over yourself. Consider as an example the habit of checking to see if a lock has been locked. Checking it once is perfectly fine. However, checking more than once is pointless and compulsive. If you were to use response stopping with this habit, you would simply refuse to allow yourself to check more than once. When you did this you would feel very anxious at first. However, after a period of time the anxiety would diminish until it disappeared. Sometimes this only takes ten or fifteen minutes. Other times it takes longer. While the elimination of a particular compulsive habit sometimes requires only one practice session, it often requires more than one. Fortunately, each practice session is usually easier than the previous one.

Recommended Activities for Lesson 6

Develop Rational Challenges for Perfectionistic Beliefs

This lesson discussed three irrational beliefs that often are the source of perfectionistic thoughts and behaviors. These include the belief that perfection is possible, the belief that a person's worth is determined by achievement, and the belief that all mistakes are terrible. Select ideas from the discussion of these beliefs that you feel are the most powerful rational challenges and summarize them on cards. Review these cards once a day until you have memorized them. Here are the cards Steffany made:

Challenges for the Irrational Belief that Perfection Is Possible

- Perfection is by definition impossible to achieve.
- Perfection is a direction, not a place.
- If my goal is perfection, I've guaranteed failure because perfection by definition is impossible to achieve.

Challenges for the Irrational Belief that My Worth Is Determined by Achievement

- Failing at a task doesn't make me a failure.
- I am valuable because every person is valuable.
- I can be mediocre and still be happy and successful in life—I don't have to be perfect or above average.
- Average is good.

Challenges for the Irrational Belief that All Mistakes Are Terrible

- Most mistakes are unimportant.
- Mistakes are gifts of wisdom.
- Mistakes are a natural part of the learning process.
- When you make a mistake, remember to use the 3-Step Approach.

Continue Using the Block Method

If you have not yet begun taking five or ten minutes every other day to use the Block Method, begin this week. Review the directions in the Recommended Activities of Lesson 5 if you are not sure how to use the Block Method. When you analyze your thoughts, identify self-talk characteristic of the perfectionistic beliefs discussed in this lesson. Be sure to use the ideas discussed in this lesson to challenge any underlying perfectionistic beliefs you discover.

Work to Eliminate Perfectionism

Do as many of the eleven activities described in this lesson as possible. Spend most of your time and energy on the first three: *Develop and Practice Rational Self-Talk that Challenges Perfectionistic Beliefs, Develop a Problem-Solving Approach to Mistakes*, and *Focus On Positives*. Review the last eight approaches and identify the ones that would be most useful. These are usually exercises that would be difficult for you. Remember, exercises that are easy, probably focus on skills you have already mastered. Exercises that are difficult probably focus on skills you need to develop. If perfectionism is a problem for you, spend two weeks with this lesson.

Be Patient and Continue to Practice

The growth you achieve while working through this program is the result of a gradual process. It is usually only noticed after you have done something in a new and more effective way. There are two reasons for this. First, you are working on attitudes and skills that are acquired and polished over time. It is much like watching a child grow. As you watch from day to day, you do not notice any difference, but, when you stand the child against a wall where past heights are marked, the child's growth becomes obvious.

The second reason progress is usually noticed after the fact is that the attitudes and skills you are developing are most effective when they are fully internalized. At first, you have to spend a lot of time and energy thinking about the skills and information you are learning. With time, they become so much a part of you that you no longer have to consciously think about them. They become as automatic as the old patterns that generated anxiety. You only notice this internalization process when you look back at an incident and realize you used the new patterns of thinking and acting without even thinking about it. It was just a natural and comfortable thing to do. This is when you know you are making these new skills and this new approach to life part of you.

An old Chinese proverb says:

"I heard and I forgot, I saw and I remembered, I did and now I understand."

All of the information, skills, and tools about which you have been reading will have little effect on your life if you do not practice using them. Knowledge alone is not enough to overcome self-defeating behaviors and thinking patterns. If you have not been following the lessons as recommended or are starting to spend less time with them, make a firm commitment now to spend as much time and energy as possible practicing the skills and using the information and knowledge you are learning. If you do not have a regular time when you study the lessons, pick a time now.

Consider Massage

Most people suffering from anxiety or stress also suffer from chronic muscle tension. Massage helps relieve chronic muscle tension and is an excellent form of relaxation. Massage is also an experience that is both very pleasurable and which only benefits you. This is especially important for people who have difficulty giving themselves permission to experience pleasure or who rarely do anything just for themselves. If you have never received a professional massage, these are two excellent reasons to do so now.

Therapeutic massage offers one additional benefit for people who grew up in a dysfunctional families where they never experienced positive touching, received little physical affection, or failed to learn how to establish healthy boundaries between yourself and others. Therapeutic massage offers an important opportunity to learn how to receive appropriate, non-sexual, positive, touching. If you come from a family like this be sure to interview potential massage therapists prior to scheduling a massage. It is important that you begin with someone you feel comfortable with. It is also likely that it may take two or three massages before you begin to relax and get the full benefit of massage.

Consider Keeping a Journal

You may find it valuable to begin keeping a journal. Use your journal to do the written activities, list problems and concerns, record insights, and keep track of progress. When you keep a journal, privacy is essential. This makes it easier to write with honesty and openness. If you write for an unseen audience you lose much of the benefit of keeping a journal. Use any kind of notebook for your journal. The main value of a journal is not the permanent record you create but the work required to create it. After several months you may decide to destroy your journal or keep it.

> The insights and behavior changes that
> result from the activities in this lesson
> form a foundation for the following lessons.
> Take your time and spend at least
> one week with this lesson.

Becoming a Positive Realist

Being a positive realist does not mean you look at the world through rose-colored glasses and ignore problems and danger. Instead, it means you face life head-on focusing on solutions and possibilities rather than on life's fearful or troublesome aspects. This lesson provides you with powerful methods for eliminating forms of negativism commonly associated with anxiety-related problems. As you use them your ability to face life as a positive realist will increase. You will find yourself dealing with people and problems more effectively and experiencing a greater sense of joy in daily living.

☐ *Negative Anticipation*

Negative anticipation is the tendency to dwell on unpleasant or fearsome events that might occur in the future. The self-talk generated by this type of worry often begins with the words "what if."

Consider Robert, who suffers from panic disorder. While preparing to visit a friend he thinks: "What if I become anxious at my friend's house?" Instead of evaluating this possibility objectively, Robert leaps to the conclusion that he will *definitely* become anxious (fortune-telling), this will be the worst thing that can happen (catastrophizing), and it will make him an utter failure in life (should/must thinking in the form of all-or-nothing thinking: I should be calm and poised at everything I do/I should be perfect and have no problems like this). The following activity can be used to challenge and eliminate negative anticipation.

Use a "Four-Step Analysis"

Whenever you notice yourself becoming preoccupied or upset with something unpleasant or fearsome that might occur, make an objective evaluation with the following Four-Step Analysis.

Determine the odds

Realistically determine the probability of the feared event actually occurring. State the odds of the event occurring as a percentage. Guard against fortune-telling which transforms a possibility into a probability. Recall your track record and consider how you have done in previous situations similar to this one. This helps you to be more realistic.

Assess the consequences

Realistically assess the consequences if your worst fears did occur. In essence, you are considering the "awfulness" of the feared event. As you do this, remember to avoid catastrophic magnification. Often, the fear of rejection and perfectionistic beliefs that generate embarrassment or shame plays a major role in your fears.

Develop a plan for preventing the feared event

Develop a detailed plan for reducing the likelihood of the feared event occurring. Be very specific as you do this. Developing rational self-talk that challenges irrational beliefs is an important part of this plan.

Develop a plan for coping with the feared event if it did occur

Decide how you could best cope with the feared event if it were to occur. As you develop your plan, avoid dwelling on how terrible it would be if the event occurred. Instead, concentrate on listing practical actions you can take. Again, be concrete and specific.

After you have completed the above steps, summarize your analysis into two or three sentences. These become coping-self statements that deal with your specific fears. If you are dealing with a major concern, write them on a card you can carry with you. Then, redirect your attention to something positive or neutral.

If you notice yourself thinking about the feared event again, recall your summary of the analysis, then, redirect your attention elsewhere. The following example shows how Robert used these steps to resolve his concern about becoming anxious at his friend's house.

Determine the odds

"I can recall many times when I have become anxious at the home of friends so this might actually happen. However, since I have been learning these new skills, I have been doing very well, so, I don't think the probability of this occurring is very high. I will give it a 20% chance of occurring."

Assess the consequences

"How terrible would this actually be? It would be uncomfortable and I would not like it, but I would be able to stand it. After all, am I actually going to be harmed or have something taken away from me? No. Becoming anxious is really not all that horrible. It's just a nuisance. My real fear is becoming embarrassed and feeling ashamed. I've been embarrassed and felt ashamed many times. I always survive and people who really matter don't care. They still like me. I also see that my fear of rejection, need to do things perfectly, and fear of making mistakes plays a major role in this fear."

Develop a plan for preventing the feared event

"Let's see, I can bring a card along that lists my anti-anxiety skills. My main problem behaviors are the tendency to hold my breath, hyperventilate, and tell myself how terrible it is to be anxious. That means the card needs to remind me to use diaphragmatic breathing and list several positive coping self-statements I like. I think I'll also take the cards that challenge perfectionism along. These have worked well in the past and will take care of any excessive physical symptoms I might experience at my friend's house. I can also have something to eat before I go since I usually do better when I'm not hungry."

Develop a plan for coping with the feared event if it did occur

If I become anxious, I can simply excuse myself for a moment and use the skills on the card. This is usually very effective. If I do become so anxious that I decide to leave, I can just tell my friend that I would like to stay but I am not feeling well. It would also be good to say I will call later.

After completing the above analysis, Robert distracted himself with household chores. After a short time, he again found himself thinking about becoming anxious at his friend's house. Since he had already worked through the above steps in detail, he now used positive self-talk in the form of a quick review of his plans and conclusions.

"Now, wait a minute. I've already thought about this and know the probability of becoming anxious is very low. I also have a plan to deal with anxiety if it does become a problem so I'm all prepared and will do just fine. If not, so what? It's no big deal. Now what else do I need to do before leaving?"

Use the "So What If" approach

"What if" thoughts and statements characteristic of negative anticipation tend to generate adrenalin and increase the amount of anxiety a person feels. An effective way to deal with them is to rethink or repeat the thought or statement, but change the "what if" into "so what if." For example:

"What if I start to breathe funny?" *becomes* "So what if I start to breathe funny?"

"What if I start to get anxious?" *becomes* "So what if I start to get anxious?"

"What if I have to leave?" *becomes* "So what if I have to leave?"

Just as "what if" thoughts generate adrenalin and increase anxiety, "so what if" thoughts tend to calm you. This calming effect can be increased by following the "so what if" thought with coping self-statements. These coping self-statements can be general ones such as those described in Lesson 3 or ones tailored to a specific fear as a result of a Four-Step Analysis.

Example: "What if I have to leave?"

Rational self-talk: "So what if I have to leave. People leave these types of events before they've ended all the time. I can then use my coping skills. If I decide to return, most of the people there won't even know I've been gone. Those that do notice won't think anything about it."

Increase Your Ability to Accept Uncertainty

Negative anticipation is frequently generated by a demand for a degree of certainty that is unattainable. Many people want a 100% assurance that what is feared will not happen. Unfortunately, the need for a 100% guarantee is reinforced by several forces in our modern world. Our modern, technological world is a relatively safe and comfortable one. Movies and television programs reinforce the illusion that all problems can be easily solved and life *should* be safe and wonderful. We don't like to look at the truth that uncertainty is a part of life. The tendency to look for someone to blame when something goes wrong implies that accidents "should not" occur. We demand that our medicines, transportation, food and everything else be 100% safe. This is impossible.

Learning to accept the inevitable danger and risks that go with life is essential in order to live fully and creatively. Use positive self-talk to convince yourself that there is often a 1-10% uncertainty factor that everyone lives with and develop the attitude of "that's just the way it is." Using the Four-Step Analysis to face your fears realistically is one way to develop this attitude. It also helps to develop the habit of looking at the positive side of uncertainty. Remind yourself that a 10% chance of a fearful event occurring means there is a 90% chance that it will not occur. In addition, you may also want to re-examine your religious or philosophical beliefs. Are you able to make some sense out of the unfortunate and unfair events that are part of living? If not, you may need to review your beliefs about life and the world that form the basis of your belief system. Having a strong spiritual rock to stand upon is often the real key to facing the uncertainties of life.

Develop Problem-Solving Skills

People with anxiety-related problems often spend much time and energy worrying when they need to make a decision. Any decision in life becomes easier if you view it as simply a problem to be solved. The five basic steps to resolving a problem are as follows:

What is the problem?

As simple as it may sound, many people fail to stop and define the problem they are facing clearly. The simplest way to do this is to state the problem in a single statement. For example, "I need to decide whether or not to go on the trip with my friend."

What are my options (choices)?

This is where many people become sidetracked. Instead of listing possible options, they slip into negative self-talk. It often helps to list possible options on a piece of paper. If you are finding it difficult to generate possible options, ask someone you trust who is knowledgeable about the problem you are facing.

Gathering information about the positive and negative aspects of each option.

This is the key to making a decision. Seek as much information as possible so the consequences of your choices are clear. Again, with complex problems you may have to consult with people you trust who are knowledgeable about the problem you are facing.

Choose the option that generates the most positive or least negative feelings.

If you have done your job well in the previous step, one option always generates more positive or less negative feelings than any of the others. If this does not occur, repeat the above steps. Once you reach this point, avoid procrastination and go ahead with that option since the anxiety generated by a prolonged conflict can be very debilitating. Use self-talk to counter the perfectionistic need for a "perfect" solution.

Follow-up (optional)

After you have experienced the consequences of your decision, take time to evaluate the actions you took. If things turned out poorly, use the Problem-Solving Approach to Mistakes discussed in Lesson 6. If things turned out well, be sure to congratulate yourself on a job well done!

Separate the Past From the Present.

People often react to the present as if it were the past even though the two are very different. This is due, in part, to the reactions triggered by conditioned response learning as discussed in Lesson 2. Harmless events trigger both anxiety and negative self-talk. When this occurs, use rational self-talk to remind yourself that while the threat you fear may have been real and important in the past, it now either no longer exists or is only a minor problem.

Barbara provides a good example of how the past can distort the present. She was recovering from panic disorder and, like many people with this problem, was very fearful of places where panic attacks had occurred in the past. Here is an example of the type of self-talk she used to challenge these types of fears.

"The threat associated with this place was real and important when I did not understand why my panic attacks occurred and I had no skills to cope with them. However, I now understand why they occurred. I also have a wide range of skills for managing anxiety which I have used successfully many times. The anxiety I am currently feeling is simply an old conditioned response habit pattern based on a threat that no longer exists. It's not dangerous. It's only an uncomfortable body sensation that will diminish with time."

Avoid Exaggerating the Importance of "Special" Items and Events

When a person exaggerates the importance of special objects or events such as a favorite cup, chair, or T.V. program, it can become the source of negative anticipation. If you have special items or events such as these, periodically use different items or enjoy different events other than your favorite ones. For example, if you use a cup other than your favorite, take time to enjoy its color, design, and feel.

☐ *Thinking and Acting Like a Victim*

The tendency to think and act like a victim is very common. People with this trait experience themselves as powerless due to the mistaken belief that they have little or no ability to exert a positive influence on events. While many people openly acknowledge they feel helpless and victimized, others think and act this way without even knowing it. The following examples of self-talk are common victim statements. Place a check by any you use.

"If only...things would be different."
"It's his (her, their, its) fault."
"He (she, they, it) made me angry (anxious, sad, etc.)."
"I've always been this way."
"I wish I could do it all over again. Then things would be different."
"That's just the way I am."
"You can't teach an old dog new tricks."
"I can't help myself."

Use the following activities to eliminate the tendency to think and act like a victim. They increase your sense of personal power and strengthen your belief in yourself and your ability to influence events in a positive manner.

Develop a Strong Belief in Your Ability to Control and Change Your Emotions

Lesson 4 describes in detail how *it is not people and events that generate emotions but the meaning you give to people and events.* This is one of the most important ideas in these lessons and needs to become a firm part of your belief system.

Whenever you notice yourself thinking or acting as if a person or event made you feel some way, remind yourself how emotions are generated. It is also useful to remind yourself that people and events can do nothing except, at worst, harm you physically or deprive you of something you want. In most cases this is very unlikely.

There are only two kinds of pain a person can experience, physical pain and psychological pain—the result of your wants and needs being frustrated or threatened. Your beliefs and attitudes about events generate psychological pain and cause you discomfort. Most of your misery about your discomfort is caused by your own distorted thinking and your constant repetition of it. As a popular saying states, "In life, pain is inevitable, suffering is optional."

Develop a Strong Belief in the Power of the Present

Many people mistakenly believe they are controlled by the past—that once something strongly influences their life it continues to determine their feelings and behavior. This idea is a false overgeneralization. Just because something holds true in some circumstances hardly proves it equally true under all conditions. For example, just because you once felt weak doesn't means you must always feel weak. Allowing yourself to remain too strongly influenced by past events causes you to cease trying. This causes the irrational belief that the past determines your future and becomes a self-fulfilling prophecy.

When you are strongly influenced by the past, feelings about people and things from the past are often transferred to the present. Going through life reacting to shadows from the past instead of current events usually results in self-defeating behavior.

For example, when Ryan was young he had an aunt who was very critical and toward whom he felt much resentment. During his early adult life he found it very difficult to deal with people who resembled his aunt in appearance or speech. Ryan finally sought help to change this reaction when he was assigned a supervisor at work who was very good natured but resembled his aunt.

Work at accepting the fact that while your past does influence you in some important ways, it has no magical, automatic effect on the present or future. Your present is tomorrow's past. Believing that today is your "point of power" helps you consider your past history more objectively and learn valuable lessons from it. This helps you avoid repeating mistakes you made in the past. Changing the present to create a better future also becomes easier.

Whenever you notice yourself doing something self-defeating and using phrases such as, "If only...," "I've always been this way," "I've always done it this way," or "I can't change," to justify the behavior, challenge your thinking with rational self-talk. Use the ideas in this lesson to challenge the idea that the past forces you to act in a certain manner. Then realistically assess your needs and wants and make a choice based on the present.

Example: Judy is very shy and usually does not look at people where she works. One day she catches herself thinking: "If only I had more confidence I could really make something out of myself."

Rational Self-Talk: "What do I mean 'if only?' I'm acting and thinking as if it's impossible for me to change. Today is the point of power in my life. I cannot change the past. However, I can change tomorrow by acting differently today even though it may be difficult at first. I want to become more confident with people so I need to practice my social skills. I am going to smile and talk to two strangers today."

Develop the Ability to Accept Frustration and Loss.

Frustrations and irritations are a normal part of daily living. Usually, they do not create catastrophes. Develop rational self-talk that reinforces the belief that you can survive quite well in spite of their existence.

One way to do this is by becoming philosophical about loss and frustration. This helps you regard it as undesirable but not as unbearable or intolerable. This, in turn, helps you let go of past negative experiences. Another important strategy to use when faced with actual physical injury, deprivation, pain, or disease is distraction. While distraction does not affect the source of the problem, it does help you cope with difficult situations after you have done what is practical to eliminate or diminish your painful circumstances.

☐ Blaming and Scapegoating

The tendency to find people and events to serve as scapegoats for one's problems and personal inadequacies is really just another form of living life as a victim. Blaming is usually accompanied by a reluctance to take responsibility for one's life and actions. The mistaken ideas that life should be fair and that achievements or actions determine worth are also frequently present.

Some blamers are very verbal and let everyone know who or what they think has caused their misfortune. Others remain silent and carry on long internal dialogues dwelling on who or what caused their misery. The following activities are designed to help you eliminate this type of self-defeating behavior.

Take Responsibility for Your Life

When you look for scapegoats and blame others for your problems, you become powerless and lose the ability to change things for the better. It is only when you take ownership of problems that you regain the ability to take constructive action. In essence, every problem you have is YOUR problem regardless of who's responsible. The solutions to your problems only come when you use your time and energy choosing effective actions instead of dwelling on whose fault or how horrible it is.

Distinguish Between Responsibility and Blame

Blaming is the condemnation of either yourself or others for inappropriate or hurtful actions. Blaming usually occurs because you are confusing inappropriate or "bad" behavior with being "bad." Use the ideas in Lesson 6 to challenge the idea that worth is determined by achievement or actions. In addition, use positive self-talk to keep yourself focused on objective problem-solving instead of wasting your valuable time and energy condemning the person responsible. As you do this, remember that a particular event usually has many causes.

Assigning responsibility for a problem or misfortune is an objective form of problem-solving. You decide what caused your misfortune without making a moral judgment about it. Your goal is simply to decide what happened so you can identify if anything can be done differently in the future to prevent the recurrence of this type of misfortune.

If you habitually condemn and blame others, you also probably turn your blaming standards onto yourself. This usually causes a considerable amount of self-loathing and feelings of worthlessness when you are "bad." This may even lead to inappropriate or self-defeating actions. Distinguishing between responsibility and blame becomes easier as you become more accepting of human weaknesses and shortcomings. Make allowances for the possibility, indeed the practical certainty, that you and others will continue to make numerous errors and mistakes. When you are hard on yourself, use self-talk such as the following to redirect your attention to problem-solving instead of blaming:

"I definitely did act in an inappropriate way. Humans beings do this. Now, what exactly did I do and how can I correct it or at least not repeat it?"

Identify and Challenge Distorted Thinking that Reinforces Blaming

One of the primary forms of distorted thinking that reinforces blaming is should/must thinking, especially the mistaken idea that life should be fair. Whenever you find yourself saying or thinking that someone or some event is unfair, remind yourself that *total fairness, like perfection, is impossible to achieve in the real world.* Because people and events are complex, there is always something different about the way you treat each person you meet. Likewise, there is always something different about the way you behave in each situation no matter how similar situations seem. The belief that life should be fair magnifies these inequalities and makes them seem much more important than they really are.

Convince yourself that injustice and inequality are facts of life. Everyone will at times act in hurtful and unjust ways for either rational or irrational reasons. Actions done with good intentions sometimes turn out to be hurtful or unjust because of a lack of knowledge or understanding. The only rational approach to living in an unjust world is to focus on needs instead of fairness. Decide if something you really need or want is being frustrated or threatened. If it is, concentrate on developing a plan to improve the situation.

Overgeneralization and magnification are two other types of distorted thinking that reinforce blaming. Whenever you find yourself condemning or blaming someone for a problem instead of using a problem-solving approach to resolve it, re-examine your self-talk and look for should/must thinking (especially in the form of all-or-nothing thinking), overgeneralization, magnification and any other form of distorted thinking you may have been using. If blaming is a major problem for you, use the block method described in Lesson 5 to analyze your thinking and practice rational self-talk. As your ability to identify and challenge distorted thinking increases, it becomes easier to stop blaming.

Learn to Deal with Negative Behaviors of Others Objectively.

One sign of emotional maturity is the ability to avoid retaliating against people who act hatefully or harm you. Becoming upset interferes with your ability to reason and correct the situation. While you cannot control the thoughts or behaviors of others, you can control your own thoughts and actions. Concentrate on identifying the most effective actions you can take to improve or at least cope with the situation.

Should/must thinking is the biggest obstacle to developing this ability. The need to punish and retaliate is often the result of focusing on how others "should" behave instead of concentrating on your main logical concern: planning actions you can take to protect yourself and, if possible, satisfy your needs. This becomes easier as your ability to identify and challenge should/must thinking increases.

Example: Albert has a brother-in-law named Sam who acts like an emotional two-year-old. One day Sam does something childish and Albert thinks: "How can he act like this? He's thirty-five and should know better. I can't stand it. He shouldn't treat people like this."

Albert's rational self-talk: "Wait a minute. Here I am expecting Sam to be reasonable and fair and treat me with respect. I know he's self-centered, unreasonable and often acts like a two-year-old. I can't do anything about that. However, I can decide how I'm going to respond in a way that protects me and fulfills my needs. I can also stop magnifying the "awfulness" of the situation. I would sure like everyone to be fair and kind, but they aren't. Now, what exactly would be the most effective way to deal with Sam's selfish and immature behavior and take care of myself?"

Another way to stay more objective when faced with negative behaviors from others is to ask yourself the following four questions.

- Do I really care what this person does?
- Does this person's actions truly affect me?
- Is it likely that this person will change if I make the effort to help him or her change?
- Do I actually have the time and energy required to help this person change?

Unless you can answer all the above with a resounding "yes," stay somewhat aloof from the errors and shortcomings of others. When you do consider it worthwhile to become involved with helping someone change, do so in an unfrantic way. Adopt a permissive, uncritical attitude. Keep in mind how difficult it is for you to change.

Recommended Activities for Lesson 7

Develop the Beliefs of a Positive Realist

This lesson discussed many of the beliefs that enable a person to face the world as a positive realist. Select ideas from the discussion of these beliefs that you feel are the most powerful rational challenges for irrational beliefs you hold and summarize them on cards. Review these cards once a day until you have memorized them. Here are samples of cards Robert, Judy, and Albert made.

Dealing With "What ifs"

- Use the Four-Step Analysis to face your fear then redirect your attention elsewhere.
- Remember that uncertainty is a fact of life—a 1% chance of a negative outcome means a 99% chance of a positive outcome.
- Stop, look, and choose actions based on present realities, not on the past.

Challenges for Victim Thinking

- People and events don't cause me to feel things; it is the interpretation I give to events that generates my emotions.
- Pain is inevitable, suffering is optional—my choice.
- Today is my point of power—make choices that bring what I want based on the realities present here and now.
- Humans can be very tough critters—I can, if I choose, tolerate frustration and loss. I don't have to let it defeat me.

Challenges for Blaming and Scapegoating

- Take ownership of your life and problems.
- People frequently act in hurtful and irresponsible ways. That's life. When this happens, focus on your response, not on how bad or awful they are.
- My parents were right—Life isn't fair. That's just the way it is.
- Don't worry about other people's shortcomings unless it effects you directly.

Practice Using the Four-Step Analysis

Do a four-step analysis with the two most important concerns you currently have. Do this analysis with paper and pencil. Create coping self-statements that summarize your analysis and record them on a card you can refer to in the future.

Increase Your Problem-Solving Skills

Think of several recent occasions when you have had difficulty making a decision, resolving a conflict, or solving a problem. List them on paper. Then review the five steps to problem-solving outlined in the lesson and identify the step or steps that were difficult or which you simply skipped. Next, list ways in which you could have completed the step or steps more effectively. Summarize your ideas on a card you can refer to in the future.

Practice Becoming a Positive Realist

After you have done the preceding exercises, review the lesson again and identify any additional approaches not covered in the above exercises that would help you become more of a positive realist. List them on a card and practice them during the time you are working on this lesson. If negative anticipation, the tendency to think like a victim, or the tendency to blame or scapegoat either yourself or others is a problem for you, spend two weeks with this lesson.

> Be sure to spend at least one week with
> this lesson. The skills and concepts
> it presents are an essential part of the
> process you are using to become
> a positive realist.

The Excessive Need for Approval

Approval, like many of the other traits discussed in these lessons, is neither good nor bad. The need for approval is essential for healthy relationships. It is only when this need is either lacking or has become excessive that it creates problems. Because the excessive need for approval is a common problem for people with anxiety-related problems, you will probably find yourself returning to this lesson many times. Each time you will find the rewards of working through the information and exercises systematically well worth the effort.

☐ *How the Excessive Need for Approval Is Expressed*

People with an excessive need for approval view themselves as being flawed in some way and thus unacceptable to others. For some, the flaws that make them unacceptable are a part of their conscious belief system. They can easily identify personal shortcomings that make them inadequate and describe them in detail. For others, the idea that they are inferior to others is a basic part of their self-image. This belief in their inadequacy generates a selective point of view as described in Lesson 4. This selective point of view causes people like this to look for and find evidence of their inferiority in whatever situation they find themselves. The process of looking for and identifying examples of their inadequacy confirms the mistaken belief that they are inadequate and unacceptable.

The mistaken belief that one is unacceptable to others usually develops in childhood. Sometimes a parent is very disapproving. Other times a child has an injury or disability which causes excessive concern for either the parent or child. It is also common for a child to simply misinterpret normal childhood events.

The belief that one is unacceptable often causes excessive concern with winning approval. This can make a person very sensitive to criticism. It is often difficult to say "no" to the demands of others since the refusal of requests might bring disapproval. The fear of rejection and disapproval can also make it difficult to deal with authority figures such as supervisors or teachers.

An excessive need for approval frequently generates an excessive empathy for others. This is usually due to the mistaken belief that others are also super-sensitive to criticism and rejection. Excessive empathy usually leads to the creation of a rigid rule that one must always be considerate, kind, sensitive, and generous. It can also cause a person to become a "rescuer" and assume responsibility for keeping friends and relatives happy.

The self-esteem of a person with an excessive need for approval is fairly unstable and dependent upon the opinions of others. Acceptance generates confidence and improved performance. Rejection shatters confidence and causes severe deterioration of performance. This often causes a person to assume a child's role toward friends, relatives, or children and constantly check to see if decisions and actions meet the approval of others.

The excessive need for approval can sometimes cause a person to attribute negative intentions to the actions of others even though there is no logical reason to do so. For example, Jim had not received a call from a friend who was busy remodeling part of his house for two weeks. Jim believed that his friend either no longer cared for him or was angry about something he had done.

Occasionally, the excessive need for approval is expressed as a need to be treated as a favorite child. When this is the case, the lack of special treatment in social situations is viewed as a slight or rejection. In extreme cases, failure to be invited or considered for an event is seen as rejection.

The following examples of self-talk reflect beliefs that are characteristic of the excessive need for approval. Check any similar to your self-talk or thinking.

"If someone important to me expects me to do something, I should do it."
"How could I be so selfish?"
"I'm not doing enough; I should do more."
"Why can't I see what needs to be done?"
"I should do what people expect me to do."
"I shouldn't be irritable or unpleasant."
"How could I be so unpleasant?"
"I shouldn't make others angry at me."
"Why did I act that way (you caused someone to become angry)?"
"I should keep people I love happy."
"Why can't I be nicer?"
"It's my fault he/she is upset."
"Rejection is the worst thing that can happen."

"I can't be happy if others don't like me."

"Why don't people like me?"

"I can't stand being alone."

"I'm nothing unless I'm loved."

"It's terrible when I'm not noticed."

"How can they be so insensitive/dense?"

"I need to be understood."

"Why can't they be more appreciative?"

"Others should show appreciation for what I do."

□ *Eliminating the Excessive Need for Approval*

Three approaches for eliminating an excessive need for approval are described below. While they may seem simple, each one takes time and practice to master. Additional activities which build on these are described later in the program when the complex issue of acceptance is discussed in relation to self-esteem and assertiveness.

Develop Rational and Realistic Views of Approval and Rejection

If you are going to include other people in your life, you will experience disapproval and rejection regularly. Sometimes this is because you have done something genuinely harmful or mean. However, much, if not most, of the disapproval and rejection you encounter has little to do with you personally. If you analyze the last few times you have received disapproval or been rejected, you will probably find the rejection had little to do with who you are or what you did. When someone reacts negatively towards you, it is often because this person is either thinking irrationally or directing emotions at you that were generated by an event which has nothing to do with you.

Consider Sharon who came home after a difficult day. Sharon noticed that her roommate, Betty, had not started dinner. Because Sharon was tired, hungry, and frustrated, she became very angry. Betty had also had a difficult day and did not take time to analyze what was happening; so she took Sharon's attack personally and felt very rejected. This is what often happens in a situation like this. However, later that day Betty took a second look at what happened and realized that Sharon's actions and rejection were due more to Sharon's hunger, fatigue, and frustration with work than to her own actions.

The next time you feel rejected, take a moment to calm down and analyze whether the person acting negatively towards you is reacting mainly towards something you did or more towards something that has nothing to do with you. Keep in mind that illness, hunger, fatigue, and excessive stress interfere with a person's ability to think in a logical and realistic manner. The negative behaviors which result from these temporary conditions often do not reflect a person's true beliefs or feelings toward you.

The perfectionistic beliefs that worth is determined by achievement and all mistakes are terrible often play a role in exaggerating the need for approval. This is especially true when one is trying to live up to a model of a "perfect person" who is *always* pleasant, rational, and understanding. When this is the case, rejection is seen as a failure. This sense of failure is even greater if the rejection is due to inappropriate actions on your part.

When someone rejects you, remind yourself that it does not mean you are worthless. When you actually do something that is unpleasant or thoughtless, separate your actions from your worth as a person. Also challenge irrational beliefs you may have about mistakes. Then adopt a problem-solving approach to the situation and think about how you can either correct the error you made or prevent it from recurring in the future. Specific ideas that can be used to challenge the perfectionistic beliefs that worth is determined by achievement and all mistakes are terrible are found in Lesson 6.

When you are rejected, remember that emotions are transitory. An emotion can only be sustained if you work very hard and constantly restimulate yourself. This is usually done by recalling and dwelling on stimulating memories or by repeating stimulating self-talk over and over. While disapproval and criticism are uncomfortable, the discomfort usually passes fairly quickly if you avoid distorted thinking and distract yourself with positive activities. So even though you may feel it's pointless to start, begin an activity you have enjoyed in the past. If you notice yourself thinking negative thoughts, redirect your attention to more positive ones.

The excessive need for approval often generates the tendency to overgeneralize and homogenize—to see everyone's acceptance and approval as both essential and equally important. Remember that one rejection will not automatically lead to a never ending series of rejections. Everyone judges you differently no matter how well or how poorly you behave. Even when someone does reject you, there are still many people who will accept you.

Develop an understanding and acceptance of the fact that you do not need the approval of everyone you meet in order to live a happy and meaningful life. Acceptance by a mail carrier, salesperson, or stranger on the street is not as important as acceptance by people close to you. While it is more pleasant and often more efficient to do business with people who are friendly and accepting, in most cases, you can still function well with people who don't like you. Only your thoughts can raise or lower your spirits. Another person's approval or disapproval has no ability to affect your mood unless you believe what was said is true. Seek out those who appreciate and accept you instead of wallowing in the rejection of one person.

In healthy relationships, disapproval is usually temporary. When you do something unpleasant or thoughtless, the other person responds in a positive way to your attempts at making amends. A relationship in which the other person is so negative, critical, rejecting, unreasonable, or unforgiving that you must behave in a demeaning or self-defeating way in order to win approval is not worth your time and energy. If you are in such a relationship, you may want to end it. If this is not possible because the other person is a relative or co-worker, consider ways in which you can protect yourself. Suggestions on how to protect yourself from negative people are given in the recommended activity titled, "Negative Friends," in Lesson 4. Suggestions on how to find positive emotional support are given in the section titled, "Emotional Support," in Lesson 3.

Rejection and disapproval are very upsetting for a person who is a perfectionist and who finds it difficult to accept mistakes. Review the sections, "Ideas used to challenge the concept of perfection" and "Learning to appreciate mistakes" in Lesson 6. If you still find it difficult to use the ideas and skills described in these two sections, work through them again along with this section.

Learn to Approach Criticism in an Objective, Problem-Solving Fashion

Criticism can be a positive force in your life. It does not need to intimidate, frustrate, or devastate you. The following four-step approach is an effective way to deal with criticism constructively. Place a check by any step you find difficult.

Use coping self-statements to maintain objectivity and adopt a problem-solving attitude.

There are two types of coping self-statements that are useful when faced with criticism. The first set includes redirecting statements that focus your attention and energy onto Steps 2, 3 and 4. Examples of this first type of coping self-statement follow.

"Remember to ask for details and evaluate before choosing a response."
"Stop taking things so personally and use your brain to evaluate what is happening and being said."
"Now don't accept any of this criticism until you have looked at it objectively."
"Don't respond until you take time to listen and evaluate."

The second set includes statements that identify and challenge any irrational ideas you have about criticism or forms of distorted thinking you commonly use when criticized. Most of the ideas in the three previous sections can be used in this fashion. Examples of this second type of coping self-statement follow.

"This criticism may be a good opportunity to learn something valuable."
"This criticism concerns only a few of my actions, not my entire being."
"While this may feel uncomfortable, it does not mean I am being totally rejected and disapproved of."
"Remember that worth is not determined by actions or achievements."

Ask for details.

In order for criticism to be useful you need details. Ask the person providing the criticism to specify the behaviors he or she finds offensive or undesirable. In addition, have this person specify actions that can be taken to correct the situation or new behaviors which can replace the old ones. If the other person is unwilling or unable to state specifics, the criticism is probably not valid and can be dismissed.

Evaluate the critic and the criticism.

Before you evaluate the criticism, consider the source of the criticism. Ask yourself the following questions:

- What are the qualifications of the person criticizing you?
- Does this person have experience or training that provides special insight?
- Have you been criticized for this particular issue before? If so, was it by several different people or by this same person on several different occasions? In what context was the present and past criticism given (in the course of an argument, friendly conversation, or what)?
- Does this person have a bias or need that might reduce this person's objectivity?

After considering the above, you are ready to decide whether or not you feel the criticism is valid. As you do this, be aware of any tendency you might have to automatically consider others as better judges of your interests than you are. If you do this, remind yourself that you know more about yourself than any other person in the world. The opinion of others is simply information which you need to evaluate for yourself before accepting or rejecting it.

If you do not feel a criticism is valid, dismiss it and get on with your life. If you feel a criticism is valid, go on to the final step.

Choose a response.

When you feel a criticism is valid, the following questions can help you decide what action, if any, would be appropriate.

- How important is the behavior specified by the criticism both to the person offering the criticism and to me?
- How satisfied am I with things as they are now?
- How hard will it be to make the changes the person specified?
- What benefits will I gain if I take the time and trouble to change my behavior?
- Will it really improve the situation if I make these changes?
- What are my chances of succeeding if I spend the time and energy required to make these changes.

If you decide that responding to the criticism is not worth your time and energy, use positive self-talk to help you accept this aspect of yourself. If you have several possible courses of action that can be taken, use the above series of questions to evaluate each alternative separately.

Strive to Do What You Want Instead of What Others Think You Should Do

Have you ever agreed to do something and then later realized it was not something you really wanted to do? Many people with an excessive need for approval find this is a frequent experience. The fear of disapproval and rejection often makes it difficult to say "no" to the demands of others. If you spend your life pleasing others, you may also lose the ability to know what it is you want in a given situation. Ignoring personal needs and wants becomes an automatic habit pattern.

There are two ways to re-establish the ability of knowing what you want. First, avoid making decisions on the spur of the moment. Postpone decisions by responding to requests with statements like, "I need to think about it," or "I'll let you know later." Second, instead of always doing what you've automatically done, get in the habit of asking yourself, "What do I really want to do in this situation?" While most people find that simply asking this question makes them aware of what it is they want, some find it takes time to know what they want. Practice delaying decisions and asking yourself what it is you want until it is easy for you to determine what you want in most everyday situations. Some people find this only takes a week while others find it takes several months.

In order to identify what you want, you need to be able to identify your emotions accurately. Lesson 4 described in detail how positive emotions are simply a message that a need or want has or will be met while negative emotions mean that you believe a threat exists or a loss has or may occur. Practice identifying your emotional reactions with simple language such as happy, excited, anxious, afraid, angry, or sad. Then, when you ask yourself, "What do I want in this situation?" use this ability to identify your emotions accurately to decide whether a need or want is being met, threatened, or if a loss might occur. This information is essential to making a good decision.

Betty, who was discussed earlier, had an experience that illustrates this process. While at work, a co-worker asked her if she wanted to go to lunch. Betty's usual response would have been to immediately say, "Yes". However, because she was working on this lesson, she said, "Let me check my schedule and get back to you in a few minutes." Betty then asked herself, "Do I really want to go to lunch with this person today?" As she asked herself this question, she noticed she was both anxious and a little irritated. She knew this meant that she must be perceiving a threat so she asked herself, "Where is the threat in going to lunch?" Betty recalled how this person was a chronic complainer. She also became aware of negative feelings she had in the past when she went to lunch and this person spent the entire time complaining about her boss and the company. Betty decided that she really did not want to go to lunch with this person and told her, "I'm sorry, I just realized I had other plans."

Recommended Activities for Lesson 8

Develop Rational and Realistic Beliefs about Approval and Rejection

This lesson identified many common irrational beliefs people hold about approval and rejection along with ideas that can be used to challenge these irrational beliefs. As you review the lesson, select those ideas that you feel are the most powerful rational challenges for irrational beliefs you hold and summarize them on cards. Review these cards once a day until you have memorized them. Here is the card that Betty made.

- Rejection is a part of life.
- While I would like everyone's approval, rejection doesn't have to defeat me.
- Most of the rejection and disapproval I encounter has little to do with me—often it is due to illness, hunger, fatigue, or stress in the other person.
- People may also reject or disapprove of me for irrational reasons—they are really angry at someone or something else; or, shadows from their past are distorting their view of me and the present.
- There will always be a few people who won't like me no matter what I do.
- Remember that disapproval is usually temporary in healthy relationships.
- If someone is so demanding I have to act in a demeaning way to win approval, this person is not worth my time and effort.
- Don't try to be so perfect—remember that you're human and will sometimes make mistakes and act inappropriately. Forgive yourself when this occurs and challenge the irrational need to be perfect.

Continue to Work with the Block Method

Continue taking five to ten minutes every other day to use the Block Method. As you analyze your thoughts, look for irrational self-talk that is generated by irrational beliefs about rejection or approval. Challenge any you find with the ideas in this lesson. Review the directions in the Recommended Activities of Lesson 5 if you are not sure how to use the Block Method.

Learn to Approach Criticism in an Objective, Problem-Solving Fashion

Develop a list of coping self-statements you can use to stay more objective when faced with criticism. Write them down and practice reciting them until you can easily recall them from memory. Then, review the four steps for responding to criticism described in the lesson until you can recall them using your own words. Spend extra time with steps that are difficult for you. Whenever you find yourself dwelling on a criticism, return to this section and work through the four steps in a systematic manner.

Strive to Do What You Want Instead of What Others Think You Should Do

The lesson listed two different ways to re-establish the ability of knowing what you want. They include postponing decisions and taking time to ask yourself what you really want. If it is often difficult for you to know what you want, practice these two techniques for at least one week. Be sure to also practice identifying your emotions with simple language as you do this. If this is difficult for you, review the discussion on the healthy management of emotions in the section titled, "Emotional Reasoning" in Lesson 5.

Take a Second Look at Nutrition and Exercise

Lesson 2 stressed the importance of proper nutrition and exercise. Examine your diet to make sure it is providing your body with the nutrition it needs. A healthy body makes the work of changing behavior much easier.

If you are not involved in any type of regular physical exercise, consider ways you could do something in this area as well. A minimum of twenty minutes of aerobic exercise three times a week does wonders not only for your physical stamina and health, but also creates a more positive mental outlook. If your ability to travel or finances are limited, there are many programs on television or in books that offer a sensible approach to exercise. If you decide to join a health spa or exercise class, remember to join one that is close to where you live or work. Having a convenient program and location helps maintain momentum in a physical exercise program.

If you have not exercised regularly for a long time, remember to begin slowly and easily. Consistency and moderation are the keys to success. Before starting a new exercise program or drastically changing your current program, it is always best to check with your doctor.

Avoid Trying to Do too Much

Considering your body as a machine with a limited supply of energy is one of the key concepts presented in these lessons. In the weeks and months ahead, there will be many times when you will experience extra stress. Some of these times are predictable, such as holidays and vacations. Others are not, such as when someone close to you is injured or ill. Keep in mind that joyful experiences such as winning money, gaining a promotion, or the birth of a child, can be just as stressful as negative ones. Whenever you encounter a period of high stress, set priorities and do less than you normally do. Doing less gives you the extra energy you need to handle the additional stress during these periods. Review the section titled, "Indications Your Body Is Tired," in the recommended activities in Lesson 5. Also, review the section titled, "Three Guidelines for Periods of High Stress" in Lesson 3.

> Spend at least one week with this lesson
> and do it as thoroughly as possible. If an
> excessive need for approval is a major
> problem for you, spend two weeks with it.

Eliminating the Self-Defeating Behaviors Commonly Associated with Anxiety

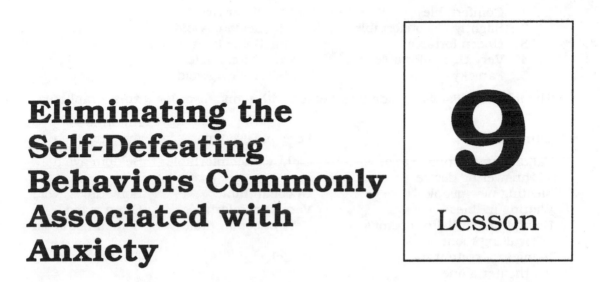

9

Lesson

Overcoming anxiety is much like working on a puzzle. Just as each piece of a puzzle gives meaning to the pieces with which it joins, each concept and skill you learn reinforces those you have already mastered. By now, you are probably beginning to see how many of the pieces of the puzzle that make up your anxiety-related problems fit together. You are now ready to explore a new part of this puzzle and begin working to overcome the self-defeating behaviors associated with your anxiety.

☐ *Behavioral Therapy*

Behavioral Therapy is an approach to psychology in which the focus is on changing behavior. The cause of a self-defeating behavior is not important. When using a behavioral approach, the first step is to identify problem behaviors you want to eliminate and develop specific, well-defined goals.

Identifying Problem Behaviors

The most common problem behavior associated with anxiety is the avoidance of specific situations, places, or objects that trigger anxiety. Make a list of situations, places, or objects you avoid because they trigger anxiety. Using the following scale, rate each item you list with respect to the level of discomfort it causes and the amount of avoidance behavior associated with it.

Level of Discomfort	Amount of Avoidance Behavior
1. Comfortable	1. Never Avoid
2. Slightly Uncomfortable	2. Seldom Avoid
3. Uncomfortable	3. Sometimes Avoid
4. Very Uncomfortable	4. Often Avoid
5. Panicky	5. Always Avoid

The following list was made by a person with panic disorder with agoraphobia.

Situation	Level of Discomfort	Amount of Avoidance
Talking on the phone to an answering device	Sightly uncomfortable	Seldom avoid
Meeting new people	Uncomfortable	Sometimes avoid
Waiting in lines	Very uncomfortable	Often avoid
Being in a dentist or doctor's waiting room	Very uncomfortable	Sometimes avoid
Being in a restaurant or theater alone	Panicky	Always avoid
Being in a restaurant or theater with friend or spouse	Uncomfortable	Often avoid
Driving on freeways	Panicky	Always avoid
Left-hand turning lanes	Very uncomfortable	Always avoid
Walking down the street by my house alone	Very uncomfortable	Always avoid
Going more than two miles from my house alone	Panicky	Always avoid

This list was made by a person with severe social phobia.

Situation	Level of Discomfort	Amount of Avoidance
Going to a theater or restaurant	Uncomfortable	Often avoid
Maintaining eye contact when talking to someone	Very uncomfortable	Always avoid
Standing in lines	Sightly uncomfortable	Sometimes avoid
Dating	Panicky	Always avoid
Meeting new people	Very uncomfortable	Often avoid
Parties or social situations with more than three people	Panicky	Always avoid

Sometimes anxiety is triggered by obsessions. Obsessions are persistent ideas, thoughts, images, or impulses that are senseless or repulsive and seem to intrude upon one's consciousness. Common examples include thoughts of harming others, violating social norms, contaminating or infecting oneself or others, and doubt about whether some action has been or will be performed. Further examples are listed in Lesson 1.

Obsessions are usually accompanied by compulsions of which there are two main types. The first includes actions intended to produce or prevent a future event or situation even though the compulsion has no realistic bearing on the event it is meant to affect. The second includes normal, rational activities performed in a clearly excessive manner. Both these types of compulsions are also called rituals. Common examples include hand washing, counting, checking, and touching. Further examples are listed in Lesson 1.

When listing obsessions and compulsions, begin by listing specific obsessions along with the amount of time you spend thinking about each one during the day. Then list any associated rituals or compulsions along with the number of times you perform each one. If your obsessions and compulsions also have associated avoidance patterns, list the specific situations or places you avoid along with the level of discomfort and amount of avoidance associated with each one. The following list was made by a person obsessed with germs and becoming infected.

Obsession:

I spend at least two hours a day thinking about germs and becoming infected. Sometimes I spend several hours when I have to be around people or travel.

Rituals and compulsions:

I wash my hands two times whenever I touch a contaminated object.
I change my clothes after being in crowds.
I shower or bathe at least twice a day.

Avoidance Patterns:

Situation	Level of Discomfort	Amount of Avoidance
Shaking hands	Very uncomfortable	Always avoid
Parties or social situations	Uncomfortable	Often avoid unless I can bathe soon afterwards
Crowded public places	Very uncomfortable	Same as the above
Public transportation	Very uncomfortable	Same as the above

If your anxiety trigger only involves a compulsion or ritual with no avoidance patterns, simply list the frequency of the behavior. Here are some examples.

"I mentally or verbally say a person's name three times whenever I think of him or her."
"I check electrical appliances at least five times after use to make sure they are switched off."
"I wash my hands three to five times each hour."

If you cannot think of any events that repeatedly trigger anxiety, the approaches described in this lesson are not appropriate for you. However, before you go on to the next lesson, spend several days observing when and where you become anxious. Carry a small notebook, and whenever you become anxious, record any thoughts or events that triggered the anxiety. If you cannot identify a specific trigger, simply describe where you are and what you were doing just before becoming anxious. With each entry, be sure to also rate the level of your anxiety. Use the scale at the beginning of this section.

Taking time to observe and record when and where you become anxious helps you identify patterns you may be unaware of. While you are doing this exercise, read through the rest of the lesson. Some of the examples may alert you to currently unknown patterns. After one week, if you cannot identify any event that repeatedly triggers anxiety, go on to the next lesson.

Developing Well-Defined Goals

Once you have identified exactly what it is that is causing your difficulty, it is time to develop well-defined goals. The importance of this second step is summarized by the popular maxim "If you don't have a goal, you'll never get anywhere."

Begin by reviewing your list of situations, objects, people, events, or thoughts that cause difficulty. For each one, list a goal you would like to achieve. These goals need to describe a specific, well-defined behavior or skill you want to develop. The approaches described in this lesson do not work well with goals stated in vague, general terms. The following examples illustrate the difference between general goals and specific, well-defined goals.

General Goal	Specific, Well-Defined Goal
I want to be able to go out by myself.	I want to be able to walk around my block alone. *Or*
	I want to drive to the mall three miles away and spend at least one hour shopping alone.
I want to be able to socialize.	I want to be able to go on a date to a movie. *Or*
	I want to go to a party or club meeting and stay at least two hours.
I want to spend less time thinking about germs and infection.	I want to go to crowded places such as a store without bathing afterward. *Or*
	I want to shake hands and touch door handles without feeling like I need to wash my hands immediately afterward.

After you have completed your list of goals you want to achieve, make another list of the benefits you will receive when your goals are achieved. Here are several benefits the people in the previous examples identified.

I will be able to:

    go on vacations with my family;
    go to dinner parties and social events;
    drive wherever I want and get to places faster;
    attend to my personal health needs which have been neglected.

I will be able to:

    go out on dates and attend parties;
    dine out and have more friends.

I will be able to:

    hold hands and be physically affectionate with my spouse;
    be more effective at work;
    go places more freely since there will be no need to bathe immediately afterward.

Thinking about these benefits is a powerful motivator which will help you continue to practice and reach your goals. If you cannot think of any benefits that are important to you, the goals you listed may not be worth the time and energy needed to reach them. This second point is especially important for people with anxiety-related problems since they often view every limitation or unusual personal characteristic as a problem. Everyone has some minor limitations and personal quirks. These only become a problem when they interfere with your life goals or deprive you of something you strongly desire.

Consider Alice, who has never driven a car. She has no real desire to drive and would gain no benefit from learning how to drive. During a period of severe anxiety it would be easy for Alice to consider her inability to drive as a problem. This would especially be true if most of her friends could drive. Alice might view her lack of skill in this area as more proof of her inadequacy and failure as a person.

Problems on your list that do not interfere with your life and which would offer no real benefits if they were eliminated are not really problems. Cross them off your list and concentrate on goals that would bring real benefits.

☐ *Gradual In Vivo Exposure*

The most effective behavioral approach to use with the types of problems discussed in this lesson is exposure. This approach is based on a simple principle: *expose yourself to a situation or object that causes anxiety until you get used to it.* Exposure can be done by actually confronting the anxiety-producing situation or object or by imagining it. When you expose yourself to the actual situation or object it is called in vivo exposure. When you expose yourself to the feared situation or object by imagining it vividly, it is called fantasy exposure. Both in vivo and fantasy exposure can be done using a slow and gradual approach called desensitization or by using a rapid process called flooding.

Gradual in vivo exposure is generally the most effective form of exposure for overcoming avoidance behavior. The four basic steps used with gradual in vivo exposure are described below.

Select a Goal and Break it into Small Steps

Look at the list of goals you made earlier in this lesson and number them beginning with the one you feel is easiest to attain and ending with the one you consider most difficult. With gradual exposure you always start with the easiest goal and slowly work your way up toward your most difficult goal. The success you achieve with the easier goals provides skills and confidence that are essential for success with the more difficult goals.

If the first goal on your list seems very difficult, divide it into several easy to reach steps. Mike had panic disorder with agoraphobia and refused to leave the house alone. He set as his first goal the ability to go to the mail box, about twenty steps from his front door. Since this seemed very difficult, he divided it into the following steps.

1. Stand on the front porch with the door open.
2. Stand on the front porch with the door closed.
3. Step off the front porch.
4. Walk halfway to the mail box and back.
5. Walk to the mail box and back.

Kathy had panic disorder but only had one avoidance pattern she considered a problem. She refused to drive alone. This problem began when she experienced a panic attack while driving on the freeway. Since she was now becoming skilled at controlling anxiety, she decided to work towards the goal of being able to drive alone across town on the freeway. Kathy's first goal was to drive to a local store alone. Since even this seemed quite frightening, she divided this goal into the following steps.

1. Sit behind the wheel alone for fifteen minutes.
2. Back the car to the end of the driveway and back.
3. Back the car into the street and back.
4. Drive to the end of the block and back.
5. Drive around the block.
6. Drive two blocks away and back.
7. Drive to the local store four blocks away and back.

Goals involving compulsions and rituals can also be divided into a similar series of small steps. Dennis developed the following series of steps to overcome handwashing associated with a fear of germs and infection.

1. Touch a door handle without washing hands.
2. Touch the floor without washing hands.

3. Touch shoes without washing hands.
4. Touch grass without washing hands.
5. Touch a car without washing hands.
6. Touch the sidewalk without washing hands.

As you reach each goal on your list, decide if the next goal needs to be broken into small steps before proceeding. The more difficult a goal seems, the more important it is to break the goal into several small steps. If you become stuck while working on a particular goal, it simply means you have not broken the goal into small enough steps.

Identify Sensations and Thoughts that Create Anxiety or Fear

Recall several times when you have been in a situation similar to the one you plan to practice. Make a list of the unpleasant physical sensations you felt at those times. Then, make a list of as many of your anxiety-producing thoughts as you can recall. Your goal is to develop a list of both the anxiety symptoms and frightening thoughts you might encounter so you can develop a plan for coping with them. Mike, mentioned earlier in the lesson, developed the following lists.

Physical Symptoms	Thoughts
Light-headedness	I'm going to go crazy
Pounding heart	This is awful, I can't stand it.
Sweating	They may come and lock me up.
Sometimes a feeling that I'm going to faint	People are going to see me like this and think I'm crazy
	If I faint I'll fall down and hurt myself.
	If I faint I won't know what people are doing or saying.

As you practice, add any new symptoms or thoughts that cause a problem to your list. Be sure to take time to develop a plan for coping with these new additions as outlined in the following step before your next practice.

Develop a List of Coping Skills

Once you identify the symptoms and thoughts that cause you problems, you are ready to develop a plan for coping with them. The main coping skills presented in the first half of the book include the following.

Relaxation response methods

If you have not yet begun developing cue-controlled relaxation using the supplemental cassettes or the scripts in Appendix 1, begin now. Cue-controlled relaxation is usually the most practical type of relaxation response to use while practicing. However, sometimes it is also possible to find a quiet place to sit or stand where you can go through a more formal method for developing a relaxation response. The muscle tensing and relaxing described in this lesson's recommended activities is also very useful.

Diaphragmatic breathing

This is a primary symptom reducing skill for many people. You may want to review Lesson 2 if you have not been using it.

Coping self-statements

If you have not been using coping self-statements, review the section in Lesson 2 that describes them and develop a list. If you have been using coping self-statements but do not yet feel skillful with them, take time to review and update your list.

Rational self-talk

Of the skills listed in this step, rational self-talk is the most difficult to learn and the most difficult to apply to anxiety-producing situations. However, it is an extremely effective skill once it is mastered. Review the basic principles given in Lessons 4 and 5 periodically.

Distraction

Distraction methods are described in Lesson 2. These skills are especially useful for coping with the intense, short-term anxiety that sometimes occurs when you first encounter a frightening situation.

When you practice, carry a small card with you which lists those specific skills you find most useful. This helps you remember to use them while you are practicing. Here is a card that Mike carried with him.

- Use relaxed diaphragmatic breathing.
- Take a moment to tense and relax.
- Use your coping self-statements.
- Externalize—observe carefully or talk to someone.
- Minimize negative self-talk.
- Watch out for magnification, catastrophizing, fortune telling, and labeling.

It is especially important to develop skill in combating the anxiety-producing thoughts you listed in the previous step. One way to do this is to substitute coping self-statements whenever you notice yourself thinking or saying anxiety-producing statements. Mike found it difficult to think of coping self-statements when he first began practicing, so he carried the following card.

- Anxiety is NOT dangerous—only uncomfortable. I can be anxious and still function effectively.
- Just take things one step at a time. There's no need to rush.
- This will only last a short time. I can handle it.
- My symptoms are usually caused by hyperventilation—they won't hurt me and will soon subside if I use diaphragmatic breathing.
- I don't have to do this perfectly. It's okay to be anxious.
- Practice will make this easier. It has already become easier for me to do many things.
- There is no need to fight anxiety. It is just adrenalin triggered by old conditioned-response habit patterns. These feelings will go away after awhile.

A second way to combat anxiety producing thoughts is to apply your rational self-talk skills to the specific problem thoughts you listed. As you review the anxiety producing thoughts you listed in the previous step, identify the type of distorted thinking each represents and write out a rational response. You may need to use the Four-Step Analysis described in Lesson 7 for some of your concerns. Once you have developed your rational responses, rehearse each one until you can easily recall it. This may take several days of practice. These rational responses become powerful coping self-statements you can use to challenge your specific concerns. When Mike did this, he developed the following rational responses for his list of anxiety producing thoughts.

Self-talk: I'm going crazy. (Labeling)

Rational response: I am not going crazy. I am only experiencing adrenalin in my system and misinterpreting what it means. I am perfectly sane and able to cope with this situation even though I may feel somewhat uncomfortable at first.

Self-talk: This is awful; I can't stand it. (Magnification)

Rational Response: This is not awful. The holocaust was awful. This is only unpleasant. I can stand it. I am alive and will continue to live.

Self-talk: People are going to see me like this and think I'm crazy. (Mind Reading and Fortune Telling)

Rational response: First of all, most of the people I meet won't even be aware of what I am doing or how I am feeling. Second, most don't care. Even if someone notices I am uncomfortable, he or she will probably have forgotten about it within five minutes. Besides, what people think is not really important. It is what I think that is important.

Self-talk: They may come and lock me up. (Fortune Telling and Catastrophizing)

Rational response: Now this is a real fantasy. The worst that could happen is I might be taken to an emergency room if I fainted. That would probably be the safest place I could be.

Self-talk: If I faint, I'll fall down and hurt myself. (Fortune Telling and Catastrophizing)

Rational response: I have never fainted so it is very unlikely that I will faint when I practice. If I use my diaphragmatic breathing it makes it even more unlikely that I will faint. If for some reason I do feel faint I can simply sit down wherever I am. People around me will either ignore me or help me. After I breathe with my diaphragm for a few minutes I will then feel fine. I might feel embarrassed, but I can handle that. No one ever died from embarrassment. It might be unpleasant but it is not really that big of a deal.

Self-talk: If I faint I won't know what people are doing or saying. (Magnification and Catastrophizing)

Rational response: This is a true statement that I am reacting to as if it were a catastrophe. There are two basic fears that are magnifying the importance of this possibility and transforming it into a catastrophe. One is my fear of losing control which causes me to want total control of both myself and everything around me. There is always the 1-10% chance of something negative occurring. Actually, the possibility of my fainting is far less than 1% because I now know how to use diaphragmatic breathing. This means I have better than a 99% chance of being fine. Even if I did faint, nothing terrible would happen.

The other fear underlying this concern is my excessive need for approval which causes me to believe that people won't like me if I faint. This is simply not true. Most people would be concerned and help me. Even if my fainting did cause some people to reject me, I can handle that. I don't need everyone's approval. I have many good friends who like me in spite of my faults. What's even more important is my own self-approval.

Practice Exposing Yourself to the Feared Situation

Once you have completed the first three steps, you are ready to begin practicing. If you have many limitations keep a record of your practice sessions. This allows you to see your progress and identify coping skills you may need to perfect. There are many formats you can use when making a record of your practice sessions. Use any that you find useful. The following format was used by Mike. The portion shown describes practice sessions he had while working on the goal of walking to the mailbox and back.

Activity: Walk to the mailbox and back.

Wed. 9/11, 2:00 - 3:00 p.m.

At first I only got half way, panicked and returned. I practiced a relaxation response exercise (progressive relaxation), reviewed my coping skills, and tried again. I was panicky but I made it three times.

Thurs. 9/12, 2:15 - 3:00 p.m.

This time I walked to the mail box and back eight times. I was very nervous the first few times but it didn't seem as bad as yesterday. I was only moderately uncomfortable the last few times. I remembered to use my diaphragmatic breathing and coping self-statements and did simple tensing and relaxing in between.

Fri. 9/13, 1:30 - 2:15 p.m.

Completed the task ten times. My coping self-statements seem to be coming more naturally now and feel more real when I repeat them. I was only moderately anxious so I spent a few minutes standing by the mail box on each trip. Tensing and relaxing and diaphragmatic breathing in between trips really helped.

Sat. 9/14, 1:00 - 2:00 p.m.

Had much difficulty when I first started and stopped after getting about a third of the way. There were several people out as it was a nice day and I felt as though everyone was watching me. I took time to tense and relax and reviewed rational self-talk on mind reading and the excessive need for approval and tried again. I made it seven times. My anxiety dropped from a high to moderate level.

Sun. 9/15, 2:00 - 3:00 p.m.

I walked down and back with no problem. I felt so good that after completing the task eight times I walked to the edge of my property and chatted for a few minutes with my neighbor. I didn't even need to use my rational self-talk or coping self-statements. My anxiety level ranged from moderate to very low.

If you have a physical disease that limits the amount of anxiety your doctor thinks you can safely experience, review your plans with your doctor. Then proceed at a speed the two of you determine is safe. You may even want to practice exposure under the supervision of someone who is familiar with your condition and trained in this technique. Fortunately, for most people anxiety is NOT dangerous; it is only unpleasant.

☐ *Guidelines for Practicing*

The following guidelines are designed to ensure your success while practicing gradual in vivo exposure. Review them often while you are working to reach your goals.

Practice Regularly.

The only way you can convince yourself that you can face the situations you fear is to practice facing them. You need to demonstrate to yourself that you can function in the feared situation no matter how you feel. In addition, it takes time to eliminate anxiety triggered by the conditioned response learning discussed in Lesson 2. For these reasons you need to practice as much as possible and practice regularly. Do not wait until you are "feeling up to it." While there are times when illness, work, or family problems prevent you from practicing, do not look for excuses to avoid practicing. Instead, make practicing one of your highest priorities.

A good general rule is to practice for at least an hour each day. If you have extensive limitations, you may need to practice more than one hour. If you have few limitations and a busy life, two or three practice sessions a week may be enough. When using fewer practice sessions, extend them to two or more hours. *You cannot practice too much.* Practice as much as your time and energy allow.

Learn to Tolerate Distress.

Anxiety is something you can tolerate; so beware of magnifying the sensations you experience when anxious. While extreme anxiety and panic are uncomfortable, they cannot hurt you. They will not drive you mad or cause any harm to your body. In fact, you have probably already experienced the worst anxiety you will ever experience.

To prove this to yourself, recall the worst episode of anxiety you have had. At that time you most likely did not understand what was occurring and did not have the skills you have been developing while working through these lessons. It was the lack of knowledge and skills that allowed your anxiety to become so intense during this episode. You now understand why this occurred and have a wide range of skills for managing anxiety effectively. As a result, it is unlikely that future anxiety will approach the level you experienced during this past episode. But even if it did, so what? You now know you can stand it and function because you have already done so in the past. You also know that it would only last for a limited period of time.

Expect Anxiety to Accompany New Activities

When you first begin a new activity, you will probably feel anxious. You may even feel panicky. This is normal and passes with time. Train yourself to expect and accept these feelings. Sometimes anxiety may even increase before it decreases. Fortunately, practicing as described in this lesson usually reduces anxiety to a tolerable level fairly quickly. Remember, much of this anxiety is simply a form of conditioned response learning as discussed in Lesson 2. As you practice, you become more and more desensitized and the skills you are learning become more reliable and more effective. Approaches that work poorly at first and reduce anxiety only slightly eventually are able to reduce even extreme anxiety quickly.

Relabel Anxiety as Excitement

The way your body reacts when you are anxious is exactly the same as the way it reacts when you are excited. The only difference is in how you interpret the feelings inside your body. An excellent example of this is the way a musician or actor feels just before going on stage. New and inexperienced performers tend to identify their feelings as anxiety while more seasoned performers delight in the excitement they are feeling. They all are feeling the same adrenalin response; the first group is interpreting it as anxiety, the second as excitement.

Identifying this extra energy in the body as anxiety causes it to interfere with your performance. However, when you start to identify this energy as excitement, it becomes a resource that makes for an even better performance. As a result, many people find it helps to label the physical sensations they experience while practicing as excitement.

This is more than just a mental game. Whenever you do something you have either never done or have not done for a long time, there is an element of excitement. In order to get in touch with this, take a moment to recall the excitement you felt as a child during your first trip to the zoo, the circus, or some other fun place. Recall also how it felt in your body. A person with anxiety-related problems tends to misinterpret this type of normal excitement as anxiety. Considering the feelings you experience as you go on the adventure of a practice session as exciting or even thrilling helps to transform them into friends and allies.

Expect Progress to be Three Steps Forward and One Step Backward

Expect occasional days when you slip back into old behaviors and find situations you thought you had conquered to be difficult. This is a normal and natural part of the learning process. When it occurs, use the Trouble-Shooting Checklist in Lesson 5 to identify what caused the temporary lapse into old patterns and what you can learn from it. Then resume practicing. Illness or fatigue usually play a major role in these periodic lapses into old behaviors; so remember the concept of the body as a machine with a limited supply of energy.

When old behavior patterns resurface because you are very tired or ill, do not become alarmed. Just view the old patterns as a message that you need to take care of your body's physical needs and apply your stress management skills more diligently. If you are working on a limitation that is especially difficult to overcome during one of these periods, break it into a series of smaller, easier activities. Keep in mind that every complex skill you have learned, from walking to memorizing the multiplication tables, took time. You frequently would have to go through a process of relearning skills you forgot or learned poorly before you mastered the skill.

Challenge Perfectionism

Sometimes people feel defeated after practice sessions because they have not done everything they set out to do. If they were especially anxious, they may even interpret the anxiety as a sign that they are getting worse. These reactions are the result of perfectionistic expectations.

There is no way for you or anyone else to know how fast you should proceed with your goals or what is best for you before you actually begin practicing. Learning the correct rate at which to pace yourself is a process of trial and error. You learn what is "too much" by doing too much. Fortunately, even when you do not accomplish all you want to accomplish, a practice session is still beneficial. Even when you only complete a small part of an activity it is still a success.

Identify and challenge your perfectionistic tendencies whenever you find yourself pushing yourself too hard and putting yourself down with statements like, "I should have known better," or "It's terrible that I can't do what I planned." Instead, tell yourself that you have successfully found your current limit and start making plans to overcome it using the methods described in this lesson. It also helps to ask yourself "What do I want to do today?," and "What would be good for me to do today?," instead of assuming you should be able to do more than is reasonably comfortable. If perfectionism becomes a major problem, spend a week reviewing Lesson 6.

Practice with as Many Factors in Your Favor as Possible

When you begin practicing new activities, arrange as many factors in your favor as possible. For example, a person practicing driving on the freeway would select a time and a section of highway where there is little traffic as a first step. It would be unwise to begin during the commuter rush hour. Only after mastering easy stretches of highway during times of light traffic would it be appropriate to begin practicing in more difficult situations.

Another important factor to consider when practicing is your physical and emotional state. Remember that you have only a limited supply of energy. If you are spending most of it coping with a cold, a family problem, or some other stress, you have less energy left for practicing than during times when you feel healthy and relatively free from outside sources of stress. During times like these, go ahead and practice but lower your expectations and plan easier activities for your practice sessions. If you are very sick or stressed, it may be wise to delay practicing for a few days in order to rebuild your strength.

In addition to the above, avoid combining your practice sessions with errands or work. Practice just for the sake of practicing. This avoids the problem of pressure that results from thinking about all of the things you "should" or "have to" do in relation to the errand or job.

Use Your Coping Skills at the First Sign of Anxiety.

Lesson 2 pointed out that coping skills are most effective when used at the first sign of anxiety. Review the card on which you listed those skills that work best for you at the beginning of each practice session so you will be sure to use them. Whenever you begin to feel anxiety rising, become aware of what you are thinking and use the rational self-talk skills to challenge any distorted thinking you identify.

Keep Pushing Yourself a Little Bit Further

Do not repeat an activity day after day because you are waiting to be completely at ease with it. Proceed towards your goals at a pace that generates a moderate level of anxiety during most of your practice sessions. Keep pushing yourself a little bit further. Whenever a practice session is accomplished easily, either extend the time you spend on the activity or do just a little more than you had planned. If day after day you are repeating activities that generate little or no anxiety, you are not really practicing. At the same time, if day after day you are panicky, you are probably going too fast and trying to do too much. When this occurs, re-examine your goal and break it into smaller, easier steps.

☐ *Other Forms of Exposure*

Although most people find gradual in vivo exposure the most effective behavioral approach, some find that one of the other forms of exposure is more effective. As you read through the other forms discussed in this section, you can decide whether or not you want to try them.

Rapid In Vivo Exposure

Rapid in vivo exposure is also called flooding. With flooding, you place yourself into a frightening situation or come into contact with a frightening object and allow yourself to experience the maximum amount of fear possible.

Alexa provides a good example of how flooding is done. Alexa was afraid of riding buses. Since she could not afford a car, this proved a major problem. She overcame this fear by spending three days riding buses. When she got on the bus for the first time, she was terrified. As the bus pulled away from the bus stop, her fear increased. After about thirty minutes her fear peaked and started to decrease. By the end of three hours, she was no longer panicky. The next day she again felt a high level of anxiety when she first boarded the bus to practice. However, it was greatly reduced and decreased more quickly than on the first day. By the third day, she experienced very little anxiety. She then started using buses regularly and had no further problems.

At first rapid exposure might seem horrible. However, it is similar to removing a band-aid from a hairy part of your body. You can yank it off quickly and be done, or you can remove it slowly, one hair at a time. While some people are willing to experience this type of anxiety and do well with flooding, most prefer the gradual approach.

Gradual Fantasy Exposure

Gradual fantasy exposure was originally developed by Joseph Wolpe who called it systematic desensitization. When used with limitations or feared situations associated with anxiety it involves the following five steps.

Select something on which to work

Begin with the first goal on your list. After you can work comfortably with it, proceed to the next one.

Allow yourself to become relaxed

Use the relaxation response method you have been practicing to develop a state of relaxation. If you have not been practicing a method, take one or two weeks to develop the ability to produce a relaxation response. Use any of the methods in Appendix 1 that work well for you.

Imagine yourself in the situation or activity

Imagine the situation or activity as vividly and with as many of your senses as you can. Create as much detail as is necessary to make it seem real to you. Then imagine yourself in the situation behaving in the way you want to behave and feeling the way you wish to feel.

Stop whenever you feel anxious

If you begin to feel anxious while doing step three, stop for a moment and use your relaxation response procedure to relax. Repeat a few coping self-statements and use rational self-talk to challenge any negative thoughts that occur.

Repeat the above steps

Repeat the above steps until you can comfortably imagine yourself in the situation you selected for at least three minutes.

If you experience excessive anxiety while doing the above steps, do the following.

Remove yourself

Spend several sessions simply imagining the situation or activity without being in it. After you can do this comfortably, imagine yourself in the situation or doing the activity.

Create an imaginary model to take your place

Imagine someone of the same sex who is very similar to you in the situation or doing the activity on which you are working. Imagine this person acting as you would like to act and feeling as you wish to feel. When you can do this comfortably, substitute yourself for the model you have created.

Increase the time

Imagine yourself in the situation or doing the activity for only a few seconds then use your relaxation response method. After you can do this comfortably, gradually increase the amount of time you spend in the situation to three minutes.

Select an easier situation

If the above suggestions do not help, work on an easier situation. Re-examine your goal and divide it into several steps.

When systematic desensitization is the only approach used, progress is usually very slow. Because of this, it is best to combine systematic desensitization with in vivo exposure. Systematic desensitization can be especially useful as a prelude to in vivo exposure when dealing with a particularly frightening situation.

Harold, who had a dog phobia, provides a good example of how systematic desensitization can be combined with in vivo exposure. Harold spent thirty minutes using systematic desensitization to imagine dogs. He began by imagining dogs walking, eating, or sleeping. Next he imagined situations where a dog was a short distance away from him. Then, he imagined a dog rubbing against him. Finally, he imagined a dog sitting in his lap. At the end of thirty minutes he was able to imagine all of these situations comfortably. At this time a real dog was brought into the room. At first the dog was kept at the opposite end of the room. Slowly, over the course of another thirty minutes, the dog was brought closer until it was placed in Harold's lap. By the end of this practice session Harold was able to hold and pet the dog without feeling anxious.

If you decide to try this combination approach, the amount of time it takes for your anxiety to decrease may be different from the above example. Some people spend several practice sessions with systematic desensitization before moving on to in vivo exposure.

Rapid Fantasy Exposure

Rapid fantasy exposure is also called implosion, flooding in imagination, or imaginal flooding. Implosion is usually done with a therapist since most people find it difficult to do this on their own. The process begins by determining a person's worst fears. The therapist then takes the person on an imaginary confrontation with those fears.

Sandra, for example, was afraid of driving on freeways. She was asked to imagine driving on the freeway during the middle of the commute rush hour. The crush of the cars, the fumes, and noise were all described in great detail. This was continued until her anxiety disappeared.

Response Stopping

Response stopping is the halting or limiting of specific compulsive behaviors for specific periods of time. Hand washing and repeated checking are examples of compulsive behaviors that can be overcome through response stopping. Response stopping is often combined with exposure since compulsions usually have associated avoidance behaviors. The following example shows how Norma who suffered from Obsessive Compulsive Disorder or OCD overcame a hand washing ritual by combining response stopping with exposure.

Norma's excessive hand washing was in response to a fear that she might contaminate her family with germs that would ultimately cause their deaths. Whenever she touched anything she considered "dirty" she would immediately wash her hands. She also had extensive cleaning rituals for most of her house.

Norma's first goal was to wash only before eating, after using the toilet, and at other appropriate times. Since she was washing every five or ten minutes when she began, this seemed like an impossible dream.

Norma made a list of things she considered dirty and ordered them from the least dirty to the most dirty. She then began having practice sessions once a day that lasted for two hours. During this time she would "contaminate" her hands with something she considered dirty and refrain from washing. She began with touching items she considered least dirty such as a light switches. As they no longer bothered her, she worked up to those items she considered most dirty such as the floor. After three weeks of practicing two hours a day, five days a week, she was able to touch the objects she considered the dirtiest without needing to wash.

Norma's next goal was to eliminate her excessive cleaning rituals. She did this in the same manner as above. She listed in order the various places in her house, starting with those she considered least important to those she considered most important. She then deliberately contaminated an area and refrained from going through her extensive cleaning ritual.

After Norma had eliminated her compulsive behaviors, she occasionally experienced the urge to return to them. Whenever this occurred, she immediately contaminated herself or the area and practiced response stopping. The need to repeat this combination of response stopping and exposure occurred every few weeks at first. However, after about six months it occurred only once every few months.

Here is a summary of points you need to remember when using response stopping and exposure to overcome compulsions:

- Practice sessions need to be longer and more frequent with compulsions than with simple avoidance behaviors. Try to have at least three practice sessions which last one and a half hours or longer each week. Four or more longer practice sessions are better when practical.
- If several compulsions are present, work with each one individually.
- When compulsions are severe, the initial period of high anxiety sometimes lasts for several days before it begins to lessen. When this is the case it is usually best to have response stopping and exposure supervised by a professional who specializes in the treatment of compulsions.
- When compulsive behavior is accompanied by prolonged or severe depression, evaluation by a psychiatrist experienced with mood disorders is essential. There is evidence that indicates people suffering from both obsessive compulsive disorder and depression may have an inherited biological predisposition to depression. When such a predisposition is present, it is important to treat the underlying biological problem in order to have success with the behavioral problems.
- Once you have eliminated a compulsive behavior, you may occasionally experience the urge to return to it when you encounter a triggering event or object. When this occurs, practice exposure and response stopping immediately.

Lesson 1 pointed out that current thought on OCD views it as a sort of neurological "hiccup" where the brain becomes stuck while performing a normal checking or grooming activity. Even so, the behavioral approach described in this section is effective for many people with OCD. However, if you have worked with the behavioral approach in a dedicated manner for several weeks and are achieving little or no results, you may need to work with a therapist experienced in using these techniques. You may also find that combining the cognitive-behavioral approach described in these lessons with the use of medication to be the key to success. At the time of this writing, two medications, fluoxetine (Prozac) and clorimipramine

(Anafranil), are showing great promise for people with OCD. Others will probably also soon be available.

If you decide to try medication, be sure to consult with a doctor who has experience working with OCD and who is knowledgeable about the current research being done with this problem. You may also find it helpful to read the books on *Obsessive-Compulsive Disorder* listed in the Recommended Reading at the back of this book.

Social Role-Playing

Social role-playing is actually a specialized form of exposure. It is used to help people with social phobia who either lack basic social skills or lack the confidence to use the social skills they do have. Social role-playing involves practicing social skills with someone who is trusted until the skills become comfortable. This person can be a trusted friend, a study partner, or a therapist who specializes in social phobia. Some of the skills that can be practiced include the following.

Greetings: Greetings range from a simple smile to standard words and phrases such as "Hello", and "How are you doing?"

Comments On Shared Experiences: Comments on shared experiences can be used to set yourself and others at ease and begin interaction in a wide variety of social situations. These experiences might include the weather, the temperature of the room, a long wait in a line, the decorations of the room you are in, or the surrounding scenery if you are outside.

Expressing An Opinion: Begin reading the papers or watching the news. Select one event each day and practice expressing an opinion about it. Listen to the conversations of others to gain ideas about how other people express their ideas. Rehearse those styles of expressing an opinion that appeal to you.

Telling A Story: People in social situations often tell stories about themselves or others. Select two or three incidents involving yourself and practice telling about them. These can either be something that happened recently or something that happened long ago.

Active Listening Skills: Active listening is a powerful social skill. It is also a skill that most people have not learned. Several basic active listening skills are described in Appendix 5.

Body Language And Voice: Practice standing and sitting with a more forceful posture. Speak a little louder and more forcefully.

In addition to social role-playing, social skills can be practiced in front of a mirror or whenever you are alone and have the time. You can even use the gradual fantasy exposure method described earlier in this lesson to practice social skills. Eventually, however, social skills need to be applied to real life situations and involve other people. When you begin to do this, be sure you follow the suggestions given in the Guidelines For Practice.

Recommended Activities for Lesson 9

Begin Eliminating Self-Defeating Behaviors

Begin using the approaches described in this lesson to eliminate self-defeating behaviors associated with your anxiety. If you have many self-defeating behaviors, this work may take many weeks, possibly many months. However, the basic principles can be mastered within one or two weeks. As you proceed through the following lessons, continue to practice regularly and review the Guidelines For Practicing periodically. If you encounter difficulty with your practice sessions, review the entire lesson to make sure you are following it accurately. If, after completing all of the lessons, you feel you need further help in applying the behavioral techniques described in this lesson, either refer to the suggested reading for additional works on these techniques or seek help from a qualified professional.

While working with this lesson, be sure to do all of the paper and pencil work it recommends. The more severe your self-defeating behaviors, the more important it is to actually write down your goals, symptoms, and coping strategies. The written work is your plan of attack for eliminating these unwanted behaviors. The more detailed and precise it is, the more successful you will be.

Reducing Anxiety by Tensing and Relaxing Muscles

When you become anxious your muscles automatically tense. It is also true that the more relaxed you are, the less anxious you feel. This is why people who have become skilled at producing a relaxation response find it an effective way to reduce anxiety. The following steps can be used to reduce anxiety by tensing then relaxing your muscles.

1. Breathe in and hold your breath.
2. As you hold your breath, tense your muscles.
3. As you breathe out, let go of the muscle tension all at once.
4. Take two relaxed diaphragmatic breaths. As you breathe out, make a conscious effort to let your shoulders drop a little and feel your muscles relax a little more than they were when you breathed in.

This simple procedure can be done almost anywhere. If a particular part of your body is especially tense, you may want to just tense and relax that part. If you have the time and it is practical, you can also go through the various parts of your body, tensing and relaxing them separately as described in the progressive relaxation method detailed in Appendix 1. Simply massaging the tensed area can also help.

Guidelines for Support People Assisting You in Your Practice Sessions

The following guidelines describe how you can be the most helpful support person possible during practice sessions.

What to do before you begin assisting in practice sessions.

- Read this lesson thoroughly so you understand the behavioral approaches being used.
- Discuss what you can do to help. Review the goals and coping strategies your friend or relative has identified so you understand what is being attempted and what skills are most helpful in reducing anxiety.
- Be realistic and fair to yourself. Do not promise more than you can deliver as far as how much time you can commit to practice sessions. If you feel overburdened you may give up or become resentful and interfere with practice sessions without realizing it.
- Be reliable. These practice sessions are very important to the person you are assisting. Do what you say you are going to do. If you don't it will probably cause much hurt and resentment in your friend.
- If it is agreeable to the person you are helping, help plan practice sessions. Your objectivity can be very useful.

What to do during a practice session.

- Remember that the person you are helping is always the best judge of what he or she can or cannot do. Your role is to assist and encourage.
- Do not pretend to know more than you do. People suffering from anxiety are highly suggestible and often make connections where none exist. Do not offer advice on food additives, vitamins, or other things you may have heard about that are "reported" to be important. Stick to the principles given in these lessons or by the therapist your friend is working with.
- Try to remain as calm as possible. Your calmness can be a powerful force for reducing your friend's anxiety.
- Avoid being critical. A person suffering from severe anxiety is supersensitive to criticism, especially during a practice session. Encourage each attempt and step towards the goal.
- Remind your friend to use the coping skills you have discussed whenever you notice him or her becoming anxious.
- If your friend becomes angry during a practice session, do not take it personally. Remember that anxiety and tension causes a person to think less rationally than usual. If this is a recurring problem, read Lesson 12 for suggestions on how to deal with anger constructively.
- Expect ups and downs and the unexpected. One practice session may go very smoothly, then the next one very poorly. This is normal. After a difficult practice session, review the Trouble Shooting Checklist in Lesson 5 with your friend. Encourage the view that the difficult period is only temporary.
- Encourage repeated practice of a new-found ability.

What to do if the person you are assisting experiences panic during a practice session.

- Remain calm and speak in a confident, friendly manner. Your calm presence is a powerful form of support.

- If you are practicing away from home, help your friend make a graceful exit and find a relatively quiet place to sit or stand as near to the scene that provoked the panic as possible where the panic can subside.
- Offer reassurance that your friend does NOT have to finish the activity to be successful. Even partial completion of the activity is a success.
- Do not discuss the anxiety symptoms being experienced at this time since this tends to make them worse.
- Remind your friend to use coping skills. Name specific skills, since it is difficult for him or her to think when panicky. Then talk about some neutral topic until the panic subsides.
- When the panic subsides, suggest a return visit to the place in which the panic occurred. Do not force your friend to go, but encourage him or her as strongly as possible while remaining positive and encouraging. Immediate re-exposure helps decrease the tendency for future avoidance.

Other ways you can help.

- Help your friend get past "stuck points" by finding in-between steps that can be taken. This is easier for you since you can view the activity more objectively.
- If you notice an old negative behavior recurring after it has been eliminated, encourage immediate resumption of exposure or response stopping practice. Do not wait until all of the symptoms reappear.
- If progress is not being made after several weeks, suggest seeking professional help.

This is a very important lesson. If
limitations or self-defeating behaviors
seriously interfere with your life,
spend two weeks with this lesson.

The Process
of Change

Change is difficult. This is true even when change produces a more enjoyable and successful life. In this lesson you explore some of the factors that make change difficult and learn how to overcome the natural human tendency to resist change.

□ *Learned Helplessness, Self-Efficacy, and Change*

In the late 1960's an experiment was performed in which dogs were given random electric shocks from which they could not escape. They developed what is called *learned helplessness*. Once they learned that nothing they did made any difference they became passive and gave up trying to escape. Later, when placed in another situation in which they could easily escape the shock, they hardly tried.

Later experiments involving humans led Albert Bandura, a psychologist at Stanford University and a leader in his field, to develop a concept he calls *self-efficacy*. The word efficacy refers to the power or capacity to produce a desired result: the ability to achieve results. The term self-efficacy refers to your belief about how well you think you will be able to cope with a specific situation. If you are confident you will do well, you have a strong sense of self-efficacy.

A person can have a strong sense of self-efficacy about one type of activity and lack a sense of self-efficacy about another. For example, a skilled musician can be confident of performing well during a concert but doubt his or her ability to deliver a simple speech at a banquet. Your belief about your self-efficacy affects your behavior in a variety of ways. It helps determine what activities you attempt and is directly related to the level of anxiety you feel in various situations.

The concepts of learned helplessness and self-efficacy help explain more fully how many of the self-defeating behaviors associated with anxiety develop and how they can be overcome. For example, Gail had a panic attack while driving. She did not understand what had happened and did not understand how her distorted thinking processes were creating the anxiety/panic cycle. As she found herself unable to escape the panic attacks, she gave up trying to drive. Gail lost her sense of self-efficacy and was in a state of learned helplessness.

As Gail went through these lessons, she learned how to prevent panic attacks by developing more rational self-talk skills and using effective coping strategies. This began to increase her sense of self-efficacy. As she practiced driving, through a gradual exposure approach, she became more and more confident of her ability to manage anxiety while driving. In essence, Gail had regenerated her sense of self-efficacy and overcame her state of learned helplessness.

Objects and situations are not intrinsically frightening. The fear and stress they evoke come from how we interpret our ability to cope with them. This is the result of a *learning process*. While it takes time, energy, and an effective method, old learning can be replaced with new learning. As you learn how to think and act in new, more effective ways, your sense of self-efficacy in various situations increases and your level of anxiety decreases.

☐ *Rationalization and Denial*

Self-defeating behaviors are often maintained because a person avoids constructive change. An example of this is a person who talks about changing but channels energy into watching television, puttering around the house, working crossword puzzles, doing non-essential chores, and other non-productive activities. This leaves little time and energy for the work of learning new skills and applying them.

When considering how you might be resisting change, remember the need for balance and moderation in your life. It is unreasonable to expect yourself to jump at *every* opportunity to use a new skill and practice *every* day without fail. On days when illness or stress is draining your energy, it is wise to reduce activities and concentrate on tasks with a high priority. You also need to schedule time for play and relaxation. However, when there is a recurring pattern of avoiding opportunities to learn or practice skills needed to overcome your problems, it usually indicates you are resisting change.

One common form of resistance is rationalizing. Rationalizing is the use of seemingly rational and socially acceptable explanations to "justify" the lack of real effort. For example, a person with many anxiety-related problems skims through the lessons pausing only to do a few of the recommended activities in a hasty, haphazard manner. This is justified by saying, "I already understand all of this, and besides, none of it really applies to me." These rationalizations allow this person to avoid spending the time and energy required to overcome the anxiety-related problems, yet still feel that some effort is being put forth.

Another common form of resistance is denial. When denial is extreme, a person refuses to acknowledge that a problem exists. With milder denial a person acknowledges that a problem exists but minimizes the importance of the problem. The person may also use rationalizations, humor, sarcasm, or put-downs to characterize the actions needed to bring about constructive change as unimportant, ineffective, counterproductive, or even dangerous.

The key to overcoming resistance to constructive change is recognizing that rationalization and denial are a normal part of human nature. As with every other human characteristic, rationalization and denial are sometimes important for survival. Rationalization and denial can be very effective coping skills when faced with unescapable pain. Two examples would be a person in a concentration camp or a child in a dysfunctional family.

At one time or another, everyone refuses to acknowledge a problem or avoids working to overcome a self-defeating behavior because they are either busy with more important life issues or because they are too frightening to deal with. Once this fact is acknowledged and accepted it becomes easier to examine your behavior more objectively and notice those times when you are doing this. When you are, do not condemn yourself or view it with alarm. Instead, accept this as a common occurrence. Then make a firm commitment to use the information in the next section to overcome this common tendency.

☐ *Six Roadblocks to Change*

There are six roadblocks that can prevent you from being successful. Each is described below along with methods for overcoming it. Whenever you notice that you are resisting constructive change, read through this section and identify the specific roadblock or combination of roadblocks generating this tendency. Then use the suggestions given to overcome it.

Change Is Often Uncomfortable

At first, new thinking patterns and behaviors feel uncomfortable and "strange." While this is less true for small changes, it can be a major roadblock for big changes. It is like buying a new pair of shoes. At first the new thoughts and actions do not feel "right." They seem foreign and do not mold comfortably to your personality.

Fortunately, you can overcome this roadblock by expecting new behaviors to feel uncomfortable at first. A person usually expects to feel awkward when learning a new skill such as skiing, sewing, or playing a musical instrument. Learning the skills in these lessons is really no different. Expect the same feelings of awkwardness. It takes time and practice to internalize new behaviors and thinking patterns. After a period of time, the new behaviors and thinking patterns become a part of you and feel as comfortable as a favorite pair of shoes. In fact, even behaviors that seem very strange and uncomfortable at first can soon feel very natural.

The Consequences of New Thoughts and Behaviors Are Unknown and Unpredictable

When you use old, familiar ways of thinking and behaving, you are fairly certain about what will happen. Even though this may cause pain, people and events are predictable. When you start to use new thinking patterns and behaviors, you begin to feel new and different feelings. People around you react differently, and events may occur in ways quite different from the past. At first, this may be somewhat frightening because you do not know what will happen as you become this new person.

One way to overcome this roadblock is to recognize what is going on and make a conscious choice:

Do I want to stay where I am and hold onto predictable and familiar thinking patterns and behaviors even though it means experiencing all of the pain that goes with them?

Or

Do I choose instead to try new behaviors and thinking patterns which, although they may be somewhat uncomfortable and frightening at first, offer a life of increased joy and fulfillment—a more effective way of living?

When making this choice it helps to remember that after you have mastered the new behavior or thinking pattern, you can always go back to your old ways. However, once you really experience the increased pleasure and fulfillment that positive changes brings, you will rarely choose to return to old self-defeating ways of thinking and behaving.

Another way to overcome this roadblock is to remind yourself that the period of discomfort experienced while learning new behaviors is usually short. The unfamiliar quickly becomes the familiar. Events that are frightening at first can quickly become old friends. It also helps to relabel the anxiety caused by your fear of the unknown as excitement. Develop the attitude that the task of changing your behavior is an exciting adventure—that the unknown is a Christmas or birthday gift waiting to be explored.

Learning Requires the Use of An Effective Method

The old saying "practice makes perfect" is not true. Practice makes *Permanent*. Consider a person trying to learn to play the guitar. If this person holds the guitar incorrectly and uses improper fingerings for the chords and notes, poor habits are developed that hinder this person's ability to play well. Likewise, when you are trying to change self-defeating patterns, you need to use an effective approach or you will be unsuccessful.

This roadblock is one of the easiest ones to overcome. The activities described in these lessons have proved to be an effective approach for overcoming anxiety-related problems. However, they are useless if they are not used. If you have not been making much progress, it may simply be because you have not been following the directions in the lessons carefully. If this is the case, continue on through the lessons but take more care to do the recommended activities. When you reach Lesson 15, plan to go through the earlier lessons again. As you repeat the earlier lessons, do the recommended activities you either skipped or did in a haphazard manner again, only this time do them as instructed.

Changing Behavior Takes Work

It takes time and effort to change the way you think and act. This is especially true for behaviors which have been repeated so many times they are now automatic. Consider the way you brush your teeth. This is a simple habit pattern, but since it has become so automatic and unconscious, like most habit patterns, a considerable amount of effort is required to change it. Before beginning to brush, you would have to remind yourself about the new method you plan to use. While brushing, your mind would wander and you would catch yourself returning to your old method. After a second reminder you would start using the new method only to forget and have to catch yourself again. And so it would go until enough time and energy had been spent to make the new method as automatic and as much a part of you as was the old method.

The key to overcoming this roadblock is to make a firm commitment to do the work required for change. During the process of changing a behavior, periodically recommit yourself to the work you are doing. It also helps to realize and accept that any major accomplishment requires a certain amount of tedious work. Dull work is more enjoyable if you focus on the results that have already been accomplished, and remind yourself often of the benefits your efforts will bring.

Self-defeating Behaviors Often Provide Important Secondary Gains

Painful behaviors often help satisfy either directly or indirectly one or more important needs. When a need is satisfied in this manner it is called a *secondary gain.* The term "secondary" is used because it indicates that this method of satisfying needs is usually not arrived at through a deliberate, conscious process. Instead, it is the result of stumbling onto advantages and using them in an unconscious manner.

To understand how this occurs, recall a time when you had an injury or illness, such as a broken leg or a bad cold. Recall any benefits you received as a result of being injured or ill which you normally did not have, such as receiving extra sympathy or attention, avoiding an unpleasant task or situation, or receiving time off from work. You probably did not hurt yourself or become ill in order to obtain these benefits. Even though the secondary gains may have been outweighed by the negative aspects of the situation, human nature is such that you probably found at least some ways to benefit from your misfortune.

The longer an unwanted event or condition persists, the more likely it is that you will learn how to obtain secondary gains from it. Sometimes a secondary gain becomes so important it can cause you to maintain a painful condition or behavior in order to continue to receive the secondary gain. This is especially true if the need is an important one and you have few or no other ways to meet it.

To identify any secondary gains you may be obtaining from a problem behavior or situation, ask yourself "What benefits do I gain from my problem behavior or situation?" Identify any ways in which your anxiety or the behaviors associated with it might help you gain attention, security, or some other benefit. Then ask yourself, "How would my life be different if this problem behavior or situation just magically disappeared?" Be aware of any feelings of regret, loss, or sadness about current aspects of your life that would be lost. Also, be aware of any feelings of anxiety or fear generated by new aspects that would be gained. These types of feelings usually indicate that a secondary gain is present.

When you identify a secondary gain, develop a positive method for obtaining the same benefit currently being obtained through the problem behavior or situation. For example, Frank was a very nervous person who had many aspirations but did little to achieve them because of his anxiety symptoms. Frank also dwelled on "catastrophes" he had experienced and used them as a method for receiving attention from others.

As Frank explored how his life would be different if he were "strong," he realized that the thought of being independent and assertive made him very anxious. As he thought further he identified two things that made him anxious. One was the thought of achieving some of his dreams. The other was a sense of doubt about whether people would be friendly and spend time with him. This helped Frank realize that one benefit of being nervous was that it allowed him to avoid taking risks. He could remain "safe" and blame his lack of effort on his anxiety symptoms.

Frank overcame his tendency to use anxiety as a means of avoiding risks by telling himself he could choose to either take a risk or to remain "safe." He did not have to use his anxiety to do this. Furthermore, he reminded himself that whichever choice he made was fine. He bolstered this type of rational self-talk with the rational arguments given in Lessons 6 and 7. He used this approach whenever he noticed himself blaming his failure to take a risk on his anxiety symptoms. This helped him make much progress in overcoming his anxiety symptoms.

Another benefit Frank gained by telling tragic stories was attention. He used two different approaches to overcome this secondary gain. First, he used rational self-talk to convince himself that the "poor you" and "how terrible" type of attention he was currently receiving with tragic stories was not really all that desirable. Even worse, people soon tired of his negative tales and began avoiding him. Next, Frank began developing social skills that allowed him to develop friendships and receive positive attention.

In a similar manner, you can always find more effective and positive ways to obtain the benefits a problem behavior provides. While this takes effort on your part, doing so removes one of the more troublesome roadblocks to change. The previous lessons have already described many approaches that can be used in this way. More are described in the lessons that follow.

Irrational Thinking Is Still Exerting a Major Influence

It is impossible to change self-defeating behaviors when the irrational beliefs and distorted thinking supporting them are exerting a major influence on your life. Identifying and challenging the irrational thinking associated with resistance to change can be done in the following manner. First, look back and identify several occasions when you used rationalization or denial to sabotage or avoid the work required for constructive change. As you do this, examine your self-talk and actions. Identify irrational thinking, then develop and practice rational challenges you can use to combat it. One of the best ways to do this is to use the Block Method described in Lesson 5. In addition, identify words, actions, feelings, or situations associated with resistance to change that can be used in the future to alert you to times when you are resisting change.

While studying this lesson, Pam realized that she often resisted change. During times like these, she would spend much of her day watching television or staring into space. She would also dwell on the past or worry about the future. Pam used the Block Method and listed the thoughts and self-talk she recalled on a piece of paper. Actually, she found she needed several pieces of paper to do this. Next, she reviewed Lessons 4 and 5 and identified the main types of distorted thinking she used during these times: should/must thinking—especially in the form of all-or-nothing thinking, overgeneralization, magnification, minimization, and fortune telling. She then wrote out rational self-talk responses and practiced them.

Pam also spent time skimming Lessons 6 through 8 and identified the first two sections of Lesson 7—"Negative Anticipation" and "Thinking And Acting Like A Victim"—as two which applied to the times she recalled while using the Block Method. Pam especially liked the section titled, "Developing A Strong Belief In The Power Of The Present" in Lesson 7. She had not really worked on this section during the week when she originally studied this lesson. So, she went back and took this opportunity to work on it in conjunction with the current lesson. Later, Pam identified two other helpful sections which had been skipped in her earlier studies— "Developing A Process Orientation" and "Scheduling Activities" in Lesson 6.

In the weeks that followed Pam found that when watching television or sitting and staring into space became a major daily activity, it was time to examine her thoughts and feelings. These two behaviors became powerful signals that alerted Pam to times when she was finding change difficult. She would then use the Block Method and review her notes on how she had challenged irrational beliefs and distorted thinking that was associated with these times in the past.

Recommended Activities for Lesson 10

Continue Working with the Behavioral Approaches in Lesson 9

Continue to apply the behavioral approaches you learned in Lesson 9 to the self-defeating behaviors you want to overcome. If you are working on many problem behaviors, review Lesson 9 occasionally. Continue this work throughout the rest of this program.

Recognizing Resistance to Change

This lesson points out that resistance to change is a natural part of human nature. This activity will help you understand how commonplace resistance to change is. Begin by listing at least two ways in which your mother, father, and the people close to you have resisted something new or different. Then spend time during the coming week observing how people around you resist change. Do not say anything about what you see or try to determine why they are behaving in that way. Your goal is simply to notice how common it is for people to resist change. Understanding how natural it is for people to resist change and seeing it in the people around you makes it easier to be more objective about times when you find yourself resisting constructive change. This in turn makes it easier to use the ideas in this lesson to overcome your tendency to resist change.

Learn to "Release"

Spend time this week considering what you might need to release from your life in order to overcome your anxiety-related problems. In particular, you might want to consider the following:

- Old attitudes which are not productive.
- Worry about your condition.
- Negative language and thinking patterns.
- Old "should" and "must" rules which do not reflect reality.
- Thinking in terms of "can't" and "have to" instead of choices.
- Distorted thinking patterns such as fortune telling and magnification.
- Relationships which are not productive.
- Worry about what others might think.
- The need to be perfect or better than you are.

Which of the above still make you feel uncomfortable, and which do you need to continue to work on? Remember, the key to success is to be able to release old, nonproductive patterns and adopt new, productive ones. Let go of the old and make room for the new.

Identify and Challenge the Ways in which You Resist Change

The following questions focus on forms of resistance common to people using this program. Consider each one carefully and answer it with Yes, Sometimes, or No.

Yes	Some-times	No	
❏	❏	❏	Have I avoided the *work* involved in overcoming my anxiety-related problems by simply going through the lessons once or twice and hoping for an "instant cure?"
❏	❏	❏	Am I still thinking in terms of unrealistic "shoulds" and "musts" and refusing to accept reality as it is, instead of thinking in terms of choices and focusing on what actions would be best to choose?
❏	❏	❏	Do I still refuse to accept what anxiety *is*—a habit pattern or condition of fear I have talked myself into by telling myself lies about what the unpleasant symptoms mean and maintained by repeating those lies over and over—and what it *is not*: a "mental illness," part of my nature that will never be changed, or my cross to bear?
❏	❏	❏	Has my fear that I will never overcome my anxiety-related problems caused me to get into the habit of just wishing things were different; and has this fear caused me to avoid making a firm commitment to working with these lessons as instructed?
❏	❏	❏	Has my identity become so interrelated with my anxiety and am I so accustomed to feeling anxious and limited that any other feelings just do not seem "right?"
❏	❏	❏	Does my anxiety give me a special place with special treatment in my family, job, or among my friends that I would lose if I overcame it?
❏	❏	❏	Am I receiving more attention from others because of my anxiety or limitations that I might not otherwise receive without those limitations (even though this attention is of a negative type)?
❏	❏	❏	What would my life be like if my anxiety suddenly just disappeared forever? Do these things somehow frighten me? Does the fear of failure cause me to stay the same and not try?

If you answered yes or sometimes to any of the above, review the section on "Roadblocks To Change." Then start to use the recommended approaches listed in that section to overcome your resistance to change.

Begin to "Normalize" Yourself

One common obstacale to overcoming anxiety-related problems is the tendency to view everything about yourself and your reactions as abnormal or sick. Every trait that humans have, both physical and psychological, can exist accross a broad range. For example, some people are short, some tall, and some in between. If you happen to be short, you probably just see it as a normal variation. In the same way, it is important to see your traits and reactions as simply normal variations of what is typical of people.

One way to do this is to use labels for yourself and your reactions that are positive rather than negative. For example, if you are the type of person who is more excitable than the average person, see yourself as being "dramatic" or having "lots of energy" rather than as "too sensitive". In essence, you are choosing to look at your traits from a healthy as opposed to a pathological point of view. This is not just a mental trick. Every trait you have has a positive as well as a negative side. While your traits have sometimes created problems, they have also served you well in many situations.

During this week, identify aspects about yourself that you have considered abnormal or sick in the past. List ways in which this trait has benefited you in the past. Also, take time to consider how this trait is expressed in others and how your expression of them is simply a variation of how this trait is expressed.

"Weird" or "Unusual" Thoughts

Occasional "weird" or "unusual" thoughts are common and normal. These can range from a fear of tearing off your clothes and going crazy to having everyone you know laugh at you. Sometimes they can even be morbid or grotesque. Most people have these thoughts from time to time. Usually, they occur when you are tired, hungry, ill, or in some other way stressed or fatigued. In fact, they are one of the symptoms listed in the Trouble Shooting Checklist in Lesson 5 that indicate your body is tired.

These types of thoughts usually disappear on their own when you are feeling better physically and mentally. If you sometimes experience "weird" or "unusual" thoughts, recognize them for what they are, simply the workings of a tired and stressed mind. Do not blow them out of proportion. Just keep substituting positive thoughts for the unpleasant ones and using your rational self-talk. Also remember that your body is a machine with a limited supply of energy and take care of yourself. Do this and these types of thoughts will probably disappear as soon as you are feeling better physically.

Challenging the tendency to resist
constructive change is an important part
of overcoming anxiety-related problems.
Spend at least one week with this lesson.

Feeling Good About Yourself

Lesson 11

Have you ever wondered why one person with only average ability is successful and happy while another person with exceptional ability is unsuccessful and unhappy? Perhaps you are this second person. A large part of the answer can be found by examining the difference in each person's level of self-esteem and self-acceptance. It is now time for you to explore these concepts and learn how to increase your level of self-esteem and self-acceptance.

☐ *Self-Esteem and Self-Acceptance*

As you matured into an adult you developed a complex set of attitudes and beliefs about who and what you are and your place in the world. These attitudes and beliefs make up what is usually called the self-concept. Your self-concept includes beliefs about your strengths and abilities, your weaknesses and shortcomings, and those personality traits you use to distinguish yourself from and identify yourself with the rest of humanity. Your self-concept influences all your hopes, aspirations, moods, and actions.

Self-esteem is a key part of your self-concept. Self-esteem is the value and respect you hold for yourself. People with a high level of self-esteem treat themselves with respect, tend to their needs in a positive manner, and stand up for their rights. Because they respect themselves, they also respect others and have a greater capacity for love. People with low self-esteem do not value and respect themselves. They ignore personal needs and frequently put themselves down. Some tend to put the needs and wishes of others first while others retreat from the world. They may feel that they have nothing to offer others or that others can do nothing for them because they are so hopeless. Any one or combination of these expressions can interfere with their ability to give and receive love and can generate anger and resentment.

Self-acceptance, a second key part of your self-concept, is closely related to self-esteem. Self-acceptance is the ability to acknowledge and own all of your parts, both desirable and undesirable. To understand self-acceptance fully, consider our acceptance of the sun and the moon. We do not try to hide or ignore the existence of the sun and the moon. Neither do we dwell on or exaggerate their good or bad qualities. The sun and the moon simply are and we accept them as a natural part of life. This acceptance allows us to minimize the negative qualities of these heavenly bodies and more effectively utilize their positive qualities. In a similar manner, people with a high level of self-acceptance consider all of their many characteristics and parts—physical, mental, emotional, and spiritual—as simply a natural part of being human. This objective acceptance allows them to make the most of strengths and minimize weaknesses.

Having a high level of self-esteem and self-acceptance does not mean you stop working at improving yourself. However, the motivation of people with low self-esteem and self-acceptance is usually very different from that of people with a high level. The first group tries to better themselves because of the mistaken belief it will make them "better" or more worthy. The second group realizes that learning about themselves and working to develop more positive and realistic behavior and thinking patterns has only one purpose—it enables them to live effectively and experience more joy and fulfillment. Self-improvement has nothing to do with their value as people.

☐ *The Development of Low Self-Esteem and Self-Acceptance*

Your first beliefs about your value or worth developed during early childhood. People with low self-esteem and self-acceptance usually experienced a real or perceived lack of acceptance during childhood. This rejection could have involved parents, siblings, teachers, peers, or relatives.

The most powerful rejection occurs when parents are so caught up in their own pain and inability to cope effectively with life that they are incapable of providing the warmth, love, and acceptance their children need. This is often the case when one or more of the various forms of abuse described in Lesson 1 is present. Children growing up with this type of rejection usually have significant problems in the areas of self-esteem and self-acceptance.

Another powerful form of rejection occurs when one or both parents have unrealistically high expectations concerning their children. This is sometimes due to the parent being a perfectionist. However, it can also be due to simple ignorance of what is appropriate for children of various ages. Regardless of the reason, children who are continually asked to perform at a skill level beyond their capability soon develop a negative view of themselves.

Sometimes parents with good intentions use parenting approaches that are very discouraging. Consider the following types of comments, which are heard all too frequently wherever there are parents and children.

Suzie is such a klutz.
Ronald is the slow one.
Why can't you be good like Mary?
Sean did such a nice job; why don't you ever do that?
Look at all the merit badges Betty has! I bet if you work hard you can do that too.
Even though Edward is eight he still wets the bed almost every night (said to a
    casual acquaintance while Edward is listening).
What a turkey! You've got your sweater buttoned up all wrong.
You're so lazy you'll never amount to anything.

Negative labeling, comparisons, humiliation, and negative criticism like the above are usually used by parents in an attempt to teach children important skills or lessons. Often, they reflect cultural and family traditions rooted in the past where people lived in a harsh, unyielding world. Unfortunately, these types of discouraging comments usually do the opposite of what is intended. Young children are not miniature adults. Lesson 4 describe how children lack many of the higher reasoning powers of an adult, have limited experience, and are egocentric. Because of this, they accept the labels and judgments of adults without question. When exposed to excessive negative labeling, comparisons, humiliation, and negative criticism, the result is usually low self-esteem and self-acceptance.

Low self-esteem and self-acceptance can also begin with rejection by friends. This is often due to a physical difference or problem or to a mental disability. However, it can also be due to a child's race, religion, political, or social background. Children can be very cruel and frequently delight in teasing a child who is different.

Repeated rejection during childhood, whether the rejection is real or a misinterpretation of events, usually leads to the mistaken belief that one is in some way unacceptable, unlovable, or of less value than others. This generates a low level of self-esteem and self-acceptance as well as an excessive need for approval. In fact, the issues and behaviors associated with an excessive need for approval discussed in Lesson 8 are closely related to, and intertwined with, those generated by a low level of self-esteem and self-acceptance.

In addition to the above, a parent with low self-esteem and self-acceptance is often present. As a child copies the parent's words and behaviors, the child mirrors the parent's sense of inadequacy.

□ *The Fear of Being Incompetent*

A low level of self-esteem and self-acceptance is often accompanied by the mistaken belief that one is in some way incompetent and does not measure up to others. When present, this belief can be a major source of anxiety. This mistaken belief is usually the result of a childhood where there were few experiences of success or mastery. Often, there was a very critical parent, continued negative comparisons with siblings, a perfectionistic parent with unreasonably high expectations, or some actual physical or mental disability. Occasionally, this belief is the result of modeling after parents who believed they were inferior because of race, religion, or social class.

People who fear being incompetent often feel like phonies or impostors when talking to someone they consider competent such as an employer, supervisor, peer, or even a stranger. They may also fear their incompetence will be exposed when dealing with authority figures. As a result, many keep a constant lookout for signs that others are noticing their incompetence. The fear that they will be unable to reach their goals is also common and can cause a problem with procrastination, the avoidance of risks, or an excessive dependency upon others. Sometimes the fear of being incompetent causes people to take statements intended as humorous literally and become anxious or upset. They may even have images of themselves as small children in world of giant adults or imagine themselves as frightened animals such as a scared rabbit or dog.

If some of the above characteristics describe you, the fear of being incompetent may be a major issue in your life. Learn to separate your worth from your achievements and develop a true acceptance of yourself. Lesson 6 discusses ways to challenge the mistaken belief that achievement determines worth. Use these ideas along with the others described in that lesson to challenge thoughts and behaviors which overemphasize the importance of achievement.

☐ *Eight Approaches for Increasing Self-Esteem and Self-Acceptance*

Eight methods for increasing your level of self-esteem and self-acceptance are described below. As you work through them, you will find they build on and reinforce work you did in earlier lessons.

Increase the Number of Positive Things You Say to Yourself about Yourself

The continued repetition of an idea tends to make it a part of your belief system. This is how most of your beliefs, both conscious and unconscious, were acquired. What you heard and thought over and over when young eventually became part of your belief system and is now what you tell yourself over and over. This principle often works in a self-defeating manner. An example of this is the tendency to dwell on negative evaluations. By selectively remembering a criticism, exaggerating it to monstrous proportions, and repeating it over and over, you make it an ever-present part of your reality. This lowers self-esteem and self-acceptance and causes you to miss valuable opportunities for growth and joy.

Increasing the number of positive things you say to yourself about yourself uses this principle in a positive, self-enhancing manner. Here are three ways to do this:

Focus on small successes and positive experiences

Whenever you do anything, no matter how small, take a moment to find something about it that was done well and focus on it. If your tendency in the past was to focus on small errors and flaws, this may be difficult at first; however, with practice it becomes very natural.

Identify and remind yourself of your strengths regularly

Develop a list of qualities or skills you possess which you consider to be positive. These need to be specific qualities you feel are accurate. Here is Ruth's list.

> I have a nice smile.
> I am well informed about current affairs.
> I am an excellent cook.
> I am a skilled pool player.
> I am very friendly.

People with a low level of self-esteem and self-acceptance often have difficulty thinking of even two or three items. If this is true for you, spend several days developing your list until there are five to ten items on it. You might find it helpful to have a friend or relative help you.

After you have completed your list, recite it two or three times a day for three weeks. This works best if you make it a regular part of your day. For example, you could recite your list while driving to and from work or while you are getting ready in the morning. If you have difficulty remembering the items on your list, carry a copy with you or post it on a wall. Whenever you think of an additional positive quality, add it to your list. After a few days of practice, begin adding successes, even tiny ones you had during the day along with examples of things you have done that demonstrate the positive qualities you have listed. Eventually, you will be able to list many positive qualities, skills, and successes without the need for your list.

Practice "mirror talk"

Develop a list of positive qualities and skills as described above. Then recite your list out loud once a day while looking at your image in the mirror. This is easiest if it is done while you are doing a regular daily activity such as combing your hair, shaving, or putting on make up. As you say each item on the list add, "And I like me." This is how Ruth recited the list she developed.

> "I have a nice smile. And I like me."
> "I am well informed about current affairs. And I like me."
> "I am an excellent cook. And I like me."
> "I am a skilled pool player. And I like me."
> "I am very friendly. And I like me."

Many people feel silly or find it difficult to face themselves with their good points and say them out loud. The more difficult this exercise is for you, the more important it is to do it until you can: 1) think of many positive qualities, skills, and successes, 2) easily and comfortably "face" yourself in the mirror, 3) sound and look like you really mean the things you are saying as you recite your list, and 4) actually ENJOY doing it.

Decrease the Number of Negative Things You Say to Yourself about Your Weaknesses

Answer each of the following questions on a piece of paper.

- What kinds of situations make you feel bad about yourself?
- What kinds of activities have you wanted to undertake but did not try because you feared you might not do them well?
- What interactions between you and another person or persons during the past few weeks or months left you with negative feelings about yourself?

Next, list as many negative labels or self-statements as possible that you said or thought to yourself about you and your behavior during or after the above events. Phrase them so they are short declarative sentences such as the following.

"I'm weak."
"I'm too passive."
"I can't do anything right."
"I'm so thoughtless."

Now review the section on labeling in Lesson 5. Add any of the negative labels that appear there to your list. Once you have completed your list, go back through and change every negative label or statement into its opposite, positive. Use phrases that begin with "I am," "I am becoming," "I am learning how," or "I can be." Here are examples which use the first two sentences on the above list.

"I'm weak."	can be changed into any of these:	"I am strong." "I am becoming strong." "I am learning how to be strong." "I can be strong."
"I'm too passive."	can be changed into any of these:	"I am assertive." "I am becoming assertive." "I am learning how to be assertive." "I can be assertive."

From now on, whenever you notice yourself making negative statements about yourself, stop and substitute new, positive labels for your actions or characteristics. To be effective, these positive statements need to be something you believe is true. It seems dishonest to say, "I am strong," when you are feeling weak. Statements like "I am learning to be strong," or "I can be strong," usually feel more truthful. You may use statements other than the ones suggested. The only rule is they to be positive and something you can believe.

Practice Giving Genuine Compliments to Others

Giving genuine compliments is an easy way to increase your level of self-esteem and self-acceptance. When you give genuine compliments, others usually feel better about both themselves and you. This in turn makes you feel better about yourself. A genuine compliment is different from praise that is general or excessive. The difference becomes clear when you examine the following examples.

Examples of Praise

You are the greatest cook in the world.
I just don't know what I'd do without your help.
You are the best-dressed person I know.
You're always so kind and generous.
You're so good.

Consider how you would feel if the above statements were made about you. On one hand, they do feel nice. However, this sort of praise is so absolute you know it's not completely true. The high standard of performance implied by these types of statements can also feel like a burden. In addition, praise like this is so vague, it does not really tell you what you said or did that was appreciated. In contrast, the following examples of genuine compliments deal with small, specific actions. You know exactly what was appreciated. This makes them easier to accept than the examples of praise.

Examples of Genuine Compliments

I really enjoyed that spaghetti.
Your mowing the lawn helped me a lot.
The color of that shirt really looks good on you.
Thank you for the flowers yesterday; I enjoyed them very much.
I appreciated your spending time with me.

Many people feel uncomfortable when complimented. This can be caused by compliments that are hard to live up to or which seem insincere, such as the examples of praise. Sometimes the person lacks experience with compliments and does not know how to respond. Often, however, discomfort with compliments is due to low self-esteem and self-acceptance. The person receiving the compliment feels unworthy, that somehow he or she is not "good enough."

If you have difficulty accepting compliments, decide which of these causes applies to you. Use rational self-talk to convince yourself that you deserve compliments. Whenever you receive a compliment, practice saying "Thank you," and nothing else. While this may be difficult at first, with time and practice it becomes easy. Eventually, compliments become enjoyable.

The ability to give and receive compliments brings several benefits. As you become more observant about what is positive in others, your ability to notice positive aspects of yourself increases. Noticing positive aspects of your environment also makes you more optimistic. All of this increases your level of self-esteem and self-acceptance.

Develop a More Realistic View of the World and Your Place in It

Becoming a positive realist is a major theme running throughout these lessons. Five ways to develop this orientation are listed below along with the location in previous lessons where each is discussed in detail.

Develop an appreciation of your own worth

You are a unique individual with a unique gift for the world. No one else has your experience or can see the world as you do. Develop an understanding and acceptance of this fact through positive self-talk, by reading encouraging books, by attending inspirational talks, and by listening to recorded audio cassettes such as those described in the back of this book.

In addition to the above, take time to review and clarify your spiritual or philosophical beliefs. How do you see yourself within the context of the world around you? What is the meaning of life? What is it that truly makes a person happy? This type of reflection is often ridiculed and seen as unimportant in a modern world that worships immediate self-gratification and the massive accumulation of things. However, it is an essential periodic activity that helps give meaning to all of the areas of your life.

If you already have a strong set of spiritual or philisophical beliefs, you know the power it has to help you see your value. If you have beliefs which helped you in the past but which you have neglected to use at this point in your life, renew your connection with them. If you have never considered this side of yourself, begin to identify how you can feed your inner need for personal meaning.

Accept that you are not responsible for the emotional reactions of others

The reactions others have to you and to the events around them are the result of their beliefs and interpretations. You do not make them happy or cause them to become upset. They make themselves happy or cause themselves to become upset. You are responsible only for your own feelings and actions. If you are having trouble accepting this, review Lesson 4 and remind yourself of the points it makes until you accept them.

Look for facts rather than opinions

It doesn't matter who's right but what's accurate. Make an effort to obtain accurate information about yourself, your problems, other people, and the various situations around you. Take time to think about your problems in a rational and logical manner. Do not accept the opinions and beliefs of others unless you have taken time to consider them carefully and they seem rational and realistic. If you have difficulty with this, review the section on adopting an objective, problem-solving approach to criticism in Lesson 8.

Eliminate distorted thinking

As you become successful at eliminating distorted thinking, you will enjoy increased success at each of the above. This often requires additional work in Lessons 4-8.

Accept your weaknesses and mistakes

Whenever you condemn yourself because of a personal weakness or mistake, remind yourself that you are not your mistakes. There is a difference between your "self" and your "behavior." Also remind yourself that your worth is not determined by your achievement. Use the ideas in the section on dealing with mistakes objectively in Lesson 6 to remind yourself that mistakes are a natural part of being human.

In addition to the above, learn to laugh at your errors and silliness. Humor is one of your greatest allies in learning to love and accept yourself. Increasing your ability to use humor in a positive manner increases your ability to use errors and mistakes as a source of wisdom. After they have served this purpose, humor then makes it easier to dismiss and leave these experiences in the past where they belong.

Learn to Refrain from Comparing Yourself to Others.

People often feel miserable and second-rate because they habitually compare themselves to others. Underlying this tendency is the mistaken belief that worth is determined by achievement. Use the ideas in Lesson 6 to develop rational self-talk that reinforces the belief that your worth as a human is a separate issue from what you do. For example, being an inferior dancer or an inferior cook does not make you an inferior person. In addition, memorize the following statement.

> "I am not inferior. I am not superior. I am simply me."

Whenever you notice yourself comparing yourself with others, recall this saying. Then, use the rational self-talk you have developed to remind yourself that your value as a human being has no relationship to others. You are unique and because of this uniqueness it is impossible to do anything exactly like someone else. You can only do things in your own style and to the best of your ability. That is good enough. If someone else does not appreciate your value and uniqueness, that is his or her problem and loss.

Work at Reducing Indecisiveness

Indecisiveness is often the result of excessive concern about what others will think about your decisions. When an excessive fear of failure is present, avoiding decisions also helps you avoid making mistakes. Here are five ways to become more decisive.

- Develop a realistic view of mistakes. Use the ideas in Lesson 6 to challenge any mistaken beliefs you still possess about the meaning of mistakes and their relationship to your worth as a person.
- If you usually rehearse your responses to others, practice improvising. Just say the first thing you think. Begin this exercise with people you find safe and in situations you find comfortable. Then gradually expand it to other areas of your life.

- Work at reducing self-criticism and adopt the attitude of "what is, is." If this is difficult, review the section on distinguishing between responsibility and blame in Lesson 7.
- Speak a little louder than you usually do. This may seem strange and you may even feel like you are yelling at people when you first start. However, most people won't notice what you are doing. As you practice speaking in a louder and more decisive tone, you will find yourself acting more decisive.
- Tell others when you feel good or bad and let them know you appreciate things they have done. Appropriate self-disclosure and the giving of genuine compliments helps to make you more aware of your feelings and increases your self-acceptance.

Limit the Number of Commitments You Make.

People with an excessive need for approval often fall into the habit of saying yes to almost every request made of them. Then, they either cannot keep all the commitments they have made, or they sacrifice their own needs and wants in order to meet them. This leads to self-condemnation and further loss of self-esteem and self-acceptance.

If you frequently overcommit yourself, limit the number of commitments you make. Make a commitment only if you are certain you are able to keep it, you are willing to make a strong effort to keep it, and you actually want to keep it. If you have a very strong tendency to overcommit yourself, limit yourself to only one commitment a day at first. Continue limiting your commitments until you are keeping commitments without resentment or regret. Then gradually increase the number you make until you reach a level that is both comfortable and enjoyable.

Use Your Imagination.

Frequent repetition of positive experiences can alter your self-concept in a dramatic and positive manner. One major difference between people with a low level of self-esteem and self-acceptance and those with a high level is the types of memories they choose to recall. People with a low level usually dwell on negative experiences and failures while people with a high level spend their time recalling and enjoying positive memories. Set aside five to ten minutes a day to recall positive things you have done and success you have achieved. Recreate these memories in as much detail and as often as possible. As you recall each positive experience, compliment yourself on your success using genuine compliments as described earlier in this lesson. Continue with this exercise until it is easy to recall success and you feel good about your self-compliments.

Recommended Activities for Lesson 11

Develop Beliefs that Build Self-Esteem and Self-Acceptance

As you review the lesson, make a list of those ideas that reinforce self-esteem and self-acceptance and summarize them on cards. Review these cards once a day until you have memorized them. Here are the cards one person made:

Self-Esteem and Self-Acceptance

- I am not inferior. I am not superior. I am simply me. And that is good enough.
- This is my world. I deserve to be here.
- I take responsibility for and own all of myself—the good and the bad.
- I work to improve myself because of the joy and fulfilment it brings—not because it will somehow make me a better person.
- I was put down a lot when I was little—those were lies from parents who loved me but who were warped by their own childhood. I am a good and decent person who deserves the best in life.
- I have often felt incompetent. All of my evaluations at work and comments from others clearly show I am very able at many things.

Notice that the last two items on the above list address personal issues. If you have identified specific events or people in your past that influenced your life in a negative way, create powerful, direct statements that challenge negative beliefs that developed in response to these people or events.

Review Rational Challenges Developed in Previous Lessons

This lesson discussed how irrational beliefs discussed in previous lessons often contribute to low self-esteem and low self-acceptance. Review cards you prepared for Lessons 6, 7, and 8. Identify those ideas that you feel will help you with this lesson and review them along with the ideas you are memorizing from this lesson.

Work at Increasing Your Level of Self-Esteem and Self-Acceptance

Do as many of the seven activities described in this lesson as possible. Spend most of your time and energy on the first two: Identify and Remind Yourself of Your Strengths Regularly and Decrease the Number of Negative Things You Say to Yourself about Your Weaknesses. Review the remaining five approaches and identify the ones that would be most useful for you. Since low self-esteem and self-acceptance are usually accompanied by an excessive need for approval, spend thirty minutes this week reviewing Lesson 8. Many of the activities in that lesson can be combined with those in this one. If low self-esteem and low self-acceptance are a problem for you, spend two weeks with this lesson.

Continue to Work with the Block Method

Continue taking five to ten minutes two or three times a week to use the Block Method. As you analyze your thoughts, look for expressions of any of the irrational beliefs that have been discussed in this and previous lessons. Review the directions in the Recommended Activities of Lesson 5 if you are not sure how to use the Block Method.

Continue Working with the Behavioral Approaches in Lesson 9

Continue to apply the behavioral approaches you learned in Lesson 9 to the self-defeating behaviors you want to overcome. If you are working on many problem behaviors, take time to review Lesson 9 occasionally. Continue this work throughout the rest of this program.

Consider Your Progress

Take a few minutes this week to consider how you have changed since you began these lessons. Do this when you are feeling good so you are reasonable and objective. Always avoid evaluating your progress when you are sick, hungry, tired, or experiencing excessive stress. As you consider your progress, answer the following questions.

How have your attitudes towards people, life, and yourself changed?
How has your approach to life and problems changed?
Is there anything you are doing now you were unable to do four months ago?

Congratulate yourself on any positive changes you identify!

Develop the Ability to Recognize and Accept "Normal" Anxiety

One of the keys to managing anxiety effectively is learning to recognize and accept "normal" anxiety. People with anxiety-related problems often fear anxiety so much that all anxiety is considered abnormal. By this point in the lessons, much, if not most, of the anxiety you experience is an appropriate response to real-life situations. There are many times when you become anxious and your anxiety has nothing whatsoever to do with your old self-defeating patterns. When you become anxious, remind yourself that anxiety is an inherent part of life. Your goal is NOT to eliminate all anxiety. Your goal is to eliminate excessive anxiety and manage the normal, everyday anxiety you encounter effectively so you can live the life you want to live.

During this week, notice how often people around you become anxious. Whenever you find yourself becoming anxious, notice how much, if not all of it, is normal and healthy. This is an important part of the process of "normalizing" yourself that was discussed in Lesson 10.

Continue to Use the Trouble-Shooting Checklist

It has been mentioned several times in the previous lessons that you may occasionally experience yourself falling back into old patterns. When this happens, refer to the Trouble Shooting Checklist in Lesson 5. Then recall how you handled these situations before and do what was successful in the past. Remember—it takes work to develop new patterns, but with time and practice they eventually become automatic. At this point in the lessons you have only spent a short time working to change thinking and behavior patterns you spent a lifetime developing. It is reasonable and probable that sometimes you will slip back into old patterns. When you do, it only means you need more work in that area. It may also mean you are overly tired and need to take better care of yourself.

What Does it Mean to Overcome Anxiety?

There is much talk in the psychological community about the need to "resolve" issues and problems. What does this mean? The common impression is that the process is somewhat like going to a medical doctor with a minor injury or illness. The doctor dresses the wound or gives you medication and after a while it is like the injury or illness never occurred. This is *not* how psychological issues are usually "resolved".

Everyone has individual psychological issues that recur during his or her lifetime. For example, it is common for individuals raised during the time of the depression to have a heightened concern about security and lots of should/must rules. These issues will be theirs for life. However, these issues do not need to interfere with their ability to have happy and successful lives.

If you have been working through the lessons as described, you have already identified many of your issues. These might be a body that reacts strongly to stress, a heightened need for approval, perfectionistic tendencies, a tendency to use certain types of distorted thinking, or any of the other issues discussed in the previous lessons. You will probably never eliminate these tendencies. They will occasionally affect your life in an adverse way. This will usually be during times when you are ill, hungry, tired, or experiencing unusual stress. They may also be triggered by people or events that resemble your past in some way as a result of conditioned responsed learning as discussed in Lesson 2.

The fact that this occurs occasionally is unimportant. What is important is to become skilled at identifying your issues, developing signals that alert you to when they are affecting your thoughts and behavior, and developing a set of skills that keeps them from interfering with your life in a negative way. It is similar to a popular carnival game where the player faces a platform with several holes. The heads of little mechanical gophers pop up out of the holes at random. The player is then supposed to hit the gopher back into the hole before others pop up. Your personality traits and personal issues are yours for life. Events will occur periodically that trigger old feelings and responses. The trick is to be like the person who becomes skilled at anticipating where gophers will pop up and hitting them back down into their hole.

Your goal is to become skilled at knowing when your "buttons" are being pushed and training yourself to respond in a way that brings you what you want in life.

> Self-esteem and self-acceptance are key
> issues not only in anxiety-related
> problems but in a wide variety of
> self-defeating behaviors. Spend at least
> one week with this lesson.

Making Anger Your Friend and Ally

Lesson 12

What do you think of when you think of anger? For most people this question brings a host of negative associations, such as frustration, hurt, loss of control, and fear. This is unfortunate since anger can be a positive, constructive force in your life when channeled appropriately. In this lesson you learn how to do this and make anger your friend and ally.

☐ *What is Anger?*

Lesson 4 describes in detail how emotions are generated through the following four-step process:

Event $\rightarrow$ Interpretation $\rightarrow$ Emotion $\rightarrow$ Action

Emotions generate actions that satisfy needs and protect us from threat and loss. They do this in two ways: by activating physical responses in the body and by producing a specific desire. The stronger the emotion, the stronger the physical response and the desire.

Anger is the emotional response triggered by an interpretation of an event that a threat is or may be present. Once triggered, anger activates the fight or flight response which prepares the body for action. This physical response is accompanied by a desire to eliminate the source of the threat.

Like all emotions, anger can exist at many different levels of intensity. Unfortunately, many people fail to recognize annoyance, irritation, or displeasure as simply low level anger. They only think of anger in terms of its higher levels of intensity like rage. Because undesirable actions often accompany more intense forms

183

of anger, anger is often considered an undesirable and negative emotion. However, anger is often the driving force behind positive actions. For example, when you ask a person to stop an activity that is annoying you, it is low level anger labeled as annoyance that is driving your actions. Whenever you assert yourself, it is anger—usually at a low level of intensity—that is providing the energy and motivation for your actions.

Anger is closely related to fear in that both are triggered by a perceived threat and both activate the fight or flight response. Anger produces a desire to meet and eliminate the threat, while fear produces a desire to escape from or avoid the threat. Because anger and fear are closely related, some people find that converting feelings of anxiety (low level fear) to anger helps them overcome self-defeating behaviors associated with anxiety. When used in this way anger provides increased motivation to meet and overcome the threat associated with the self-defeating behaviors. Relabeling the physical symptoms generated by anxiety as anger also enables these people to view their physical symptoms as a source of strength instead of as a sign of weakness.

☐ *The Threats that Generate Anger and Fear*

Lesson 4 describes in detail how human beings are unique in that they have no instinctive fears. By the time you are an adult, everything you identify as a threat is something you have learned. Furthermore, once a threat is identified, the key that determines whether you respond with fear or anger is your perception of how well you can meet the threat. This is also based on beliefs and thinking patterns you have learned. If a threat seems unmanageable, it triggers fear. If it seems manageable, it triggers anger. Often people alternate between fear and anger as their perception of both the situation and their ability to cope with it changes.

One notable exception is a situation where the threat seems unmanageable and from which escape seems impossible. One person will experience paralyzing fear and another intense anger. No one knows exactly how or why these reactions occur although it probably has deep biological roots in our evolutionary past. In this sense we respond like a cornered animal: we either freeze or attack.

Another interesting aspect of the interpretation process that generates anger is the nature of threats in our modern world. In ancient times most threats involved physical needs and were concrete—you could see, touch, smell, or feel them—such as a wild animal, a hostile neighboring tribe, or a long drought. Concrete threats such as being fired from your job or threatened on the street still exist. However, most of the everyday threats we experience in our modern, technological society involve psychological needs. These needs are usually partially or totally abstract, such as a sense of personal power, pride, love, self-respect, or a sense of belonging and significance. This aspect of anger is dealt with more thoroughly later in the lesson when inappropriate anger is discussed.

☐ *Actions Generated by Anger*

The various responses people have when angry are summarized below. This list starts with what are usually the most undesirable response patterns and ends with what is usually the most productive one in everyday life. As you read through the list, remember that all anger patterns are learned. Because these patterns become automatic they often seem unchangeable. However, because they were learned, they can be replaced with new patterns if you use an effective method and are willing to do the work required to bring this about.

- Violent, destructive and/or harmful actions
- Tantrums: Verbal and/or physical
- Hurtful or critical remarks, sarcasm, or teasing
- Sulking/pouting
- Passive aggressive behavior: Behavior that causes problems for the person you are angry with but which seems unintentional such as forgetting something important or being late.
- Hurtful or destructive fantasies: Daydreaming about what you would like to do to the person you are angry with.
- Suppression: Knowing you are angry but pretending not to be angry.
- Repression: Being angry but being unaware of your anger.
- Constructive action: Action that reduces the threat with the least amount of harm or discomfort to both yourself and others.

The energy and motivation generated by anger and expressed through the actions listed above can be focused in one or more of the following four directions.

- It can be ignored through suppression or repression.
- It can be directed at an identified external threat.
- It can be turned inward and directed at a real or imagined personal weakness or inadequacy.
- It can be directed at someone or something unrelated to the threat which generated the anger.

An example of each of the above is given in the following situation. Four different people have lost their money by putting it into a faulty candy machine. Don never allows himself to become angry and so suppresses his anger and walks off trying to be calm even though he is very irritated. Deborah first directs her anger at the machine and kicks it. Then she directs it at the fact that she has lost money and goes looking for someone who can refund it. Mark turns his anger inward at his perceived inadequacy and begins to put himself down with comments such as "I'm so stupid. These things never seem to work for me." A few minutes after losing her money, Linda has several harsh comments for a co-worker who does not merit them.

☐ *Appropriate vs. Inappropriate Anger*

Anger is an appropriate response when a real threat exists. The action it generates is appropriate when that action brings about the reduction or elimination of the threat with the least amount of discomfort or harm to yourself and others.

Anger can be inappropriate in two ways. The first is when anger is felt even though no real threat exists. For example, a person with good intentions says in a positive manner that your shirt looks nice and you become angry. The second is when anger is felt at a level of intensity too high for the threat that is present. An example of this is a person who goes into a rage when a shoelace breaks.

Anger felt when there is no real threat or at an excessively high level is usually the result of irrational thinking. This can be due to irrational beliefs which are part of a person's basic belief system or to a temporary reduction in the person's ability to think in a logical and rational manner. Both of these issues are discussed further in the next section. The actions generated by anger are inappropriate when they bring unnecessary pain to yourself or others.

☐ *Minimizing Inappropriate Anger*

This section presents six approaches you can use to minimize the amount of inappropriate anger you experience. Once you have done this, you will have taken a major step towards the goal of making anger your friend and ally.

Protect Your Ability to Think in a Logical and Rational Manner

A major source of inappropriate anger is the loss of your physical ability to think rationally. Remember, the brain is a physical organ. Anything that interferes with its ability to function interferes with your ability to interpret events accurately. Common factors that interfere with the brain's ability to function are hunger, fatigue, illness, excessive stress, and drugs. Inappropriate anger is much more likely when one or more of these factors are present. In fact, Lesson 3 pointed out that increased irritability and emotionalism are often early warning signs that you need to use stress management principles. A discussion of these principles along with suggestions for staying functional during times of high stress are given in Lesson 3. Setting priorities and taking care of yourself as suggested in that lesson helps to maintain your physical ability to think and assess possible threats accurately.

Challenge Mistaken Beliefs About Anger

There are two common mistaken beliefs about anger: the idea that anger is in some way a "bad" emotion, and the idea that anger always results in undesirable behavior. Sometimes these mistaken ideas are the result of direct instruction. Children are often told very directly that anger is not an acceptable emotion. Here are some common examples:

"Don't get angry at me!" (a command from a parent or adult)
"You shouldn't be angry at your brother or sister."
"Only dogs get mad."
"It's not ladylike to be angry."

Sometimes a child's anger is ignored or discounted with comments such as, "You're not really angry." A child may also come to the mistaken conclusion that anger is "bad" or "dangerous" if a parent always suppresses anger and rarely expresses irritation. Sometimes a child learns this lesson by living with an adult who is very explosive. In this case the child may need to stay calm in order to be spared the wrath of the adult. A child might also make a conscious decision never to be like the explosive adult, and thereby develop the habit of suppressing anger.

If any of the above describes your childhood and you rarely or never allow yourself to experience anger, review the following ideas daily until they become a firm part of your belief system.

- Events will occur every day that cause you to become angry. This is normal.
- Anger is an appropriate response to a situation when a real threat exists.
- Feelings just *are*. What is important is not *what* you feel but how you *respond*.
- Anger can be directed to become a positive force behind constructive actions.

Minimize Distorted Thinking and Irrational Beliefs

All of the forms of distorted thinking and irrational beliefs discussed in the previous lessons can cause you to feel threatened when no threat exists and generate anger. This is especially true for events that violate your should/must rules. Roy is a good example of this. He had a rigid belief that people should always be fair. Whenever Roy was in a situation where someone acted unfairly, he would become extremely angry even when the situation was trivial. As Roy learned to challenge this rigid rule, he was able to focus on how he would respond when events were unfair instead of becoming angry and reacting against the fact that something is not fair. In a similar manner, as your ability to challenge distorted thinking and irrational beliefs increases, the amount of inappropriate anger you experience will decrease.

Build a High Level of Self-Esteem and Self-Acceptance

If you find it difficult to accept your human weaknesses and limitations, personal weakness and limitations become a threat and generate inappropriate anger. The best way to overcome this type of inappropriate anger is to use the approaches described in Lessons 8 and 11 to develop a high level of self-esteem and self-acceptance. People with a high level of self-esteem who accept their human frailties are not threatened when their limitations are noticed. As a result, they concentrate on what they can do, and feel no remorse or anger over what they cannot do.

Identify Sensations and Emotions which Have Been "Taboo" in the Past and Deal with Them More Directly

A taboo sensation or emotion is one you believe you must never experience. Often, this is an unconscious belief. For example, Janet had a strong need to be in control of herself and any situation. The experience of being weak or helpless was taboo. Whenever she perceived herself as being helpless or out of control, Janet found herself becoming angry. This did not help the situation. However, the physical feeling of strength generated by the anger created the illusion that she was powerful and in control. She could also ignore her weaknesses and inadequacies because she was busy being angry. Other emotions and sensations which are frequently covered by anger include fear, guilt, shame, embarrassment, confusion, and sexual sensations.

Emotions other than anger can also be used to hide taboo sensations. Anxiety and depression are two common ones. For example, John had strong sexual taboos and became very anxious whenever forbidden sexual feelings were experienced. John's anxiety helped distract him from the fact that he was experiencing sexual feelings.

Whenever an experience, emotion, or sensation is hidden by anger or any other emotion it interferes with your ability to think rationally. Since most of your energy is used to generate and maintain the secondary emotion, little mental energy is left to deal with the world in a realistic, here-and-now fashion. This usually causes you to act in an automatic, self-defeating manner.

Identify any *recurring* situations which usually result in inappropriate anger. These are situations in which you hurt someone you love, lose something you value, find it difficult to explain yourself or understand what you are experiencing, or in some other way act in a self-defeating manner. After you have identified this type of recurring situation, the next step is to identify the forbidden emotion or sensation beneath the anger. Here are two ways to do this.

- Look at the recurring situations you have noticed in an objective manner and complete the thought, "I am acting as if..." This may suggest possible emotions or sensations. You might even pretend you are watching an actor in a movie and try to guess at what the character might be feeling in that situation.

- Identify the feeling you experienced just before the anger. You can do this either during or after one of the recurring situations you identified. The emotion or sensation just before the anger probably is *not* the forbidden feeling you are seeking. However, it can help you identify the taboo feeling. Ask yourself, "What does this feeling remind me of?" This question may trigger a memory of a painful experience in your past. The emotion or sensation felt during this past experience is probably the one you are avoiding.

Craig was living in a foreign country with his wife. During the first few months he noticed that he would become angry and sarcastic whenever they went shopping together. Using the above techniques Craig looked at his behavior and found he was acting as if his wife "should" know the local customs. He also found the feelings he experienced just prior to his anger reminded him of times when he was very embarrassed as a child and young adult. Craig realized he was embarrassed because he did not know the local customs. After this realization, Craig only had to become aware of the embarrassment he felt when shopping with his wife and his anger would leave. He still felt embarrassed, but he was now able to respond in an appropriate manner. With time the embarrassment faded.

You will know you have succeeded in identifying a hidden feeling when your anger vanishes. The emotion or sensation hidden beneath the anger simply replaces it. While this feeling may be uncomfortable, you are now able to utilize all of your mental abilities to deal with the situation more effectively.

Whenever you uncover a taboo emotion or sensation underneath inappropriate anger, identify the irrational beliefs which cause it to be taboo. Identifying and challenging these irrational beliefs makes the feeling more acceptable. With practice you stop converting the "forbidden" feeling into anger.

Learn to Release Resentments.

Resentment is a re-stressing process where a past hurt is recalled and you tell yourself things about that event that make you angry over and over. Gaining skills in releasing resentments allows you to free energy tied up in resentment so it can be used constructively. You also cease to be victimized by negative feelings and gain a sense of accomplishment, freedom, and control. Whenever you find yourself nurturing a resentment, explore each of the following areas. One or more will probably provide the key for releasing the resentment you are experiencing.

Weigh the seriousness of the offense and ask yourself, "Is holding onto this resentment really worth it?"

No matter how justified a negative feeling is when first experienced, continuing to nurture and re-experience it has tremendous physical and emotional costs for you. When carrying a resentment, you are the ultimate source of your own misery and stress. Resentment rarely affects the object of the resentment. It is the person carrying the resentment—you—who suffers the negative consequences of resentment.

Identify actions you can take which would improve the situation or satisfy the unmet need that is generating the resentment

Resentments involving someone you deal with regularly indicate that a need is not being met. Identify the need and decide what action would be appropriate. Can you approach this person and discuss ways to improve the situation? If not, is there a symbolic way in which you might vent your feelings such as writing a letter which is never sent? Consider each action that occurs to you and weigh the risks and benefits each offers. If any seem promising, make a decision as to when and where you will carry it out.

Examine the situation or event from the other person's perspective—there may be a very good reason for this person's behavior

Was the other person physically ill or tired? Did this person have important concerns or problems that had nothing to do with you but which prevented this person from dealing with you in a more rational way? Is it possible this person was busy RE-acting to events and people from the past which had nothing to do with you but which made it impossible for this person to deal with you in a rational manner? Does this person have irrational beliefs and expectations which generate irrational behavior?

Examine your beliefs and expectations and determine if they are rational and realistic

How "should" this event have taken place. Create the proper or ideal situation or sequence of events and interactions. As you do this, use the following questions to identify irrational beliefs and expectations. Do you have an exaggerated need for people to act "correctly" or for events to be "fair"? Perhaps you have an excessive need for approval, a perfectionistic tendency, or some other exaggerated personal need which has been frustrated. Are you accepting people and events as they are and deciding how best to respond to them or are you refusing to accept reality and demanding that people and events somehow be different from what they are? Are any of the forms of distorted thinking or irrational beliefs discussed in this or previous lessons still playing a role in your resentment?

Identify secondary gains you may receive from this resentment

Does this resentment allow you to continue punishing someone or to receive some special reward, benefit, or attention you either do not know how to obtain or are afraid to ask for directly? Perhaps you have difficulty accepting responsibility for your feelings—that you are the ultimate source of your stress and misery—and rather than accept and acknowledge that the anger or hurt you felt was the result of your expectations and beliefs and your responsibility, you play the role of a victim. Does this resentment allow you to feel sorry for yourself without having to take responsibility for changing the situation as you continue to resent the other person for "making" you feel that way?

☐ *A Four-Step Approach for Dealing with Anger*

The following four-step approach can transform anger into a friend and ally. In most situations it takes less than a minute to use. If you have difficulty responding in a positive manner when angry, identify the step or steps you fail to use. Then review the steps daily until they become an automatic part of your behavior.

Stop and "cool down"

When anger first flashes you lose much of your ability to reason logically and rationally. The first response you choose is often an ineffective one. In addition, taking action when anger first flashes usually makes you angrier. The ancient advice of counting to ten when angry has stood the test of time. Fortunately, in most situations it takes only a few seconds to regain your ability to reason. When you are very angry, take a "time out" and excuse yourself. Take as long as you need to cool down so you can think rationally.

Identify the source of your anger

Ask yourself, "Why am I angry?" Usually, this is all it takes to identify the source of your anger. If this doesn't work, ask yourself, "How am I threatened by this?" or "What do I want?"

Check to see if your anger is appropriate

Most anger is a mixture of appropriate and inappropriate anger. The easiest way to determine whether your anger is mostly appropriate or mostly inappropriate is to ask yourself, "Is my anger appropriate for this situation?" Asking yourself this question allows you to become aware of times when there is no real threat or when the intensity of your anger is too high for the threat which is present. As discussed earlier, this is most often due to illness, fatigue, hunger, or excessive stress. When your anger is mostly inappropriate, delay all action until you have time to identify the source of the inappropriate anger. If your anger is mostly appropriate, go on to the next step.

Take positive action

Your goal is to minimize or eliminate the threat you face with the least amount of harm or discomfort to yourself and others. Most people already have many skills they can use to take positive action. This might involve taking action to protect yourself, developing a plan that will enable you to satisfy a need or want, choosing a new goal, or asserting yourself. Each of these and other possible actions you can take are explored in detail in the lessons that follow.

☐ *Suggestions for People Who Habitually Suppress Anger*

Anger has two important functions: it tells you when needs are threatened or unfulfilled, and it provides energy and motivation for overcoming threats and satisfying needs. If you habitually suppress anger, you have a reduced awareness of when needs are threatened or unfulfilled. It may also be difficult to take actions that satisfy your needs. As was discussed in Lesson 3, when important needs are denied, they generate stronger and stronger emotions that can trigger a physical reaction, an inappropriate emotional response, or self-defeating behaviors.

One common self-defeating behavior associated with the habitual suppression of anger is periodic blow ups. When you suppress anger you are ignoring important needs. Eventually, the emotions generated by the ignored needs become so strong you explode. Unfortunately, this type of anger usually causes you to act ineffectively. If you don't blow up periodically, the ignored needs may generate resentment, anxiety, depression, or passive-aggressive behavior.

Recurring anger that is continually suppressed can keep the fight or flight response activated. When this response is kept activated for prolonged periods of time the muscle tension and over production of hormones associated with the fight or flight response can interfere with normal body functions, such as digestion and your ability to fight disease. Shoulder, head, and back aches can also occur.

It might seem that the habitual suppression of emotions is always undesirable. This is not so. Throughout human history the ability to ignore certain basic needs and suppress emotions has helped people survive harsh environments. Since most people in the past died relatively young and were primarily concerned with physical survival, the negative effects of suppressing emotions were of little importance. A pioneer family living on the prairie, serfs farming a king's estate, or a group of nomadic hunters needed to put most of their time and energy into physical survival. Sharing work and meeting physical needs were far more important than meeting emotional needs.

It has only been in recent times and in select countries that the common person enjoys increased health and longevity along with a large degree of economic and political freedom. People in this environment do not spend as much time and energy meeting physical needs, as their ancestors. In fact, the satisfaction of emotional needs and "quality of life issues" often is a more important aspect of modern relationships than the meeting of physical needs. The result is the habitual suppression of emotions now interferes rather than helps.

Do not misinterpret what has just been said to mean that today all suppression of emotions is undesirable. It is often important to suppress emotions temporarily in order to deal effectively with a pressing situation, such as a medical emergency or an important business meeting. Situations like these require immediate decisions and actions. The feelings generated by these events are best dealt with later. This type of occasional, temporary suppression of emotion is often appropriate. However, the constant, habitual suppression of emotions like anger usually becomes self-defeating.

If you habitually suppress anger, you need to become skilled with the three parts of effective emotional management described in Lesson 3. Here are four ways to do this:

Increase your ability to identify your emotions accurately

Ask yourself periodically, "What emotion am I feeling?" Do this until it becomes easy to identify the various emotions you experience. As you do this, avoid words that describe your mental state or events such as frustrated, helpless, confused, or stressed. Instead, use words that identify true emotions. Several examples are listed below.

Words that Describe Positive Emotions

at ease	delighted	happy	pleased
calm	excited	joyous	proud
comfortable	exhilarated	loving	relieved
content	glad	passionate	satisfied

Words that Describe Negative Emotions

afraid	depressed	frightened	irritated
angry	disappointed	guilty	miserable
anxious	discontent	hate	repulsed
bored	embarrassed	hurt	sad

If you find it difficult to identify what you are feeling, develop physical or behavioral indicators you can use. A physical indicator can be any recurring physical response triggered by an emotion. Common examples for anger include tight shoulders, a clenched jaw, and increased agitation. Behavioral indicators can be identified by recalling how you have acted in the past when angry. Common examples include not talking to loved ones, isolating yourself, and increased or decreased productivity. Make a list of your indicators and memorize it.

Increase your ability to identify accurately your needs and wants

Habitual suppressors often find it difficult to know what they want when confronted with a request or the need to make a decision. Delay making decisions. Take time to ask yourself, "What do I want?" If you are not sure, list the choices you have in your mind and tune into the emotions each choice generates as you consider it.

Increase your ability to develop and carry out plans that enable you to satisfy your needs or wants in an appropriate and realistic way.

When habitual suppressors identify what they want they often find it difficult to take positive action. For many, this is because they lack assertive skills. If this describes you, take extra time with the following two lessons that described assertive skills in detail. The other major force that often maintains the self-defeating behaviors characteristic of habitual suppressors are the excessive need for approval, low self-esteem, and low self-acceptance. If this is true for you, review Lessons 8 and 11 which discusses these issues in detail.

❏ *Suggestions for People Who Anger Easily*

The tendency to anger easily is a learned behavior that helps people gain social power. People try to avoid upsetting a person with a quick temper so this person often gets his or her way. At the same time, a quick temper makes it difficult to have healthy relationships. Most people try to avoid a person with a quick temper. This usually lowers self-esteem and increases the need for control in the quick-tempered person. This can cause other types of self-defeating behaviors.

A quick temper usually comes from growing up with a quick-tempered adult. The adult's behavior is passed on to the child by way of example. Sometimes a child is taught to be aggressive directly by parents who say things such as, "It's a dog-eat-dog world. Take everything you can get and be sure you win." A quick temper can also develop in a child with weak or overindulgent parents. This child learns that throwing temper tantrums is an effective way to get what is wanted. As the tendency to throw a temper tantrum continues into adult life, it becomes self-defeating. Sometimes, having a quick temper helps a child survive a harsh environment or a social setting where a quick temper is valuable.

If you anger easily, work in the following three areas.

Learn to delay action when angry

Take time to stop and cool down when you are angry. The angrier you are, the longer you need to take. Remember, you can control your temper if you choose to do so.

Develop a wider range of emotional responses and identify "taboo" feelings

Do the exercise titled, "Increase your ability to identify your emotions accurately," in the section for people who habitually suppress anger. Then identify emotions you consider as a sign of weakness. Refer to the section on taboo emotions earlier in the lesson. People who anger easily often find that "weak" feelings such as confusion, helplessness, and sadness are unacceptable. Use positive self-talk to convince yourself that these taboo feelings are normal and healthy.

Develop assertive skills

There is a big difference between being assertive and being aggressive. If you anger easily, you probably confuse the two. If you often rely on aggressive behavior to resolve conflicts, you need to develop a wide range of assertive skills that can replace your aggressive behaviors. These skills are described in detail in the lessons which follow.

☐ *Dealing with Anger Directed at You from Others*

The first and most important step in dealing effectively with anger directed at you from others is training yourself to avoid taking their anger as a personal attack. Most of the anger you encounter has little, if anything, to do with who you are or what you have done. Anger from others is usually due to one of the following factors:

- A temporary reduction in the angry person's ability to think rationally and increased emotionality due to hunger, fatigue, or illness.
- The angry person's deep seated irrational beliefs and expectations.
- Displaced anger that is being directed at you from a source which has nothing to do with you.

The best approach to use with displaced anger is often to distance yourself from the angry person so you will not be an easy target. Another approach is to describe in an assertive but tolerant manner what you perceive. For example, you could say to a co-worker who had a difficult meeting and who is now acting aggressively towards you, "I know Bob gave you a real hard time this morning, but now it seems like you're taking it out on me even though I'm on your side." At this point most people back off.

In the occasional instances where you have actually done something that is a real threat or hardship for the other person, separate your behavior—what you did—from who and what you are. This enables you to remain more objective and problem-centered. Silently acknowledge and identify your needs but put them on hold temporarily until the other person has cooled down. Remember, an angry person is usually an irrational person.

The following approach is usually effective in turning the anger and attack from another person into a problem-centered discussion. It works equally as well for when you have actually done something to anger someone as for when displaced anger is being directed at you from an unknown source. Again, the key to making it work is to avoid taking the others person's anger personally.

Begin by allowing the other person to express his or her anger freely

Adopt an understanding and non-judgmental attitude. Avoid interrupting or contradicting the sender. Do not defend, justify, or rationalize your actions or position. Concentrate on reflecting the other person's concerns. This helps to dissipate the intense energy of "hot" anger so the other person can become more reasonable. As you do this, begin to ask for the specifics of legitimate problems or criticisms.

As the angry person becomes more problem-centered and calmer, become more focused in your questioning

The clarification skills described in Appendix 5 are the most effective way to do this. If you are unskilled with them, develop skill by practicing clarification skills in friendly situations with people you know.

Once the angry person has calmed down, if it is appropriate, begin legitimate problem-solving

Frequently there is no need for further problem-solving. This is especially true when the other person's anger was triggered by something that had little or nothing to do with you. If a problem does exist and the other person is very angry, break off your discussion until a later time. This gives the person time to cool down and become more rational.

The above approach works well for the occasional angry confrontations we all encounter. If you are in an ongoing relationship at work or home with someone who constantly uses an angry or aggressive style, you may also want to consider the following:

- How important is this relationship to me? Do I have other alternatives?
- Is there any way I can minimize my contact with this person?
- If there is no way to avoid this person, a "walk away" strategy may be appropriate. Simply walk away whenever this person becomes aggressive. Deal with this person only when he or she is relatively calm and rational. With some people it is best to just walk away without saying anything. However, with most it is best to make a short statement such as, "I'm not willing to talk with you when you're so angry. I will discuss this with you later after we have both calmed down."

If you are in a relationship with someone who may become violent, do what is necessary to insure your safety. If you have an immediate need for help call the police. There are also many excellent shelters and crisis intervention centers around the country. They are usually listed in both the white and yellow pages of your telephone book. If you cannot find one, call either a local hospital or your county's mental health service and ask for help in locating one. These agencies can also recommend support groups and counseling resources where you can receive individualized help for dealing with your situation. Additional resources are listed in Appendixes 2 and 3. Seek help if you need it.

□ *The Fear of Losing Control*

The fear of losing control can take many different forms. Since an authority figure may dominate you or make you do something you do not want to do, the fear of losing control is sometimes expressed as a fear of authority figures. Occasionally it even generates a master-slave mentality when in situations where there is a hierarchy. For example, a supervisor or teacher may be viewed as an unfriendly master who needs to be either placated or overthrown. Other common forms for this fear include a fear of losing control to illness, relationships, or financial problems.

The fear of losing control is a major contributing factor in the development of both the anxiety/panic cycle and many avoidance reactions. It is usually not the panic attack that is feared, but the consequences of losing control during the panic attack. Likewise, when a place or situation is avoided, it is usually not the specific place or situation that is feared but the consequences of losing control of oneself or events in that place or situation.

The excessive concern with control is usually the result of growing up in an environment where helplessness and lack of control were major issues. Often this involves a domineering parent. Another frequent pattern is a child who has been unable to get a consistent response from parents and therefore lives with constant ambiguity. This often involves parents who are chemically dependent. As adults, children from this type of environment usually find uncertainty and ambiguity very difficult. The sense of helplessness or lack of control can also be due to physical, sexual, or mental abuse as well as growing up where there is war or social upheaval.

Anger is only one response people have to the fear of losing control. Many people simply avoid situations where they feel they have no control. Others follow a rigid set of rules for how they should behave and how tasks should be performed. Some make excessive requests when in social situations such as adjusting lighting and heating or putting limitations on what can be discussed or done. Actions like these often cause people like this to be seen as controlling and manipulative. A small number gain a sense of control by giving up all control.

Many different types of irrational assumptions can generate the fear of losing control. Examples of self-talk which reflect these irrational assumptions are listed below. Place a check by any which are similar to how you think or talk.

- I have to be my own boss.
- Rules and regulations imprison me.
- I have to be free.
- I can't stand it when others tell me what to do.
- I have to do what is right (which means be perfect) in order to maintain control.
- Asking for help is a sign of weakness and loss of control.
- If I let someone get too close, he or she may come to control me.
- Others are always trying to control me.
- If I give in to others, they win and are controlling me.

- Conforming means losing control.
- One must remain independent in order to avoid losing control.

Study the following list of rational arguments and select those which best challenge the irrational beliefs you checked. List the arguments you select on a card and memorize them. Be sure to add any others you may think of in addition to those listed.

- There is nothing over which you have absolute control. The universe is such that every event is affected by many different factors. While some factors may exert a greater degree of influence than others, no one factor is totally responsible for any one event.
- A reasonably healthy adult who is thinking rationally can easily resist the influence of other people in normal situations if he or she so chooses.
- Using rational self-talk skills and facing life as a positive realist allows you to stop and look at the people and events you encounter and make choices. This is the most effective way to exert control over your life.
- There is always some uncertainty in any activity. However, the odds for success in most endeavors are usually overwhelmingly in your favor.
- Choose to view the 1-10% chance of failure or misfortune as a 90-99% chance of success and fulfillment.
- True freedom requires structure and an ability to work within the rules and limitations of nature and society. For example, a skilled musician practices the basic skills of his instrument and learns the rules of music so well he can freely improvise on any song; a skilled politician knows how to work within the system to achieve his goals.
- Every human has limitations and weaknesses. Knowing how to ask for and accept help when it is needed is the most effective way to get what you want.
- Acknowledging and accepting limitations is the first step in minimizing their influence on you.
- Blind rebellion against rules or social convention actually limits your freedom and the amount of control you have over your life.
- Rules and social conventions are simply a means for allowing people to co-exist and achieve their life goals. For example, traffic laws are simply rules which allow many people to use public roads and drive safely.
- Conforming to social norms is often an effective and convenient way to achieve what you want.
- Giving up the illusion of control is the way to freedom.
- Compromising with others is often the best way to fulfill your needs.
- True intimacy requires you to be vulnerable at appropriate times with the appropriate people. If you refuse to be vulnerable you will never experience true intimacy and doom yourself to a life of loneliness.

After you develop rational arguments that challenge your irrational beliefs, identify triggers—specific actions, words, phrases, or situations you can use to know when the fear of losing control needs to be challenged. Here are some examples of triggers Laura identified:

Phrases

> I should be able to do it myself.
> I can't get too close.
> Who do they think they are by telling me how to do things.
> I have to do this right.

Situations/Behaviors

> Inappropriate anger and condemnation towards myself or others when I am not completing a task as I think it "should" be done.
> Anxiety and a feeling that I need to get away when talking about personal matters or when in intimate situations.
> Anxiety, anger, or resentment when I do not know something and need to ask for help at work.

Laura recalled her rational arguments whenever she caught herself saying the above phrases, in the above situations, or doing the above behaviors. She found this helped reduce both the anxiety and inappropriate anger she experienced. It also helped her accept limitations and events over which she had little or no control.

Recommended Activities for Lesson 12

Examine the Roots of Your Anger Patterns

The following exercise takes ten to twenty minutes. Use paper and pencil when you do it.

1. List the ways in which your parents expressed anger.

2. What did your parents say and do to you when you became angry as a child?

3. Were your brothers and/or sisters told the same things and treated in the same way when they became angry? If not, what did you think and feel when they were treated differently? Did you make any resolutions as a result of this different treatment? If so, are those resolutions still valuable today or are they interfering with your life?

4. What made you angry as a child? What did you do when you became angry?

5. What makes you angry as an adult? What do you do when you become angry?

6. Is there anything about your present anger patterns you would like to change? If so, how will you do this? (You will find it easier to answer this final question after you have studied this lesson. You can then select from the activities it describes which would be most appropriate for reaching your goal.)

Use Rational Self-Talk to Minimize Inappropriate Anger

The following exercise takes about ten minutes. Use paper and pencil when you do it.

1. Recall a time recently when you experienced what you believe was mostly inappropriate anger—anger that is too intense for the threat that triggered it or anger that is occurring when no real threat is present. Describe the event briefly.

2. Recall and list as much of your self-talk that occurred just before and during this event as you can.

3. After you have listed all the self-talk you can recall, identify any distorted thinking or irrational beliefs which are present. Then develop a rational response for each one.

4. List any additional things you could think or do that would help minimize this type of inappropriate anger.

5. Take a moment to imagine yourself using the rational self-talk and new behaviors you listed in a future situation similar to this one. This final step is most important. Rehearsing desired behaviors greatly increases the chance that you will use them in the future.

Special Issues

This lesson addresses three special issues: the tendency to suppress anger, the tendency to become angered easily, and the fear of losing control. If any of these issues is a major problem for you, be sure to spend time studying the section that applies to you and do the exercises it recommends.

Spend at least one week with this lesson.
If inappropriate anger or suppression of
anger is a major problem for you, spend an
extra week with this lesson.

Lesson

Standing Up for Yourself

Conflict arises whenever the satisfaction of your needs and wants interferes with those of someone else. Since everyone's needs and wants are different, conflict is a natural and healthy part of all human relationships. If you find this type of normal conflict difficult, it can be a major source of anxiety. This lesson shows you how to resolve conflicts in a way that is both effective and satisfying. Gaining skill in resolving conflicts positively, reduces the anxiety associated with them and produces more enjoyable relationships.

☐ *Three Basic Types of Behavior*

When faced with conflict you can become non-assertive, aggressive, or assertive. Understanding the difference between these three different approaches is the first step to effective conflict resolution.

Non-Assertive Behavior

The goal of non-assertive behavior is to avoid conflict. When you are non-assertive you place the needs and wants of others ahead of your own. You allow others to make choices for you and take advantage of you. When most or all conflict is approached non-assertively, it is called general non-assertiveness. When non-assertiveness is restricted to a limited number of situations it is called situational non-assertiveness. Situational non-assertiveness is much more common than general non-assertiveness. Situational non-assertiveness usually involves authority figures, such as supervisors, teachers, and parents or people you are close to, such as a friend or spouse.

One common myth is non-assertive people are always "passive." While passive people are usually non-assertive, people who are active and enjoy interacting with others can also be non-assertive. Whenever you do not stand up for your rights or do not work to satisfy your needs and wants because they conflict with the rights or needs of others, you are being non-assertive. While this is appropriate in some situations, the frequent, habitual use of non-assertive behavior usually causes loss of self-respect and self-esteem. It is difficult to think well of yourself when your needs are not being met and others are disregarding your dignity and rights.

Non-assertiveness sometimes results in passive aggressive behavior. This is "getting back" at someone indirectly such as by forgetting an important commitment or being late. When people are unable to fulfill needs and wants in a direct manner, they sometimes resort to sulking or crying. Others develop a "see-saw" pattern in which they swing back and forth between non-assertive and aggressive behavior. People with a general non-assertive pattern often blame others for their problems and refuse to take responsibility for the quality of their lives. They may even play the role of martyr.

Whenever you choose non-assertive behavior, you choose definite irritation within yourself instead of possible irritation to others. Because a non-assertive response encourages unwanted behavior from others, it blocks improvement in undesirable situations. In fact, it guarantees that relationships and events will remain the same.

Aggressive Behavior

The goal of aggressive behavior is to gain control or power. When you are aggressive, you express needs and wants freely but in a hostile, tactless, or angry manner. You stand up for your own rights and work to satisfy your needs and wants. However, the rights, needs, and wants of others are ignored whenever they interfere with what you want.

In most situations, aggressive behavior is equally as self-defeating as non-assertive behavior. People who are the object of aggressive behavior usually feel like they are being attacked. Sometimes this intimidates them and they do what the aggressive person wants. Other times, aggressive behavior causes others to become hostile and resist cooperating with or helping the aggressive person. In either case, aggressive people are usually avoided. As a result, aggressive people are often as troubled about their inability to make or keep friends as are shy people. Sometimes, after mistreating others or failing to solve an interpersonal conflict in a satisfying manner, they feel guilt and dejection.

Assertive Behavior

The goal of assertive behavior is to resolve conflicts in a way that is satisfying for both you and others. When you are assertive you express problems, feelings, needs, and wants in a way that is both self-satisfying and socially effective. You respect the rights and dignity of both yourself and others. There is a personal focus on "reasonable compromise" rather than on winning. Solutions are sought which will make everyone feel good.

Many people think that aggressive and assertive behavior are the same. The confusion may come from the fact that much is said in books and workshops about changing non-assertive behavior into assertive behavior while little is said about changing aggressive behavior into assertive behavior. Assertive and aggressive behavior both involve expressing yourself freely, standing up for your rights, and working to satisfy your needs and wants. However, an aggressive approach ignores the rights, needs, and wants of others while the opposite is true of an assertive approach.

One common roadblock to being assertive is anger. The angrier you are, the more aggressive you will be. Another common roadblock to assertiveness is irrational thinking. There are many irrational beliefs about assertiveness that can keep you from asserting yourself. These are explored in the next section. Irrational thinking that blocks assertiveness can also be generated by an excessive need for approval, a fear of being incompetent, or a fear of losing control.

Two common myths often associated with assertiveness are: being assertive is always the best way to resolve a conflict, and assertive people can get whatever they want. While an assertive approach is usually best, it is not always the most appropriate or most effective way to resolve a conflict. There are occasional situations where aggressive behavior is appropriate, such as when there is imminent danger to life or property, or when a person or group will only respond to an aggressive approach. There are also occasional situations where non-assertive behavior is appropriate. These usually involve situations where the cost of asserting yourself in terms of time, energy, or resulting negative consequences outweighs the benefits you would receive.

As you become more assertive, you find assertiveness occasionally makes situations worse. At other times it has no effect. However, in most situations, an assertive style is the most effective and gratifying way to bring about positive change. Even when no change takes place, you usually feel better for having spoken up. The main question to consider when deciding whether you want to be assertive is, "Do I wish to risk the possibility of irritating others, or do I choose to definitely irritate myself by holding my feelings in and doing nothing?" In making that choice it helps to remember that *when you use a truly assertive style, those who matter won't mind, and those who do mind seldom matter.*

☐ *Common Irrational Beliefs about Assertiveness*

Many different types of irrational beliefs can keep a person from being assertive. These irrational beliefs are usually concerned with the "worst possible" outcomes of being assertive. Several common ones are listed below. The first seven generate non-assertive behavior. The last five generate aggressive behavior. Check any that reflect how you have felt during conflicts.

- If I assert myself, others will become angry or upset with me.
- If I assert myself and people become angry or upset, I may not be able to handle the situation.
- It is wrong and selfish to refuse the requests of others. If I allow myself to be selfish in this way it makes me a "bad" person.
- I must avoid asking questions or making statements that might make me look stupid or ignorant.
- Assertive people are cold and selfish. If I'm assertive I'll be so unpleasant people will not like me.
- I prefer others to be open and straight forward with me. However, if I'm straight forward and open with others, I will hurt them.
- If what I do hurts others, I am responsible for their feelings regardless of my intentions and how I acted. (Common variation: I should be able to find a way of acting that will not hurt others.)
- If I "give in" in any way it means the other person has "won" and is taking advantage of me.
- My solutions and methods are best. If they are not accepted I am a failure.
- In many ways people are my adversaries. They are trying to put me down and take away what is mine. I must always be on guard and fight to have things go my way.
- I must always be strong. If I compromise it means I am weak.
- I always need to be in control. If others get their way it means I am not in control.

Your beliefs about assertiveness and the behaviors you use to resolve conflicts developed during childhood. Answer the following questions and explore how these beliefs and behaviors developed.

- How did each member of your family handle conflict?
- How did the adults in your childhood train you to deal with conflict?
- What were you told about conflict? (for example, don't rock the boat, people won't like you if you're nasty, ladies never yell, gentlemen don't fight).
- Did your brothers and sisters receive the same training and the same messages you did? If not, how was it different?
- How did you get what you wanted directly (for example, by asking or taking)?
- How did you get what you wanted indirectly (for example, by hinting, whining, sulking, or having someone else ask for you)?
- Did you learn how to get what you wanted in any other ways?
- Which of these methods do you use today to get what you want?
- What types of messages or statements do you repeat to yourself when you are in conflict with others?

As you identify your irrational beliefs about conflict and being assertive, develop rational self-talk responses you can use to challenge them.

☐ *Your Rights and Responsibilities*

To be assertive, you need to believe in both your individual rights and the rights of others. This balance between rights and responsibilities is summarized below. Rights are shown in standard type; responsibilities in italic. As you read these rights and responsibilities, check statements which make you uncomfortable or which do not reflect your normal behavior.

❏ I have the right to be treated with dignity and respect.

I have the responsibility to treat others with the same dignity and respect I desire from them.

❏ I have the right to decide what is best for me.

I have the responsibility to allow others to decide what is best for them.

❏ I have the right to have and express my own feelings and opinions.

I have the responsibility to express those feelings and opinions in a way that does not insult or put others down.

❏ I have the right to ask for what I want and need.

I have the responsibility to allow others the right to refuse my request even though I might not like being refused.

❏ I have the right to say "NO" without feeling guilty.

I have the responsibility to allow others the right to say "no."

❏ I have the right to be listened to and taken seriously.

I have the responsibility to listen to others and take them seriously.

❏ I have the right to make mistakes.

I have the responsibility to accept the consequences of those mistakes.

❏ I have the right to all of my human weaknesses and limitations without guilt or shame.

I have the responsibility to allow others their weaknesses without ridiculing or resenting them.

❏ I have the right to do what is necessary to protect my physical and mental health even though this sometimes requires non-assertive or aggressive behavior and discomfort in others.

I have the responsibility to do this in a way that causes the least amount of harm to both myself and others.

If you checked any of the above statements, identify the irrational beliefs that makes them difficult to accept. Then develop rational self-talk you can use to challenge your irrational thinking. If you are frequently non-assertive, memorize the above rights and practice reciting them until they become comfortable. If you are frequently aggressive, memorize and practice reciting the above responsibilities.

□ *The DERN Approach: An Effective Assertive Method for Resolving Conflicts*

The DERN approach is an effective four-step assertive approach you can use to resolve most conflicts. DERN stands for the words: describe, express, request, and negotiate. These words describe each of the four steps used in this approach.

Describe the problem behavior or situation.

Express your feelings.

Request the changes or actions you want.

Negotiate for a mutually satisfying solution.

Before you assert yourself, ask yourself "What do I want?" and "What is keeping me from getting what I want?" After you answer these questions, you are ready to use the DERN approach. Often, you will only need to use the first three parts of the DERN approach to effectively assert yourself. The best way to use these three steps is to create a D.E.R. script. Detailed guidelines that describe how to create each part of a D.E.R. script are given below.

D - DESCRIBE the problem behavior or situation.

Describe the other person's behavior or actions objectively. Example: "You have been late three times this week."

Avoid vague words or descriptions. Example: "Sometimes you are so irresponsible."

Focus on one well-defined behavior or problem that you want to deal with now in specific, simple terms. Example: "The car needs a tune-up."

Avoid generalizing for "all-time." Example: "You never take care of the car."

Describe specific times and places where the problem occurs in a short, clear manner. The description should clarify the situation, not complicate it. Example: "I have asked three times during the past week to be shown how to operate the duplicator, but I still have not been shown."

Avoid mind-reading or psychoanalyzing the other person by guessing at his motives, goals, attitudes, or intentions. Example: "You seem to be afraid of teaching me how to operate the duplicator. You must want to be the only one who knows how to do it."

E - EXPRESS your feelings

Express feelings and opinions as your own without blaming the other person. Example: "I am really frustrated when this happens."

Avoid denying or holding your feelings in.

Keep your wording low-key and aim for emotional restraint rather than dramatic impact. Example: "That really annoys me."

Avoid unleashing emotional outbursts. Example: "I'm truly outraged at such behavior. People like you should be shot!"

Express your feelings in a positive manner. Example: "It makes me very unhappy when you refuse to speak to me."

Avoid words that ridicule or shame, along with swear words and labels such as "dumb," "selfish," and "idiotic." Example: "You're cruel and heartless to treat me like this."

Stay focused on the specific offending behavior rather than on the whole person. Example: "When I see a mess in my work area it really annoys me."

Avoid attacking the character or personality of the person. Example: "If you were capable of organizing your time you'd be able to get things done and things wouldn't always end up in my work area."

R - REQUEST *the changes or actions you want.*

Make a direct, clear and explicit request for a change or action. Example: "I need you to be here by no later than 3:15 today."

Avoid only implying or hinting that you'd like a change. Example: "It would be nice to be surprised today."

When dealing with behavior, request only a small change. "I need this area to be kept clean."

Avoid asking for major changes in a person's character or personality. Example: "You need to learn how to be neat and keep things orderly."

Request only one or, at MOST, two changes or actions at one time. Example: "Would you give me a five-minute warning before you want to leave?"

Avoid demanding many changes or actions. Example: "I want you to stop asking me to leave at the last moment. And don't be so picky when we're out in public. That reminds me, I've been meaning to tell you..."

Describe the specific actions you want stopped and those you want to see performed. Example: "Please keep the door closed and be as quiet as you can in the morning."

Avoid asking for changes or actions in vague or general terms. Example: Please be more considerate in the morning."

Consider whether the other person can meet your request without suffering large losses. Can you reasonably expect the other person to agree to your request? Example: "Please do not smoke in the car while we drive to work."

Avoid asking only for your own satisfaction while ignoring the other person's needs. Example: "You need to stop smoking and air out this car."

A D.E.R. script is usually most effective when each part is only one or two sentences long. While your goal is to describe your perceptions and feelings accurately and make a clear request, this is best done with as few words as possible. The following three examples shows how this can be done using the above guidelines.

Example 1: Asking For Help

Situation: Sophia had just returned to work after a period of unemployment. During this time she assumed a major portion of the household chores. These chores were too much to continue doing after she returned to work. Sophia's goal was to have her spouse assist her more.

DESCRIBE the problem behavior or situation.

"Since I returned to work two weeks ago, you have continued to do the same amount of work around the house that you did when I was out of work."

EXPRESS your feelings.

"I am feeling overwhelmed and cannot continue to do all of the chores I did when I was not working."

REQUEST the changes or action you want.

"I would like you to help me with the daily dishes, weekly vacuuming, and watering the yard and garden. Will you help me and do these chores?"

Example 2: Saying "No" To Unreasonable Behavior

Situation: Ramon had a friend who was constantly dropping by without first calling despite many hints that he would like the friend to call first. This occurred two or three times a week and the friend would stay for two or three hours each visit.

DESCRIBE the problem behavior or situation.

"For the past month you have been dropping by two or three times a week to visit without calling me first. You then stay for two or three hours to visit."

EXPRESS your feelings.

"I value our friendship but am becoming frustrated and annoyed because I never know when you are coming and there are things I want to finish that are being left undone."

REQUEST the changes or actions you want.

"I would like you to start calling before you drop by."

Example 3: Asking For Understanding

Situation: Mia was recovering from agoraphobia. She was working on a regular basis with in vivo exposure and had overcome most of the avoidance behaviors that had developed during the time she was agoraphobic. She was feeling very good about her progress but still had one major goal left: driving by herself. Mia's spouse wanted her to start driving by herself as soon as possible and was beginning to become very critical about the amount of time it was taking for Mia to reach her final goal.

DESCRIBE the problem behavior or situation.

"During the past few weeks you have asked me at least once a day when I am going to start driving by myself."

EXPRESS your feelings.

"I feel that I am under a lot of pressure whenever we talk about my driving. I also feel hurt because it seems like I'm not given any credit for all of the effort I've put forth and all of the progress I've made in other areas."

REQUEST the changes/actions you want.

"I would like you to stop asking me when I will start driving by myself and let me follow the exposure plan I've developed at my own pace. This will help me reach this goal more quickly and make it more enjoyable to talk with you."

A complete D.E.R. script is often used to set the stage for the final phase of the DERN approach—negotiation. This is illustrated in Examples 1 and 3 above where the D.E.R. scripts used by Sophia and Mia flowed into a negotiation phase. However, sometimes a D.E.R. script is used to set limits as was done by Ramon in Example 2. Ramon was not willing to negotiate on his need to have his friend call before visiting. Even when this is the case, a D.E.R. script is usually the best way to state your perceptions and needs clearly and objectively.

When dealing with simpler problems, it is often only necessary to use one or two parts of the D.E.R. approach. Often, a simple and direct description of a problem is all that is needed when the solution to a problem is obvious. For example, saying, "That cup leaks," will prevent most people from using a defective cup. If you have a specific action you want taken, add a request such as, "That cup leaks. Please use the blue one instead." The combination of a clear description with a direct but polite request can be used to resolve many simple everyday situations. Here are two more examples:

"This shirt was not sewn properly (Describe). I would like to return it (Request)."

"Greenback Lane is under construction and the traffic is backed up (Describe). Let's go by way of Madison Avenue (Request)."

The best way to become skilled with D.E.R. scripts is to create written scripts and rehearse them. The advantage of a written script is you can check it against the guidelines given earlier and revise it if does not follows the guidelines. When you reciting your scripts, pretend that you are actually talking to the person for whom it is meant. Try to look and sound assertive as you rehearse your script. Continue practicing like this until it is easy for you to create effective D.E.R. scripts. With time and practice D.E.R. scripts become your normal way of stating your perceptions and making requests.

The main roadblock to using D.E.R. scripts is strong emotion. Whenever you are angry or upset, take time to regain control of yourself so you can think rationally. If you are extremely upset, you may have to go someplace where you can be alone in order to cool down. As you cool down, you will find the creation of a D.E.R. script helps to focus your thoughts on constructive actions.

The Final Step: Negotiate

The fourth step of the DERN approach, negotiation, is usually required when you are working with complex or persistent problems. When this is the case, you will be a more effective negotiator if you consider the following before you begin negotiating.

How important is this issue?

Decide what a specific change in the other person's behavior or a specific action is worth to you. How much discomfort will you experience if the situation continues unchanged and what benefits will you experience if your request is met?

What are you willing to do?

In most situations it is unreasonable to demand that only one person change or act. The concessions you are willing to make are your "bargaining chips" during a negotiation session.

What might this person ask for?

Most of the time you know the person with whom you will be negotiating. Considering this person's past behavior reduces the chance of being caught off guard by surprise maneuvers.

Will the other person be willing to negotiate with me in good faith? If not, what negative consequences (punishments) can I use?

Fortunately, most negotiations do not require the use of negative consequences. However, when they are required it is important that they be something you are both willing and able to carry out. Exaggerated or unrealistic threats you can't or won't carry out usually backfire.

Once you have considered the above, you are ready to negotiate. Negotiations are essentially a five step problem-solving session. These steps are described below.

Describe the problem or difficulty you are having and state your request

The best way to make your needs and wants known in a way that causes the least amount of resistance is to use a D.E.R. script.

Identify the other person's perceptions, needs, and wants

As soon as you finish delivering your D.E.R. script, the other person will probably state his or her perceptions, needs, and wants. The best way to understand this person is to use active listening. Active listening is different from passive listening where you just listen to a person without much response. With active listening you reflect feelings, clarify points which are unclear, and periodically paraphrase what was said. By doing this, you know that you heard what was said accurately and you communicate that understanding to the other person. If this is difficult for you, Appendix 5 describes how to develop three basic active listening skills. These skills are easy to learn and are essential for successful negotiations. They also prove beneficial in many other areas of your life.

Shifting between stating your ideas and listening to the other person usually continues throughout the entire negotiation process. The better you are at shifting between these two opposite but complementary activities, the more successful you will be at negotiating.

Generate possible solutions

After everyone's needs and wants are identified, it is time to generate possible solutions. One way to do this is "brainstorming." Brainstorming is a technique used by government and business professionals as well as by scientists. Everyone involved in the negotiation session offers as many possible solutions as possible. Avoid evaluating solutions while you are in the process of generating alternatives. Evaluating solutions as they are suggested stifles the creative process of thinking up new and different ways of resolving a problem.

Evaluate possible alternatives and agree on the best solution

After several possible solutions have been suggested, evaluate them for practicality, the degree to which they satisfy everyone's needs, and the degree to which they are agreeable to everyone involved. During this phase avoid focusing only on your needs. Keep both the other person's and your own needs in mind. At the same time, avoid feeling responsible for taking care of the other person's needs to the exclusion of your own.

The best solution is one which leaves everyone feeling satisfied. Avoid solutions that cause people to feel that someone has won and someone has lost. Your goal is to make everyone have a feeling of being a winner. While this is not always possible, the closer you come to reaching this goal, the greater the chances are that the solution you arrive at will work.

The best way to arrive at a solution which is agreeable to everyone is to think in terms of "competing needs" rather than in terms of "competing solutions." Sometimes a person has already decided upon a "correct" or "best" solution before negotiating. This person then tries to use the negotiation session to sell this solution. This usually doesn't work. One way to avoid this trap is to remember that there are usually many different solutions for a given problem that would satisfy everyone's needs and wants. The challenge is to identify them.

If none of the proposed solutions are adequate, do more brain storming. If everyone is stuck, take a break; then start again. Taking a break is especially helpful when strong emotions have been generated.

It is sometimes necessary to encourage a person to cooperate and negotiate in good faith. Usually, the best way to do this is to concentrate on positive consequences the other person will enjoy when the problem is resolved. In a business setting you might stress the increased savings or productivity that will result. In personal relationships you might stress increased closeness, additional free time together, or your personal appreciation for the other person's consideration. In some cases you may even want to offer rewards for the changes or actions you want. For example, doing some of the other person's work in exchange for help with your project. If you offer rewards, select ones that are appropriate for the person with whom you are dealing. Avoid rewards that only you would find desirable or which you can't deliver. If you decide to try rewards, you may even want to ask what this person would find rewarding.

Only resort to negative consequences when positive ones have failed to win cooperation. If you decide to use negative consequences, be sure they are ones you are both *willing* and *able* to carry out. If none are available and the other person remains uncooperative, an assertive approach may not be appropriate for this problem.

Restate the agreement and, if appropriate, formalize it

Once an agreement has been reached, restate it so everyone understands what they have agreed to. Do not let embarrassment or discomfort over an emotionally sensitive problem pressure you into ending your negotiation session too quickly. If you fail to restate your agreement, you and the other person may walk away with a different understanding of the agreement.

If you think the other person may try to back out of the agreement later, formalize it in writing. In counseling this is often done when working with couples or with parents and children. Even when you trust the other person, it is usually best to formalize business agreements in writing. This can be done through a simple memo, an exchange of letters, or a formal contract.

Whenever you reach a mutually satisfying solution through a negotiation process, thank the other person for agreeing to change or take action. If you have been negotiating with a person who has been difficult to deal with in the past, suggest that future conflicts or problems be handled in a similar manner. Avoid bringing up new problems at this time as this could jeopardize the gains you have just secured.

□ *"I Language"*

When you review the various examples in this and the following lesson, you will find that assertive people usually speak using "I messages". An "I message" is a statement that tells the listener what you see, think, feel, or want in an objective manner that does not assign blame or put the listener down. A statement that assigns blame or puts the listener down is often referred to as a "you message". Here are some examples of each.

You Message: "You're making so much noise it's driving me crazy. Why can't you be more considerate?"

I Message: "I would really like some peace and quite for a while. Would you do that in the other room?"

You Message: "Look at this kitchen. You're such a slob. When are you going to be more responsible?"

I Message: "I need you to clean up the things you used in the kitchen so I can cook."

Recommended Activities for Lesson 13

Challenge Irrational Ideas about Being Assertive

Identify irrational ideas you have about conflict and being assertive and develop rational self-talk responses you can use to challenge them. Actually write them down on paper. Refer to earlier lessons if this is difficult. Once you have developed your rational responses, memorize them. Whenever you are in a situation where you are finding it difficult to assert yourself, recall the rational responses you developed.

If you are often non-assertive, memorize the list of rights and recite them daily until they become a firm part of your beliefs. If you are often aggressive, memorize the list of responsibilities and recite them daily until you find it easy to respect the rights of others.

Practice Creating and Rehearsing D.E.R. Scripts

During this week, create and rehearse at least five different D.E.R. scripts. These scripts can be for current situations or for ones which have occurred during the past few weeks. Write out each script so you can compare it with the guidelines given in the lesson. If your scripts do not follow the guidelines, rewrite them so they do.

In order to develop skill in delivering your scripts, have practice sessions during which you pretend you are saying your script to the person for whom it is intended. The more difficult you find this sort of practice, the more you need to do it. You can practice creating and rehearsing scripts while driving, doing housework, or in any other private situation. Include practice sessions in front of a mirror so you can actually see what you look like as you deliver your script. The most powerful type of practice is to rehearse with a study partner you trust. During all of your practice sessions, work at making your tone of voice and body language match the assertive words you are using. In essence, you are desensitizing yourself to assertive behavior so it does not seem strange or frightening.

Do not begin using your D.E.R. scripts in real life situations just yet. Wait until after you have completed Lesson 14. With this lesson your focus is on learning how to create and deliver D.E.R. scripts. Create scripts for as many different types of situations as you can. Then rehearse them until it is easy to act in a confident, assertive manner. Developing skill at creating and delivering D.E.R. scripts is important preparation for Lesson 14.

Evaluate Your Negotiation Skills

Recall several situations where you negotiated for a change in someone's behavior or for something you wanted. Review the five-step negotiation process described in the lesson and identify actions you could take to improve your next negotiation session with someone. Mentally rehearse those actions until you find them easy to use during actual negotiations. If you feel your listening skills are weak, read Appendix 5 and do the exercises it outlines.

Develop Skill with Simple Requests and Statements that Violate Your Rights and Dignity

There are many subtle ways in which a simple statement or request can violate your rights and dignity. People who are non-assertive often do not even recognize them. Many others recognize them but find it difficult to respond with an appropriate assertive reply. Eight common situations that violate your rights or dignity are listed below along with possible assertive replies. As you read each one, notice that an assertive reply is one that is not angry or hostile. It is one that is calm and polite but shows the other person you do not allow your rights or dignity to be disregarded.

Type of Statement or Request	Example	An Effective Assertive Reply	Example
Being put on the spot.	"Are you busy tonight?"	Answer with a question which requests the reason.	"What did you have in mind?" "Why do you ask?"
Receiving unwanted advice	"If I were you..." Or "You should..."	Deny the "if" and affirm you are the one that has to make right decisions for yourself.	"That might be right for you but..."
Violation of privacy.	"Maybe I shouldn't ask, but..."	Set your own limits; OR answer with a question which requests the reason.	"I really don't care to say." "Why would you want to know that?"
Vague remarks or criticism.	"You have been so defensive lately."	State your own opinion with a *simple* response; OR ask for concrete examples.	"I don't think so." "Exactly what have I done that makes you say that?"
Insulting labels for your behavior.	"That's a dumb thing to do."	Refuse to accept the label.	"I don't think so."
Having the worth of your choices questioned.	"Do you really think that shirt suits you?"	Emphasize your right and ability to make personal judgements.	"Yes, I think it suits me just fine."

Negative predictions based on observations of your personality.	"You're not assertive enough for the job."	Ask for clarification of the observation; OR affirm your ability to judge your own strengths and abilities.	"In what way do you think I am not assertive enough?" "That may be how you see it, but I think I'll do just fine."

If you have difficulty in asserting yourself in these types of situations, do the following.

- Make a list of simple statements and requests you have encountered which violated your rights and dignity or which made you uncomfortable. Record the response you made to each statement.

- If you did not like your response, develop an assertive reply using the above suggestions. You can get many other useful ideas by listening to assertive people you know respond to similar situations. If you know someone with a positive assertive style, ask this person how he or she would respond to situations that are difficult for you. Record any responses you like. As you do this exercise, remember that a given situation can have many different assertive responses that would be appropriate.

As you do this exercise, remember that it is only meant for situations where your dignity and rights have been violated by simple statements or requests. More complex conflict situations or problems require a D.E.R. script or the full DERN approach.

> As with past lessons, take your time and
> do the exercises in this lesson as
> thoroughly as possible before going on
> to the next one.

Lesson

Staying On Track

Now that you have learned how to describe what you see, feel, and want with a D.E.R. script, you are ready to learn how to stay on track when others try to resist your assertive efforts. You are also ready to explore when and where it is more appropriate to be non-assertive or aggressive than assertive.

☐ *Seven Common Tactics that Can Sabotage Your Assertive Efforts*

A person who does not want to be bothered with you will use one or more of the following tactics to resist your assertive efforts. This is usually not a deliberate, malicious attempt to beat you down. Instead, it is usually an automatic behavior the other person learned early in life as a way of self-protection. From time to time you also use these tactics to resist the demands of others and to protect yourself. There is nothing wrong with this. However, the next time you notice yourself using one of these tactics, decide whether you could accomplish the same goal more effectively by using the assertive skills discussed in Lesson 13.

Avoiding Discussion of Your Request

The first and most direct way to avoid dealing with your request is to simply postpone the discussion. Two different approaches can be used to overcome this tactic: push to discuss your request immediately, or have the other person specify a time and place where it can be discussed. If you push to discuss your request immediately, you may find an assertive approach called, "yes, but" helpful. Agree with the other person, then say, "but" to emphasize your need or perception.

Occasionally, it is useful to specify the consequences of not discussing your request. Here are examples of each of these approaches.

"Some other time, I'm busy."   "I realize you're busy, but this is very important and won't take long."

"I'm too tired to talk now."   "I can understand that; however, before I let you go I need to know when we can talk about and resolve this problem."

"I don't have time to think about that now."   "It really won't take long, and if we don't discuss this now much time will be lost because of the problems it will cause."

A second and more indirect method to avoid dealing with your request is to sidetrack the discussion with irrelevant comments or questions. There are three different ways to overcome this tactic: ignore the distraction, dismiss the distracting comment with a short statement, or give a quick answer. After using one of these approaches, repeat your request and continue towards your assertive goal.

"You're lovely when you're angry."   (Comment is ignored) "What I need is..."

"By the way, Mr. Smith came by yesterday."   "That's not important now; however, as I was saying, we do need to decide on..."

"Don't you have work to do?"   "Yes, but it can wait until we're finished. As I was saying."

Challenging Your Description

A person will sometimes try to sidetrack you from your assertive goal by challenging your description of the problem behavior or situation. Concentrating on specific behaviors and actions minimizes the chances of this occurring. However, if you have specified behaviors and actions and your description is still challenged, do not become sidetracked by arguing who is "correct." Instead, turn the challenge aside by acknowledging that your perception is different from the other person's then repeat your request. The "yes, but" approach is often an effective way to do this.

"That's not the way it happened."   "I can see that we have very different ideas about what happened. In any event, I need..."

"You've got it all wrong."   "That may very well be the case, but I still feel it is important to..."

Refusing to Accept Responsibility

Sometimes a person tries to avoid taking action or discussing a problem by refusing to accept responsibility for either the creation or resolution of a problem. Here are four common ways in which this is done.

Blaming

There are two types of blaming: you are blamed for the problem behavior or situation, or the problem is blamed on something other than you. Blaming is similar to challenging your description in that it centers on your description of the problem behavior or situation. Since the problem is seen as being caused by you or someone else, the other person views him or herself as having no responsibility to take corrective action. The most effective way to deal with blaming is to avoid focusing on who is to blame and concentrate on your request.

"You didn't tell me to do that."	"That's true. However, I still need..."
"You forgot to remind me."	"That's not the issue. What I want..."
"The freight company always seems to mess up."	"I can see the problems that would cause, but I still need..."

"Everybody Does It"

Using the argument that "everybody does it" justifies a refusal to consider your problem seriously. The "yes, but" approach can be used to counter this tactic in either of two ways: acknowledge this view without endorsing it then repeat your request, or redefine the situation in terms of your individual needs.

"Everybody drives fast."	"That may be; however, I am very uncomfortable when we are going this fast and I would like..."
"You're the first person to complain about my writing."	"That may be, but I find your writing very difficult to read and would like..."

Reinterpreting

A person will sometimes reinterpret the problem behavior or situation in such a way that there seems to be a misinterpretation or lack of information on your part. When this happens, a simple exchange of opinions or information often achieves your goals. However, people can also reinterpret their behavior as being based on good intentions and therefore excusable. When this happens, use "yes, but" to acknowledge the other person's stated good intentions and repeat your request.

"I wasn't really serious."	"That may be, but I feel..."
"I was trying to help you."	"That may have been your intention, but I think..."

Psychoanalyzing

A person may try to redefine the problem behavior or situation in terms of a "psychological problem" you possess. This is often someone who knows you well or who has some knowledge of psychology. Psychological explanations like these are usually inaccurate and are often a subtle put-down. It is easy to become sidetracked by this tactic since the explanation offered may sound logical or deal with an issue that concerns you. Avoid becoming involved in an argument over the explanation. Simply affirm your own ability to assess your actions and personality then press on with your request.

It seems you're becoming very paranoid."

"I think my behavior is perfectly normal. Now as I was saying..."

"You've been getting pretty uppity since that assertive workshop."

"I have been finding it easier to express myself. In any case, I need..."

"You've just got an inferiority complex."

"I can understand how you might feel that way, but I still feel..."

Triggering Guilt or Embarrassment

Here are four common tactics that can sabotage your assertive efforts by triggering guilt and embarrassment.

Tears

Tears can be very manipulative. Do not allow this form of "water power" to make you feel guilty about sticking up for your rights. If crying interferes too much with your D.E.R. scripts, write it out as a letter or memo that can be read in your absence.

"You're making me feel like an awful shrew."

"I'm sorry you choose to feel that way. However, I feel..."

Offended martyr

Another guilt producing tactic is to play the offended martyr. A martyr frequently makes accusations or describes your behavior as being "mean" or "cruel." Refuse to accept this interpretation and redefine your behavior objectively. Then persist in your assertive efforts. Avoid becoming sidetracked by arguments over your motives and remain focused on what you want.

"You're so mean to talk to me like that."

"I am not being mean; I am just describing what I see. Now what I want..."

Physical symptoms

A person might use distressing physical symptoms as an excuse to avoid discussing your request. If you assume responsibility for causing this person's physical symptoms, your guilt can also prevent you from confronting this person in the future. Deal with this tactic in the same manner as you would postponing/sidetracking. Either negotiate a specific time to discuss the problem or press to discuss the matter now in spite of the physical symptoms. If the physical symptoms interfere too much with your D.E.R. script, send a letter or memo that can be read in your absence.

"Let's not talk now, I'm getting this terrible headache."

"When do you think you will be feeling better?"

Or

"I'm sorry to hear that, but this won't take long."

Excessive Apologies

Do not feel guilty or embarrassed if a person begins to offer excessive apologies upon hearing your description of a problem. Simply accept the other person's apology and continue with your request.

"I'm so sorry! I should have never let that happen. How could I be so thoughtless."

"I'm glad you're sorry and I accept your apology. Now I feel we need to decide how..."

Intimidation

Intimidation is one of the more difficult tactics to overcome because it often triggers strong negative emotions inside of you. This can cause you to either back away from your assertive goal or adopt an aggressive style that leads to a fight. In either case, you fail to get what you want. When you are going to deal with an intimating person, take time before the meeting to do the following: review both your rights and responsibilities, identify and develop effective rational challenges for irrational thinking associated with this person, develop and rehearse a D.E.R. script, and identify and practice the specific approaches described in this lesson that would be the most effective with this person. Here are the five common types of intimidation.

Verbal abuse/name-calling

There are many forms of verbal abuse such as sarcasm, criticism, jokes, ridicule, insults, and swearing. The most effective approach to name-calling is to ignore it and continue pressing for what you want. If you do choose to redefine an inaccurate or slanderous remark, do so in a restrained way as you do not want to become involved in a fight that sidetracks you from your assertive goal.

"You must be losing your grip."

(Comment is ignored) "Furthermore, I think..."

"What makes a nit-wit like you think you can tell me what to do?"

"I am not trying to tell you what to do. What I am trying to do is solve the problem of..."

"You're acting like Wonder Woman."

"You may think any way you want, but I need..."

Hostile or negative body language

Sometimes people use their face, body, or tone of voice to convey the message that your assertive approach is angering, boring, or hurting them. Deal with this tactic by either commenting on the non-verbal message or by ignoring it and continuing with your assertive efforts. If you comment on a non-verbal message you may need to switch to your listening skills before continuing.

The other person looks very upset and unhappy.	(Non-verbal message is ignored) "Now about the problem of..."
The other person frowns and looks angry.	"You seem angry about what I am saying."

Interrogation

Some people are very good at bombarding you with questions that sidetrack you from your assertive goal. There are two ways to deal with this: give a quick response or dismiss the questions and requests for justifications as either irrelevant or unimportant. In either case you then quickly return to your request.

"Do you really think this is necessary?"	"Yes. What I want is..."
"Why is it so important to you?"	"I do not have to justify my feelings."
	Or
	"That's just the way I feel."

Debating

Some people are very adept at using superior knowledge or logic to overwhelm others. When you are making a request, there is one thing that is always more powerful than knowledge or logic—your feelings. You do not need to justify or logically explain them. Simply state that while you understand they seem illogical, it is the way you feel. Then proceed to press for your assertive goal.

"You are being totally illogical."	"You are exactly right, it is illogical. However, I still feel very strongly..."

Postponing a Decision

Sometimes a person appears ready to listen and agrees to negotiate but then postpones making a decision. This type of procrastination is actually a subtle form of non-negotiation. If you are not sure whether a postponement is sincere or merely a procrastinating tactic, grant one postponement before using one of the two following assertive approaches.

Set a deadline for making a decision without further delay

If the person tries to put you off again when the deadline arrives, you are dealing with a non-negotiator. Approaches to use with non-negotiators are described in the next section.

Insist on a tentative immediate agreement with the provision for further negotiation

Your basic message is, "I want a temporary agreement now. Then, unless you discuss and agree upon a different solution by..., the agreement we make now goes into effect." A variation of this approach is the conditional contract. Use a conditional contract when the other person insists on a consultation for an expert opinion. Anticipate the possible opinions that might be obtained and plan your actions accordingly. Your basic message is: "If the expert's opinion is X, we will..., if it is Y, we will..." Make sure you agree on a specific time to obtain the consultation and set a deadline for the final decision. Remember, you have the right to be present at any consultation which affects you and to hear the consultant's advice directly rather than from the person with whom you are negotiating.

The Non-Negotiator

Most people respond positively to the approaches you are studying. However, anyone who continues to use the tactics discussed in this lesson to avoid or sidetrack your negotiation efforts is a non-negotiator. In addition to using the previous tactics, tough non-negotiators may also resort to one or more of the following four tactics.

There is no problem

With this tactic the non-negotiator refuses to accept that a problem exists. If this person has some regard for your feelings, emphasize your feelings and how important the problem is for you.

"I just don't see what all the fuss is about."

"I know you don't believe there is a problem here, but I do and I feel very strongly about..."

All solutions are unacceptable

Sometimes a non-negotiator continues to find all proposed solutions unacceptable. Try turning the task of developing an acceptable solution over to the other person. When you do this, set a deadline for this person to have one or more reasonable solutions ready to discuss.

"Frankly, none of these ideas is good enough."

"Well then, why don't we take a break and see if you can come up with some ideas which might be acceptable. How about meeting again after lunch to discuss them?"

The "price" for change is too high

Sometimes very aggressive or hostile people make unreasonable demands in order to meet your request. Try pointing out the unreasonableness of the demands. As you do this, emphasize both your feelings and the importance of the problem.

"That's what I need from you if this report is going to be on time."

"I really feel that is unreasonable. This is a very important problem that requires us to cooperate in order for it to be resolved."

A refusal to negotiate

Some non-negotiators refuse to even discuss your problem. If this occurs, focus on the other person's refusal to negotiate and use your assertive skills to get a commitment to discuss your problem.

If you have tried positive approaches and the other person continues to be a non-negotiator, two basic options remain: use a more aggressive approach and specify negative consequences you will take if the problem is not resolved or attempt to resolve your problem through one of the three non-assertive approaches discussed in the next section. If you decide to specify negative consequences, consider the consequences of your actions carefully along with both your *ability* and *willingness* to carry them out.

☐ *Five General Approaches for Resolving Problems and Conflicts*

Five general approaches can be used to resolve problems and conflicts. One is assertive, one is aggressive, and three are non-assertive. In order to be effective in life, you need to select and use the most appropriate approach for the situation you face. Sometimes a person will not use a particular approach because of a lack of skills. Other times a person has irrational beliefs which makes an approach unacceptable. Whenever an inappropriate approach is used to resolve a problem, the result is unnecessary stress and discomfort. For example, Judy refused to withdraw from a very negative job situation even though other jobs which paid equally well were available. For her, changing jobs was interpreted as failure and was totally unacceptable. She continued to try and change working conditions where she was even though improvement was hopeless and she experienced severe physical problems due to the stress.

As you read each of the following descriptions, be aware of any negative reactions you have. If you notice any, take a moment to identify the beliefs generating them. In addition, if you identify any approach you seldom or never allow yourself to use, list the beliefs that prevent you from using it. Whenever you identify irrational beliefs, develop rational self-talk responses you can use to challenge it.

Conform

The first non-assertive approach for resolving conflicts is to conform. You simply comply with the demands of others and go along with a situation without making any effort to change it. Conforming is often the best approach to use when the amount of discomfort you feel is small and the act of asserting yourself would either produce little results or result in more stress and conflict than is produced by having your needs and desires go unfulfilled. Three common types of situations where conforming is appropriate are: "no-win" situations involving inflexible bureaucracies such as the Internal Revenue Service, situations where you are in conflict with a person with higher rank or authority than you such as a judge or your boss, and situations in which you value another person's friendship and the issue involved is not very important to you.

When you choose to conform, you can reduce your discomfort by re-examining your beliefs and expectations about the situation and becoming more philosophical. This often requires you to identify and challenge should/must rules associated with the situation. While conforming is sometimes the best way to resolve a conflict, it is self-defeating when used as your main method of dealing with conflict. A person who continues to ignore needs and wants tends to experience more and more frustration, anger, and resentment. When not expressed directly, these feelings may be expressed inappropriately or create internal stress that slowly eats away at you both physically and mentally.

Withdraw

A second non-assertive approach for resolving conflict is to withdraw. You retreat from the problem situation and make no further attempt to resolve the conflict. This is an appropriate approach when other approaches are not working and you are experiencing stress and conflict that is or will become a destructive force in your body or daily life.

If you find it difficult to withdraw from no-win situations, use rational self-talk to convince yourself that withdrawal is often the best way to solve a problem that cannot be resolved through any other approach. Remind yourself that it is impossible to master every situation and successfully overcome every problem you face. As you use this type of rational self-talk, examine your beliefs. If you find it difficult to withdraw from no-win situations it may be because you consider the act of withdrawing as a sign of failure. This self-defeating attitude is often generated by a combination of perfectionistic, all-or-nothing thinking and the mistaken belief that worth is determined by achievement. A review of Lesson 6 will help you challenge this type of irrational thinking and convince yourself that knowing your limits and withdrawing when you have reached them is a sign of wisdom.

If withdrawal is one of your main methods for dealing with conflict, learn to be more assertive and stand up for your rights. Review the rights listed in Lesson 13 until they are a firm part of your belief system. Create and rehearse D.E.R. scripts until they become easy to create comfortable to deliver.

Select a Substitute Goal

A third non-assertive approach is to select a substitute goal. When it is necessary to withdraw from a no-win situation or when an assertive goal is unattainable, you select a new goal. While this might seem like an obvious approach, many people find it difficult. This usually is because they have perfectionistic, all-or-nothing thinking patterns and should/must beliefs that causes them to consider anything less than their first choice as unacceptable.

Selecting a substitute goal is often the best approach to use when dealing with a non-negotiator and you are either unwilling or unable to carry out negative consequences that would force cooperation. For example, Terry's co-worker had poor work habits that interfered with Terry's job. This person refused to recognize there was a problem or negotiate with Terry. Terry did not want to push the issue too hard since his supervisor did not want to get involved. Therefore, he decided to focus on a new goal of protecting himself from this fellow employee. Terry did this by reducing the amount of time he interacted with this person and by writing memos that put on record what was occurring whenever this person's poor work habits interfered with Terry's work. This minimized the effect this person had on Terry and his job.

The selection of a substitute goal can also be effective when personal goals are creating tremendous stress or disappointment. For example, Rose wanted very much to become a surgeon but did not have the grades or ability. She finally decided to satisfy her desire to be in medicine by becoming a physical therapist.

Become Aggressive

It is often appropriate to become aggressive when life or property is threatened or you are dealing with someone who is irrational or emotionally immature and will only respond to an aggressive approach. Unfortunately, this approach is either over-used or used at inappropriate times by many people. Some use an aggressive approach as their main method of meeting every day needs and resolving conflict. Others "see-saw" back and forth between an aggressive approach and one of the non-assertive approaches described above. This second group uses a non-assertive approach until the frustration and resentment resulting from denying needs and wants builds to a point where they can no longer be denied. An aggressive approach is then used in an attempt to satisfy the needs and wants. The aggressive approach is also sometimes used to punish the person or persons viewed as being responsible for the deprivation.

If you use an aggressive approach as your primary method for resolving conflict, spend additional time developing assertive skills and learning to channel anger into constructive actions as described in Lessons 12 and 13. If you see-saw back and forth between non-assertive and aggressive behavior, spend additional time building self-esteem, becoming more in touch with your feelings, and developing assertive skills as described in Lessons 11, 12, and 13.

Become Assertive

In most situations it is best to ask for what you want in a polite, direct manner and resolve conflicts through the negotiation process described in Lesson 13. Working with the guidelines and exercises in these lessons is enough to enable most people to develop a more assertive style. However, if asserting yourself is very difficult, consider doing additional work with a book on assertiveness, attending one or more assertiveness workshops, or possibly even working with a therapist.

☐ *When Is an Assertive Approach Most Effective?*

The best way to decide when an assertive approach would be effective is to think in terms of how much "power" you have. Power, in this sense, is the ability to influence others to act in the way you would like them to act.

Your assertive skills are most successful in situations where you have more power than the other person. This usually involves people who are providing a service or selling something such as sales clerks, repairmen, and waiters.

A more difficult type of situation involves people who have the same amount of power as you. Examples of these are friends, relatives, people who cut into line ahead of you, or people who smoke in a stuffy room. These types of people can sometimes be tough to deal with. However, most will respond positively if you use an assertive approach.

The most difficult type of situation arises when the other person has more power than you. These types of people are usually authorities in law, business, or government such as judges, police officers, teachers, corporate bureaucrats, and doctors. While these types of people are often the most frustrating to deal with, they also usually respond positively when assertive skills are used.

If you are not sure about whether it would be best to assert yourself in a particular situation, ask yourself the following questions.

How irritating is this?

Take a moment to tune into yourself and determine the amount of discomfort you are feeling. Remember, discomfort signifies a need or want is being frustrated or threatened. The more discomfort you feel, the more important the need or want is and the more important it is to take action.

What is irritating me?

The next step is to determine what need or want is being frustrated or threatened along with the source of this frustration or threat. If you are not sure, delay action as you may do more harm than good.

What can I do to satisfy that need or want or at least make it known?

Once you know what you want, decide who has the power to help you achieve it. Then identify the approach that has the greatest chance of success. This is the point at which many people become sidetracked by a desire to punish the person causing the discomfort or by a need to win. Winning usually means proving you have more power and control than the person causing the discomfort. Both of these detours tend to be self-defeating exercises. Even when you succeed in winning or punishing the offending person, the victory is usually empty since you probably failed to satisfy your original want. You can help minimize the tendency to become detoured by keeping your assertive goal in mind. Keep asking yourself, "What do I want? What is the best way to achieve it?"

☐ *What to do When People Fail to Keep Their Agreements*

Sometimes you think you have resolved a problem with others; then they fail to keep the agreement. When this happens, consider the following.

Were the rewards or negative consequences you promised sufficient motivation?

If you only offered rewards, you may need to strengthen those rewards or consider negative consequences. If you said you would carry out negative consequences, do so. Some people need to know you are serious before they will act. Be willing to give people a second chance before considering them as a non-negotiator.

Are reminders needed because this person is naturally forgetful or very busy?

When you are dealing with issues that are important for you but unimportant to the other person, you may need to train this person to remember to carry out the agreement you made. This is especially true if this person is naturally forgetful or very busy with other activities. Since it is better to win cooperation than force submission, use cues or reminders in a friendly, encouraging manner rather than in a way that is felt as a put-down or punishment. Also, remember that the closer the reminders are to the time the behavior or action is to be performed, the more effective they will be. While you may need to give several reminders at first, keep in mind that your goal is to have the other person learn to keep the agreement without being reminded.

Are one or more automatic behaviors interfering with this person's ability to keep the agreement?

This is especially important if your request requires this person to change a deeply ingrained behavior such as asking the person not to smoke or swear in your presence. When this is the case, adopt a tolerant attitude similar to what a sympathetic teacher has towards a struggling student. If the other person has made reasonable and well-intentioned attempts, reward this partial fulfillment of the agreement. Keep in mind how difficult it is to change many of the automatic behaviors you have been working on. If sufficient progress is not made after a reasonable length of time, decide whether the other person is willing to spend the time and energy needed to change and whether you have the time, energy and willingness to continue assisting in this process. If not, consider an alternative solution.

Is there a factor you have overlooked which greatly influences this person's ability to keep the agreement?

Illness, work-related activities, and personal relationships are common factors that can keep a person from keeping an agreement. If you identify a factor like this, re-analyze the problem, develop a new script, and try again. As you negotiate a new agreement, be sure to address the problem created by the factor you have identified.

If you have considered the above, made a reasonable effort to resolve your conflict assertively, and have made little or no progress, you are probably dealing with a non-negotiator. When evaluating behavior pay more attention to what a person does than to what a person says. Past behavior is usually the best predictor of future behavior. The only exception is a person who is working in a systematic and dedicated manner to change old patterns as you are doing with this program. Be wary of entering into an agreement with someone whose track record indicates this person is untrustworthy and fails to keep agreements. If you make an agreement with a person like this, decide what you will do if the agreement is broken before you begin negotiating.

☐ *Resolving Conflicts with Businesses and Sales People*

If you use the following guidelines, you will find that your assertive skills will usually work well in situations where you receive defective merchandise or poor service.

- Identify the correct person to deal with, someone who has the power to help you.
- Lodge your complaint privately or quietly if in a public setting.
- Register your complaint as soon after you notice the problem as is possible.
- Be sure to have any and all receipts, supporting paper-work, or defective merchandise readily available for inspection.
- Keep in mind the various elements of the DERN approach. While all of the guidelines are important, the four most essential ones to keep in mind are: make only one complaint at a time, avoid statements that may make the other person defensive, avoid apologizing for your complaint, and be specific as to what happened and what you want without generalizing with words like "always" or "never." Remember, with simple problems only the Describe and Request parts of a D.E.R. script may be required; with more complex problems all four parts of the DERN approach will probably be needed.
- Only complain about actions or defects which you think can be changed or corrected.
- Try to stay friendly as you register your complaint and say something complimentary about the other person or the situation. This helps to minimize defensiveness in the other person.

Recommended Activities for Lesson 14

Continuing Developing Basic Assertive Skills

Continue developing skills presented in Lesson 13 which you feel are weak. These might include any of the following:

- Creating D.E.R. scripts.
- Responding to simple situations that violate your rights.
- Enhancing your listening skills.
- Developing negotiation skills.

If asserting yourself is difficult, continue reviewing the list of rights and responsibilities in Lesson 13 each day. Also be sure to challenge irrational ideas you have about being assertive whenever you are using your assertive skills.

Practice the Skills Used to Overcome Sabotaging Tactics

Recall instances where it was difficult for you to assert yourself and identify the specific tactics other people used to sabotage your assertive efforts. Develop a D.E.R. script for situation and begin rehearsing it. As you rehearse, imagine the other person interrupting you with the specific tactics this person used in the past. Then practice using one or more of the approaches suggested in this lesson for overcoming each tactic.

You can practice overcoming resistance from others while driving, doing chores, or just about anywhere. However, if it is difficult for you to use the skills described in this lesson, spend time practicing with another person. As you do this, switch roles at times. Let your practice partner deliver your script as you pretend you are the person with whom you wish to be assertive. This allows you to see how your practice partner uses the skills you are studying. It also shows your practice partner how to role play the person you have in mind when it's your turn to deliver your script. It is also effective to practice in front of a mirror. This helps you develop gestures and expressions that are assertive.

Begin Using Your Assertive Skills

Begin using the assertive skills you are developing. As you begin, remember to start with as many factors in your favor as possible. Learning to be assertive is similar to learning to play the piano. Just as a piano student begins with easy pieces and gradually works up to more difficult works, start with small conflicts or needs, master them, then go on to more difficult ones.

Have a Review Session of the Day's Problems and Conflicts

At the end of the day, spend a few minutes reviewing the problems and conflicts which occurred that day along with how you dealt with them. Do this daily for as long as you are working on developing your assertive skills. As you review your day, identify alternative approaches that might resolve similar conflicts or problems more effectively in the future. Practice skills you failed to use but would like to use in the future. You may even want to plan regular practice sessions for skills which are difficult. This type of review and practice increases your ability to use assertive skills in similar future situations.

Avoid using this review as an opportunity to condemn yourself because you "failed" to handle each situation in the "best" way or as it "should" have been handled. Remember that you handle each and every situation as best you can at the time it occurs. True, you sometimes forget to use some of your skills, but that is only human and is to be expected.

Developing assertive skills takes time and practice. Spend at least one week with this lesson—longer if asserting yourself is difficult.

Continuing Your Growth

Lesson 15

This is the final lesson in the program. However, it is far from the end of your journey. As you choose and carry out one of the plans described in this lesson, you will probably find that your ability to manage anxiety effectively will continue to increase for many months to come. So you have not really come to an ending, but to the beginning of a new life.

☐ *Evaluate Your Progress*

The rate at which people working through these lessons overcome their anxiety-related problems varies greatly. By this lesson, some feel they have completely overcome their self-defeating behaviors and are managing anxiety effectively while others feel they have only just begun. Most are somewhere in between. Three different plans have been developed for continuing your growth. However, Before you read about the plans, stop and complete the Post-Evaluation at the end of this lesson. This evaluation helps you systematically evaluate the progress you have made so you can choose the best plan for you.

☐ *Three Plans for Continuing Your Growth*

Now that you have evaluated your progress, you are ready to choose a plan that will help you continue to increase your knowledge and skills. Read each of the following statements and place a check by the one that best describes your current progress.

❑ *Plan A:* Excessive anxiety is no longer a major problem in my life. I have reduced anxiety to a manageable level and have overcome most or all of the self-defeating behaviors formerly associated with anxiety. Any remaining anxiety-related problems are now minor and do not seriously interfere with my ability to function effectively and enjoy life.

❑ *Plan B:* I have made progress in overcoming my anxiety-related problems. However, I still have self-defeating behaviors and reactions associated with anxiety which are interfering with my ability to function effectively and enjoy life.

❑ *Plan C:* I have made little or no progress in overcoming my anxiety-related problems OR I feel that I was making progress but am now "stuck" and making little or no progress.

Read the plan that corresponds to the statement you checked and follow the directions it gives. If you cannot decide which statement best describes you, read each plan and use the one that best fits your needs.

Plan A: For People Who Feel Anxiety No Longer Seriously Interferes with Their Lives

Some people reach this point after one time through the lessons, others after working through the lessons two or more times. Some need the help of a professional therapist to reach this point. It really doesn't matter how long it took or whether you worked alone, with a friend, a group, or a therapist. You have now reached the point where anxiety is no longer seriously interfering with your life. Stop and congratulate yourself! You have accomplished one of the most difficult tasks there is: changing the way you think and act.

As time goes by, the skills you have developed become even more effective. This does not mean that you will eventually handle all problems and conflicts you encounter perfectly; no one does that. However, you now have a much greater understanding of yourself and a much wider range of skills to deal with life than the average person. To insure your continued growth, devote some time and energy to reinforcing the new behaviors, attitudes, and ways of thinking you learned while working through the lessons. This prevents stagnation and the possibility of slipping back into old patterns. Four different ways in which this can be done are described below.

Schedule a monthly review of the lessons

Spend at least one hour a month reviewing the lessons. Concentrate on only one lesson during this review. As you review the lesson, identify skills where further work is needed. Make a conscious effort to strengthen any weak areas you identify in the weeks that follow by using the exercises described in the lesson. Select different lessons for each review session so you eventually review the entire program. Continue this practice for at least six months.

Review your coping cards at the first sign of old behaviors

Save the various summaries of key concepts and coping self-statements you made while working through the lessons. When you notice yourself returning to old patterns, review the cards that challenge those specific behaviors or thought patterns.

Do supplemental reading

Read at least one book from the recommended reading list every two months. Select books which deal with your weakest areas. Remember to take your time as you read these books. It also helps to read each chapter twice: once for the big picture, and once for detail. This is the best way to absorb the information and skills presented in a self-help book. Continue this practice for at least a year.

Use classes, workshops, or support groups to reinforce and further the progress you have made

Attending a class or workshop is an excellent way to reinforce concepts and skills. Personal growth classes and workshops are held at churches, hospitals, colleges, the adult education division of local school districts, and counseling centers. While there are many excellent programs available throughout the country, there are some of dubious quality. Therefore, it is always best to check on the credentials and experience of the person presenting the workshop. It also is best to stay away from programs that promise a "quick fix." If it sounds too good to be true, it probably is.

If you experienced physical, sexual, or emotional abuse as a child, come from a family where there was substance abuse, have experienced a traumatic experience, or have an emotional or physical problem, you will find it valuable to become involved in a support group that addresses your specific issues. Appendix 3 provides guidelines for locating a local support organization that is right for you.

The time and energy needed to continue your growth decreases as time goes by. Some people find they can keep their momentum going and continue progressing by doing two or three of the above activities. Others need to do all four. If you are doing well and continuing to apply your skills effectively, you are probably doing enough. If you are slipping into old patterns and failing to use the skills you learned from these lessons, you probably need to spend more time reviewing and practicing. Taking time for these activities becomes easier if you remember that the time and energy you spend with them is returned to you many times over as your ability to live more effectively and enjoy life increases.

Plan B: For People Who Have Made Progress but Who Still Have Important Anxiety-Related Problems

If you are feeling disappointed or consider yourself a failure because you have worked through the lessons and still have anxiety-related problems, stop and challenge the perfectionistic thinking behind these thoughts and feelings. Many people find that, anxiety continues to seriously interfere with their lives after completing the lessons. Usually, this is simply because their anxiety-related problems are the result of many different, deeply ingrained beliefs, thinking patterns, and behaviors. You spent years developing these self-defeating habits. It is unreasonable to believe that the short time it takes to work through the lessons once is enough to completely change a lifetime of learning. People with numerous deeply ingrained self-defeating beliefs and habits often require a year or more to internalize all the material presented in these lessons. Many find they need to work through the lessons two or more times. This is especially true for people who experienced physical, emotional, or sexual abuse as children.

As you challenge negative thoughts and feelings you have about your progress, be especially aware of should/must thinking, overgeneralizations, and magnification/minimization. Focus on the progress you have made and remind yourself that there is no one time when you "should" or "must" overcome all of your problem behaviors. You are progressing at your own rate—a rate best for you. Keep in mind that it takes time to learn new concepts and skills. Change is usually a slow process. The process of change is illustrated in the following little story.

Five Short Chapters on Change

*Author Unknown**

Chapter I: I walk down a street and there's a deep hole in the sidewalk. I fall in. It takes forever to get out. It's my fault.

Chapter II: I walk down the same street. I fall in the hole again. It still takes a long time to get out. It's *not* my fault.

Chapter III: I walk down the same street. I fall in the hole again. It's becoming a habit. It *is* my fault. I get out immediately.

Chapter IV: I walk down the same street and see the deep hole in the sidewalk. I walk around it.

Chapter V: I walk down a different street.

* This version of the story appeared in the ABIL Newsletter. ABIL (Agoraphobics Building Independent Lives) is a large non-profit organization headquartered in Richmond, Virginia.

Once you have developed rational self-talk that challenges negative thoughts and feelings, it is time to make a firm commitment to continue your journey. Plan B is simple: start with Lesson 1 and work through the lessons again in order. As you do this, you have two basic goals. First, work at deepening your understanding of concepts you either missed or did not understand fully the first time through. Second, practice skills you either skipped or did not learn thoroughly due to lack of time, understanding, or commitment. The best way to reach these goals is to follow these suggestions:

- Take your time with each lesson. Spend two or three weeks on a lesson if you feel you need it.
- Be sure to read each lesson at least three times—more if you are having difficulty with the concepts.
- Do as many of the exercises you skipped as possible. Also be sure to repeat exercises which were a challenge for you when you did them previously.
- When a lesson deals with an area that is especially troublesome, supplement it by reading one or more of the books listed for that topic in the Recommended Reading.

Many people find it difficult to follow the above guide-lines because they either are too busy or because they find it difficult to use written lessons. If this is true for you, put a check by any of the following ideas that could help you give the lessons the time and energy they deserve.

- Establish a regular time to work with the lessons. Make this scheduled study time as important as your regular meals. If you follow a written calendar, record your study times on the calendar.
- Remind yourself that you can make the most progress when you are feeling good and your life seems to be running smoothly. It is during these times that it is easiest to look at yourself objectively and do the activities listed in the lessons.
- If you have difficulty with written material, consider obtaining the audio cassettes described at the end of the book.
- Find a study partner or group that can help you keep motivated and use the lessons as they are intended to be used.
- Consider working with a therapist who is skilled with anxiety-related problems.

Most people who use Plan B are surprised at the amount of information that was missed on their first or even second time through the lessons. There are several reasons for this. The amount of information you can absorb and the number of skills you can master in a given amount of time is limited. The more anxiety is interfering with your life, the more difficult it is to learn the concepts and skills in the lessons. Because you have made progress in reducing the amount of anxiety you experience, you now have more energy available as you go through the lessons again.

Each lesson contains more information and describes more skills than can be mastered in one to three weeks. The lessons are intentionally written in this fashion since the specific skills and information that are important differ from person to person. The information and skills important for your continued progress at this time are also probably different from those that were important when you first began.

Because the concepts and skills presented in the lessons are interconnected, it is easy to miss some or much of what is presented. Full mastery of a concept or skill in one lesson often requires the mastery of concepts and skills in others. Now that you have studied the ideas and practiced the skills in later lessons, you have an increased ability to apply the ideas and skills presented in earlier ones. Likewise, your increased understanding and skill with the earlier material helps you as you repeat the later lessons.

Plan C: For people who have major anxiety-related problems and feel like they are blocked and unable to progress.

If you are reading this plan you have either not made much progress since beginning the lessons or made some progress then became blocked and ceased progressing. Before going any further, read and answer the following questions.

- Did you spend at least one week on each lesson?
- Did you work through the lessons in order, reading each lesson at least three times?
- Did you do most of the recommended activities for each lesson?
- When doing recommended activities, did you take care to do them in the way you were directed to do them?

If you answered "no" to any of the above, your lack of progress or feeling of being blocked is probably due to using the program incorrectly. If this is the case, do not feel bad or condemn yourself. Many people do this when they first work through the lessons. Many have never worked with printed lessons like these and lack the reading and study habits needed to use the lessons effectively. If you fit into this group, follow Plan B and work through the lessons again.

Another common reason for difficulty is the presence of a factor that causes you to resist change. If you think this might be the case, review Lesson 10 and identify the source of your resistance. Then follow the suggestions given in Lesson 10 for overcoming that particular source of resistance.

If none of the above seems to apply to you and you are feeling that you are stuck and not progressing, seek help from a professional therapist. Appendix 2 describes how to find one.

Post-Evaluation

List any medications you are taking and the usual dosage per day.

Medication: Dosage:

Use the following scale to indicate how much control of your life you feel now (circle one):

(no control) 1 2 3 4 5 6 7 8 9 10 (complete control)

Read the following items. Then choose a number from each of the three scales to indicate how frequently you experienced this problem during the past month, how much discomfort it caused, and how much it interfered with your life. Rate each item with respect to how it affected you during the past month. If you have *not* experienced a particular symptom during the past month, simply check n/a (not applicable). Use an additional sheet of paper if you need to.

Frequency of Occurrence (Freq)	Level of Discomfort (Disc)	Degree to which it inter-feres with your life (Inter)
1-Never occurs 2-Seldom occurs: once a month or less 3-Sometimes occurs: 2-6 times a month or once per week 4-Often occurs: 2 or more times per week but not daily 5-Always occurs: one or more times daily	1-Comfortable 2-Slightly uncomfortable 3-Uncomfortable 4-Very Uncomfortable 5-Panicky	1-No interference 2-Slight interference 3-Moderate interference 4-Considerable interference 5-Severe interference

A. *Physical Symptoms*

	n/a	Freq	Disc	Inter
Shortness of breath (dysnea or smothering sensations)				
Choking				
Palpitations or accelerated heart rate (tachycardia)				
Chest pain or discomfort				
Sweating				
Dizziness, unsteady feelings, or faintness				
Nausea or abdominal distress				
Feelings of unreality (depersonalization or derealization)				

	n/a	Freq	Disc	Inter
Numbness or tingling sensations (paresthesia) usually in the fingers, toes, or lips				
Flushes (hot flashes) or chills				
Others:				
Others:				
Others:				

B. Fears Associated With Anxiety

People with anxiety-related problems often think about one or more of the fears listed below. Use the preceding scales to rate each one that applies to you. If you have not thought about a particular fear during the last month, simply check n/a. Use the spaces provided to list specific examples of what you fear. For example, if you fear losing control, exactly what is it you fear you might do?

	n/a	Freq.	Disc.	Inter.
Fear of becoming seriously ill or dying				
Fear of going crazy				
Fear of losing control and doing something that might harm or embarrass myself or others				
Others:				
Others:				
Others:				

C. Panic Attacks

Panic attacks are episodes of intense apprehension, fear, or terror characterized by four or more of the physical sensations or fears listed in items A and B. (for example, shortness of breath, accelerated heart rate, dizziness, and the fear you are dying.) If you have experienced panic attacks during the past month, use the preceding scales to rate their frequency, discomfort, and degree of interference. If you have not experienced panic attacks check n/a.

n/a _____   Frequency of Occurrence _____

Level of Discomfort _____   Degree of Interference _____

D. Episodes of Severe Anxiety

If you have experienced episodes of high anxiety other than panic attacks during the past month (three or fewer sensations or fears listed in items A and B). Use the preceding scales to rate them. If you have not, check n/a.

n/a _____   Frequency of Occurrence _____

Level of Discomfort _____   Degree of Interference _____

E. Triggering Events/Situations

List any events or situations that have been associated with anxiety or which triggered recurring anxiety during the past month. Then use the preceding scales to rate each one on frequency, discomfort, and degree of interference. If you completed the Pre-Evaluation, be sure to also list the situations you listed in Section E of the Pre-Evaluation and re-rate them with respect to the past month. Since situations like these are often avoided, also rate each one on how often you avoided it during the past month using the following Avoidance Scale (Avoid).

1-Never avoid   3-Sometimes avoid: 1/4 -   5-Always avoid: 3/4 - all
                                      1/2 of the time   of the time
2-Seldom avoid: 0 - 1/4 of   4-Often avoid: 1/2 -
   the time   3/4 of the time

If you have always avoided a particular situation during the past month (5), rate the level of discomfort in terms of how much discomfort you think you would experience in this situation and the degree of interference in terms of how much the avoidance of this situation interferes with your life. Rate the frequency for situations you always avoid at 1 unless it is something you had to face in spite of your best efforts to avoid it.

Situation	Avoid	Freq	Disc	Inter

F. Compulsions

People with anxiety-related problems sometimes develop compulsions. These are actions which are ritualistically repeated in order to neutralize or prevent some dreaded event or situation. However, the compulsive behavior is either unconnected in a realistic way with what it is designed to neutralize or prevent, or it is clearly excessive. Repeated hand-washing in response to a fear of contaminating oneself or others is an example of a common compulsion. Other common compulsions include counting, checking, and repeated touching. List below any compulsions you have along with the average number of times you performed the compulsive act EACH DAY during the past WEEK. Then rate it with respect to the degree of interference it has on your life using the same scale you used in the previous sections. If you do not have compulsions, skip this section.

Compulsion	Average No of times/day	Interference

G. Global Rating: Anxiety

Use the following scale to rate the *overall* progress you have made since beginning these lessons in reducing the amount of daily anxiety you experience (Items A, C, and D). Circle the number for the rating that best describes your current evaluation of your overall progress. If you completed the Pre-Evaluation, review it and compare the responses to those on this evaluation before making this rating.

1	2	3	4	5
Complete Improvement	Much Improvement	Improved	Slight Improvement	No Improvement

H. Global Rating: Self-Defeating Behaviors

Use the following scale to rate the *overall* progress you have made since beginning these lessons in overcoming self-defeating behaviors associated with anxiety (Items B, E, and F). Circle the number for the rating that best describes your current evaluation of your overall progress. If you completed the Pre-Evaluation, review it and compare the responses to those on this evaluation before making this rating.

1	2	3	4	5
Complete Improvement	Much Improvement	Improved	Slight Improvement	No Improvement

Feedback Form

I would like very much to hear about your experiences with these lessons. Knowing the problems you faced, the successes you achieved, and the changes you would suggest provides me with valuable information I can use when making future revisions. Simply photocopy the form on this page and mail it to me at the following address:

Reneau Peurifoy
c/o LifeSkills Publications/Tapes
P.O. Box 7915
Citrus Heights, CA 95621

1. In general, what did you like about the lessons?

_____

_____

_____

_____

_____

_____

2. In general, what didn't you like about the lessons?

_____

_____

_____

_____

_____

_____

3. What lesson(s) or technique(s) did you find most helpful? How?

_____

_____

_____

_____

_____

4. What lesson(s) or technique(s) did you find least helpful? Why?

_____

_____

_____

_____

_____

5. What changes would you recommend for future versions of the lessons?

_____

_____

_____

_____

_____

6. If you have any other comments you would like to make about the lessons, do so here:

_____

_____

_____

_____

_____

Methods for Developing a Relaxation Response

1
Appendix

The term relaxation response was coined by Herbert Benson and is used to describe a state of deep muscle relaxation that is triggered by some set method. There are many different methods that can be used to trigger a relaxation response. They range from meditation and hypnosis to autogenic training and biofeedback. This appendix begins with a brief description of four of the most popular methods for producing a relaxation response. This is followed by two detailed scripts which can be recorded and used for practicing the various methods. The two scripts include wording that show how to associate your relaxation response with a cue in order to develop cue-controlled relaxation.

☐ *Progressive Relaxation*

Progressive relaxation is the oldest of the "modern" approaches to deep relaxation. It was first formalized by Edmund Jacobson in 1908 and is based on the principle that a muscle will become more relaxed after it is first tensed. Progressive relaxation takes practice to master so expect only limited success when you first begin. However, with regular practice, most people find they can eventually use it to relax their entire body fairly quickly.

1. Pick a time and place where you will not be disturbed and lie or sit in a comfortable position.

2. Close your eyes and breathe in a relaxed manner while you scan your body and notice how the various muscle groups and joints feel. As you do this, identify the parts that are most tense.

3. Tense and relax one muscle group at a time. Begin with the feet and slowly work your way up to your head and face. Before moving from one muscle group to the next do a complete breathing cycle, breathing in and out in a relaxed manner. Use moderation as you tighten and relax each muscle group, especially neck and back muscles where excessive tightening might result in a strain or injury. Some people also find that over-tightening the toes or feet can sometimes result in muscle cramps.

    The more difficult it is for you to relax, the more you need to take additional time and work with smaller groups of muscles. For example, tighten and relax the toes on the left foot first then the right foot. As you become skilled with this process, you can shorten it by combining muscle groups, such as tightening the toes on both feet at the same time.

4. When you have completed tensing and relaxing the muscle groups in your entire body, stop for a moment to feel how much more relaxed you are than when you began. Identify those areas where tension remains. If you wish, you can switch to a counting or visualization process to deepen the relaxation you have produced.

□ *Breath Counting*

Counting backwards is a common relaxation technique. It is found on cassette tapes designed to produce a relaxation response as well as by therapists teaching relaxation response techniques to clients. Breath counting is an effective adaptation of this approach for a person working on his or her own.

1. Pick a time and place where you will not be disturbed and lie or sit in a comfortable position.

2. Close your eyes and begin counting backward from 50. Time each count in the following manner to match your breathing. After you *exhale*, notice that you don't have to breathe in again immediately and can rest comfortably for a few seconds. For some people this may only be one or two seconds. For others it may be as long as twenty seconds. Count during this peaceful time when the lungs have paused and the body is still. Count one number for each cycle of breathing in and out.

    As you practice breath counting, you will probably find that you occasionally lose track of the number you are counting. This is normal. When this occurs, simply resume counting from the last number you can remember. If 37 is the last number you remember counting, resume your count with 36. If you wish to spend more time with this exercise, start counting at a higher number such as 75 or 100. One advantage to this method is that, with experience, you can estimate how long it will take depending on what number you begin with.

3. After completing your countdown, you can either return to your normal alert state or spend additional time developing your relaxation response by switching to one of the other methods.

As with progressive relaxation, breath counting often takes several practice sessions before it begins to produce results. However, once you become skilled with it, it can be not only a good method for producing a relaxation response, but it is also an effective centering technique that can be used when your mind is whirling with many different thoughts or concerns.

□ *Focal Point Technique*

There are numerous types of religious and secular meditation practiced around the world. Many of them offer effective methods for producing a relaxation response. The following method is an adaptation of the one developed by Herbert Benson after he studied many different types of meditation.

1. Pick a time and place where you will not be disturbed and lie or sit in a comfortable position.

2. Close your eyes and choose a center of focus. This is a word or phrase that helps shift your mind from logical, externally-oriented thought to an internal, passive center of focus and stops mind wandering when it occurs. The most common focal point is a word such as "one," "calm," or "relax." However, a short phrase can also be used such as "relax and be at peace." Many people like to use words or phrases that have a spiritual or religious meaning such as, "God is with me" or "I am being watched over."

   People who are very visual find it useful to develop a secondary focal point in the form of a mental image that forms a background for the use of the word or phrase that has been chosen. Examples include a mental image of a calm lake or a religious figure. Some people prefer a focal point that allows them to keep their eyes open, such as a candle, picture, or statue.

3. Repeat your word or phrase each time you exhale. As you do this, adopt a passive attitude. This is the most important element of this method. Avoid concern about how well you are performing the technique and adopt a "let it happen" attitude. Your mind will occasionally slip away from its concentration on the word or phrase you have chosen. When this happens, don't panic or abandon your practice. This is normal and to be expected. It does not mean you are performing the technique incorrectly. Simply redirect your mind to your breathing and continue repeating your chosen word or phrase after each exhalation.

4. Practice for 10 to 20 minutes then open your eyes and resume your normal activities. You may open your eyes to check the time but do not use an alarm.

□ *Fantasy*

This is another technique that is widely used on cassettes presenting relaxation response techniques and in therapy. It is often referred to as imagery or visualization. However, these two terms are somewhat misleading since they imply that you must "see" what you are fantasizing. This is unfortunate since many people who are poor visualizers incorrectly conclude that they cannot use fantasy techniques. Anyone who can imagine people, places, and events can use fantasy techniques whether they actually see anything in their mind or not. While the following fantasy procedure can be used by itself, it is frequently combined with progressive relaxation and counting techniques.

1. Pick a time and place where you will not be disturbed and lie or sit in a comfortable position.

2. As you breathe comfortably, close your eyes and imagine something peaceful and enjoyable. The types of places and activities you can use for a fantasy are only limited by your imagination. They can range from the seashore or mountains to a mythical garden. Be as creative as you want. Go on an imaginary journey or visit with real or imaginary friends. Recall a pleasant memory or do the impossible and fly on a cloud if the mood strikes you. This is your mind and your imagination. You have complete control and can make up any rules you choose. If unpleasant thoughts occur or your mind wanders, simply redirect them back to your chosen fantasy.

    When using fantasy, remember that it is based on a simple principle: whenever you imagine an experience vividly, you trigger the physiological responses that accompany it in real life. A simple example of this is the tension you feel when watching an exciting movie. Since your goal is to have your muscles relax, choose something relaxing. Exactly what you choose to imagine is unimportant as long as it is relaxing and enjoyable, will hold your interest, and can be created in detail. The more vividly you create the situation, the stronger will be the physiological responses that are triggered. The best way to do this is to involve as many of your senses as possible. For example, if you are imagining a hidden beach, imagine the warmth of the sun, the sound of the surf, the taste and smell of the salt air, and as many other details as possible.

3. After 10 to 20 minutes, open your eyes and resume your normal activities.

□ *Relaxation Response Scripts*

The following two scripts provide you with a detailed example of how the four methods described in this appendix can be used to produce a relaxation response. They also show how the different methods can be combined and associated with a simple physical cue to develop cue-controlled relaxation. Begin with the first script and record it on a sixty minute audiocassette tape exactly as written. If you prefer, you may have someone you know who has a soothing voice record it for you. When reading the script, use a slow, calm pace and pause where indicated by a series of three dots (...).

After you have recorded one of the scripts, pick a time and place to listen to it when you will not be disturbed. Sit or lie with your hands and feet uncrossed so there is free circulation of the blood and assume a comfortable position. It often helps to remove shoes or apparel that might interfere with your physical comfort. Then, start the cassette and follow the recorded directions. While many people like to work with one script at a time, others prefer to record the second script on the reverse side of the cassette. This allows them to alternate between the two scripts during each succeeding practice session without the need to rewind the cassette each time.

You will probably find your mind wandering while listening to a recorded script. This is especially true after you have used it several times and know what to expect. When this happens do not be concerned. Your goal is to produce deep relaxation. Whether you stay focused on the words of the script or let your mind wander is unimportant as long as you are producing a relaxation response.

With time you will find that simply recalling the different steps in the script will begin to produce a relaxation response. When you develop this ability, you will have a powerful tool for calming yourself in anxiety producing situations.

Script 1: Progressive Relaxation And Fantasy Techniques

In this script progressive relaxation is used to start your relaxation response. Fantasy is then used to deepen your relaxation and create a "special place." Having an imaginary special place is a useful tool for many anxiety-producing situations. It not only provides you with an additional method for producing relaxation and calming yourself, but it is also a valuable form of distraction.

Script

In just a moment, it will be time to begin developing your relaxation response through a process of progressive relaxation. By placing the first two fingers and thumb of either hand lightly together and keeping them in this position during this process, you will develop a very effective anchor, a simple physical cue or signal that can be used to activate your relaxation response whenever you feel yourself becoming anxious or tense.

Now, take a moment to settle down into where you are sitting or lying and take a few relaxing breaths... Close your eyes as you take these relaxing breaths so you can experience more fully the sensation of the air moving in through your nose and traveling down deep into your lungs...

Let the muscles of your rib cage relax... as your diaphragm invites the air inside... and the area below your stomach lifts and expands gently... notice how the air seems to just trickle out... as the diaphragm releases and moves gently... and easily... back into its soft... relaxed... flattened position... then, after a brief pause, the whole process is repeated so effortlessly...

As you continue to breathe in this soothing manner... take a moment to scan your body and become aware of any areas that seem tense and tight... notice also any areas that are relaxed and loose... after you have done this, move your attention to your left foot...

As you breathe in, tense the muscles in your left foot and hold both the breath and the tension for a few seconds... then, as you exhale, release the tension and allow your foot to relax completely... now do the same for the right foot... tense as you inhale and hold your breath for a few seconds... then exhale and release all of the tension...

Now, allow yourself to breathe in... and out... as you relax and prepare to shift your awareness to your left leg... and when you're ready, tense the left leg... hold it a moment... then let go as you exhale... now do the same for the right leg... tense as you inhale and hold for a few seconds... then release as you exhale...

Now take time once again to breathe in... and out... in a relaxed... easy manner... taking the air way down deep inside... letting it flow out slowly... comfortably... Now become aware of your buttocks... and as you inhale, tighten the muscles of your buttocks... hold it a few seconds... and when you're ready to let go, exhale and release the tension there...

And when you are done... take time to become aware of little sensations that let you know you are beginning to relax as you breathe in and out in a way that is just right for you... taking in just the right amount of air... becoming more and more aware of the pleasure of deep relaxation...

Now become aware of your abdomen and stomach... as you inhale, tense this area and hold it along with your breath for a few seconds... then release as you exhale and note the pleasant differences you are beginning to experience... and when you are done... continuing to breathe in... and out... so peacefully... calm and controlled...

Now directing your attention to your chest and shoulders... tense this area where so much anxiety and stress is stored as you breathe in and hold your breath for just a few seconds... now let go and release as you exhale... and take time once again to breathe in... and out... gently... easily...

Now become aware of your left hand and arm... make a fist with your left hand as you breathe in and tense both the fist and arm... hold it a moment then release the fist and relax the arm and hand completely as you continue to breathe in... and out... peacefully... calmly... now direct your awareness to your right hand and arm... make a fist with your right hand and tense it along with the arm as you breathe in and hold it for a moment... and when you're ready... breathe out completely and release the fist... relaxing the hand and arm... letting go of all the tension...

And again taking time to breathe in... and out... as you now move your awareness to your neck... another area where tension is sometimes stored... and as you finish a relaxing breath, tense the neck as you breathe in and hold your breath for just a few moments... then exhale all at once and release the tension there...

Now resting again... taking another relaxing inhalation... breathing at the most comfortable pace you can... in the most comfortable way possible... and when you've completed taking this relaxing breath, move your awareness to your face and head... as you breathe in, tense all of the muscles in your head and face and hold it... and when you're ready, let go... let go of all the tension in your body and in your mind...

And as you continue to breathe easily... and relax more and more... take a moment to scan your body and become aware of how much more relaxed you are than when you started... and if your body wants to readjust, to settle even more deeply, just allow it to do so as you continue to breathe out tension... breathing it out through your fingers... through your toes... just like sand pouring out your fingers... out your toes... just letting go and allowing your body to settle even more easily... just like settling into a thick white cloud... allowing the cloud to carry you so comfortably... so peacefully... so securely... all of your body so loose and limp and relaxed... just like a rag doll... all that's important right now is your own increasing sense of relaxation and peace... your own feelings of comfort and safety...

And now, imagine and create in your mind a very special place... a place of your choosing... one where you can feel at peace and secure... where you can experience re-creation and renewal... this can be a place where you have been to before, or one to where you have always wanted to go... maybe a place you have read about or seen in a movie, or that someone has told you about... it can even be a place that only exists in your mind... your special place can be any kind of place you wish... one that is just right for you... where there is comfort and contentment...

And as you find your special place... a place that's security... comfort... and contentment... let yourself really take it in... whether it's the coolness of a breeze... the sounds of birds... clouds drifting by... the colors of sunlight filtering or sparkling... or whatever is there...

And you may find that you want to be the only one there; or, you may want to have a special friend or relative there... you may even want to create a special person to share your special place... at times, you may want to change your special place in some way or even create a new one... and that is perfectly fine... this is your special place... you can do whatever you want to here... and as you take some time now to enjoy the comfort and peace and security of your special place... just let your mind wander and drift to wherever it wishes...

(Allow one to three minutes of silence before continuing with the rest of the script. If you have the know-how, you can record some relaxing music during this portion of the tape.)

Spending time in your special place brings an inner peace and strength that allows you to face the world with new energy and confidence. Any time you wish to return to your special place, you can do so by simply closing your eyes and taking a moment to relax. You will then be able to return to your special place and renew your energy and confidence and replenish yourself. Knowing that you now have this special place allows you to face the world in a positive new way...

From now on, placing the first two fingers and thumb of either hand together signals your mind and body to relax deeply, calm and controlled, and to experience the same feelings of relaxation... peace... and security that you are feeling now.... Your eyes may be open while you are experiencing these positive feelings and you will be able to more effectively do whatever it is that you are doing....

Now, in just a moment I will begin counting from one to five. With each count you will become more and more alert. At the count of five you will feel bright, alert, wide awake, and refreshed. Your body will have a feeling of well-being throughout your arms, your legs, and your entire body. I will now begin counting... one... just floating back so easily to this time and space... two... your muscles beginning to stir... three... move your toes and fingers slightly as you become more and more alert... four... your eyes getting ready to open... five... opening your eyes as you're ready, you feel alert and rested as though you just awoke from a refreshing sleep... now take a deep breath, fill up your lungs, and stretch.

Script 2: Variations On Breath Counting and Focal Point Technique

This script uses a combination of counting and focal point techniques. Since your rate of breathing varies depending upon how relaxed you are, the countdown pace on a script that is to be recorded needs to be independent of your rate of breathing. However, the idea of using a countdown to focus your attention and trigger a relaxation response is essentially the same as in breath counting. The initial spot on which you focus in this script and the word or phrase you repeat in the middle of the exercise are variations on the focal point technique. External focal points like the spot teamed up with counting or breathing techniques are very useful in anxiety-producing situations.

Script

In just a moment, it will be time to begin developing your relaxation response through a process of progressive relaxation. By placing the first two fingers and thumb of either hand lightly together and keeping them in this position during this process, you will develop a very effective anchor, a simple physical cue or signal that can be used to activate your relaxation response whenever you feel yourself becoming anxious or tense.

Now, take a moment to settle down into where you are sitting or lying and take a few relaxing breaths... Close your eyes as you take these relaxing breaths so you can experience more fully the sensation of the air moving in through your nose and traveling down deep into your lungs...

Make yourself comfortable and find a spot a little above your eye level to fix your attention on... it can be any type of spot... perhaps an interesting object... a shape... an area... a color... anything that appeals to you... now, as you continue to look at that spot, allow your eyes to go into a soft focus... not really concentrating hard, but rather, just using the spot as a center of focus in a soft, easy way... now inhale deeply through your nose and hold it for just a moment... then exhale all at once through your mouth...

As you now take a second deep breath, notice the tension in your chest... and as you again exhale all at once through your mouth, feel the release as you start to really relax... now, take a third deep breath... hold it a moment... then let it all out and notice how good your body is beginning to feel...

Continue to focus your attention on the spot as you now breathe in... and out... evenly... and regularly... relaxing more and more deeply... and as you continue to focus on the spot, your eyes may water a little... your eyelids may even flutter a bit as they begin to feel very heavy... and these are all good signs that you are ready to relax completely...

And as you continue to focus on the spot, your eyelids become increasingly heavy... so heavy that you want to close them... now, on a very comfortable... relaxing exhalation... just allow them to close... keeping your eyes closed now allows you to move into a deeper... and deeper relaxation... as you now move your attention to your hands and continue to breathe very easily and comfortably... calm and controlled... breathing all the way from your abdomen...

And as you focus on your hands, you begin to notice a very pleasant and interesting sensation... beginning maybe in your right hand... maybe in your left hand... perhaps even in both hands... you may feel this sensation in the back of your hands or perhaps in your fingers... a feeling of lightness... or increased warmth... perhaps a coolness... or a sensation of heaviness... very often a feeling of pleasant tingling... any one or combination of these feelings is a good sign that your muscles are relaxing and letting go... causing your blood vessels to expand a little and allow just a little more blood to flow to your skin as your entire body moves into deeper and deeper relaxation...

And you can just allow that pleasant sensation to begin to spread throughout your body... calm and controlled... more and more relaxed with every exhalation... breathing in comfort and peacefulness... breathing out all the tension as you allow a very natural process of deep relaxation to carry you deeper and deeper... very calm, pleasant feelings... nothing to do but allow it...

And you can go even deeper now as I count from ten to one... your relaxation doubling with every number... ten... just allowing a very natural process of deep relaxation to carry you even more deeply inside... even more peaceful and relaxed... nine... more and more comfortable... eight... relaxing calm and controlled... just allowing yourself to float and drift... seven... nothing important but the increasing sense of comfort and peacefulness... six... even deeper... five... halfway there... continuing to go even deeper with every exhalation... four... and you can allow yourself to go deeper and deeper... drifting comfortably... three... so peaceful... so comfortable... so secure... two... relaxing deeply... nothing to bother... nothing to disturb... the deep relaxation proceeding on its own... completely relaxed right now... one...

And in just a moment you will have time to go even deeper into this pleasurable state of deep relaxation by using a word or phrase as a focal point... this can be any word you choose that is relaxing and comfortable... you might like the word "calm"...

or the word "relax"... you might even want to use a short phrase such as, "I am centered and calm"... it can be any word or phrase you choose...

And you will repeat your word or phrase once every time you exhale... and if you choose, you may also imagine a special place while you practice saying your word or phrase on every exhalation... and with every exhalation... and every repetition of your word or phrase... your relaxation will increase... deeper and deeper... and now you have time to say your word or phrase on each of your exhalations.

(Allow one to three minutes of silence before continuing with the rest of the script. If you have the know-how, you can record some relaxing music during this portion of the tape.)

From now on, placing the first two fingers and thumb of either hand together signals your mind and body to relax deeply, calm and controlled, and to experience the same feelings of relaxation... peace... and security that you are feeling now.... Your eyes may be open while you are experiencing these positive feelings and you will be able to more effectively do whatever it is that you are doing....

And now it is time to return to the outside world. In just a moment I will begin counting from one to five. With each count you will become more and more alert. At the count of five you will feel bright, alert, wide awake and refreshed as if you awoke from a peaceful sleep. Your body will have a feeling of well-being throughout your arms, your legs, and your entire body. I will now begin counting... one... just floating back so easily to this time and space... two... your muscles beginning to stir... three... move your toes and fingers slightly as you become more and more alert... four... your eyes getting ready to open... five... opening your eyes as you're ready, you feel alert and rested as though you just awoke from a refreshing sleep. Now take a deep breath, fill up your lungs, and stretch.

Guidelines
for Selecting
a Therapist

2
Appendix

When seeking therapy remember that a given therapist does not work effectively with every type of person or problem. In order to find a therapist with a personality and an approach that is effective for you, talk with at least three therapists before choosing one. There are several ways to obtain the names of therapists who work with anxiety-related problems. Several good sources for referrals are listed below. If you are unable to locate a suitable person from these sources, you might try encouraging a local mental health professional whom you like to develop a specialization in anxiety disorders. Many professionals working with anxiety disorders were recruited by people with anxiety-related problems.

Referral Sources

- Friends who have had therapy
- Your family physician or health maintenance organization
- The Anxiety Disorders Association of America's *National Treatment Directory for Phobias and Related Anxiety Disorders* (see Recommended Reading)
- Local professional societies such as organizations of psychiatrists, psychologists, marriage family therapists, and social workers
- Medical schools, universities, and other major research and clinical centers
- Local mental health associations

After you have obtained the names of three therapists, give each one a call. When talking with each therapist, begin by describing as quickly and as simply as possible your symptoms and the behaviors you want to eliminate or change. Many people find it helpful to have written notes to keep them focused. Next, ask the questions listed below. A good therapist welcomes questions about his or her treatment approaches

255

and understands the importance of finding someone who matches your personality and problem. As you talk with each therapist, be sure to ask for an explanation whenever you do not understand what is being said. Two qualities you definitely want in your therapist are a willingness to answer questions directly and the ability to explain things clearly.

Are you licensed?

Licensing varies from state to state. In California, for example, there are four different types of state licensed psychotherapists. They are:

Psychiatrists: These are medical doctors (M.D.s) who, after their basic training in medicine, specialized in psychiatry.

Psychologists: These usually have a doctorate (Ph.D.) in psychology.

Marriage and Family Therapists: These may also be called Marriage, Family, and Child Counselors. They usually have a masters (M.A. or M.S.), sometimes a doctorate (Ph.D.), in counseling or psychology.

Social Workers: Social workers who conduct individual therapy are often referred to as Clinical Social Workers. They usually have a masters (M.A. or M.S.), sometimes a doctorate (Ph.D.), in social work.

While licensing does not guarantee competence, it does indicate that the state's standards of education and training have been met. When discussing licensing with a therapist, it is a good idea to ask what requirements needed to be met in order to be licensed in your state. Since some states do not issue licenses in all of the above categories, you can also ask whether the therapist is a member of a professional association. If so, ask what requirements needed to be met in order to join the association.

How much experience or training have you had with my type of problem?

If at all possible, try to find someone who has experience dealing with the type of problem you are experiencing. If the therapist has little or no experience with your type of problem, it is best if the therapist at least has some specific training which deals with it.

What is your basic approach to treatment?

This is probably the most confusing part of therapy since there are many different therapeutic approaches, each with its own set of terms. With anxiety-related problems, it is best to find someone familiar with both cognitive therapy and a form of behavioral treatment known as in vivo exposure (also called contextual therapy and travel or exposure therapy). Cognitive therapy involves the learning of specific techniques for changing the way you think. In vivo exposure concentrates on going into difficult situations and using specific behavioral and cognitive techniques to cope with the frightening feelings and thoughts as they occur. The goal of in vivo exposure is for the anxious thoughts and feelings to diminish and finally disappear as experience and skill are gained.

Cognitive and behavioral approaches are often combined with other forms of treatment such as psychopharmacologic treatment (the use of medications), psychodynamic therapy, and hypnosis. Therapists who use a combination of these approaches usually tailor them to the needs of individual clients.

Does the standard course of treatment have a fixed length? If so, how long is it and are there provisions for follow up?

Many therapists who work with anxiety disorders have a basic program which lasts from 8 to 20 weeks. This type of program may be a group or individual program or may combine both group and individual therapy. Programs like this often feature group or individual in vivo exposure with either a therapist or trained paraprofessional.

What is your definition of success with my type of problem, and based on that definition, what is your rate of success?

With anxiety-related problems two major areas of importance are the reduction of anxiety symptoms and the elimination of self-defeating behaviors such as avoidance patterns.

How much does treatment cost and is any of it reimbursable by health insurance?

Is it possible to speak with former clients?

Once you have chosen a therapist and have had two or three sessions, you will want to decide whether the therapist's personality and style seem right for you. It is best if you can answer most of the following questions with a "yes."

Do I feel:

- That it's safe to say whatever I want when I am with the therapist?
- More hopeful and positive about myself at the end of most therapy sessions?
- What the therapist says makes sense to me and seems relevant to my problems?

Did the therapist seem:

- Comfortable with me?
- At ease rather than stiff and formal?
- Flexible and open to new ideas?
- Genuinely concerned about me?

During our sessions, does the therapist:

- Take time to establish a set of goals for my therapy that I am able to understand; and is the therapist willing to use these goals to make periodic evaluations (every 4-6 weeks) of how the therapy is going and to set new goals if it seems appropriate?

- Encourage the feeling that I am as good as he or she is and treat me with respect rather than as if I am sick, defective, or about to fall apart?
- Admit limitations rather than pretend to know things he or she does not know?
- Answer direct questions in a simple, straight-forward manner?
- Find it easy to admit when he or she is wrong and apologize for making errors or for being inconsiderate?
- Welcome and encourage my viewpoint when I disagree with him rather than reacting negatively or telling me that I am resisting.
- Allow me to direct the conversation if I want to do so?
- Act as if he or she is my consultant rather than the manager of my life?
- Show empathy and caring and give value to my feelings and thoughts?
- Reveal things about him or herself either spontaneously or in response to my questions and do this without bragging or monopolizing the conversation?

While it is important to find someone you are comfortable with, it is also important to remember that your goal is to eliminate or change behaviors that concern you. *Do not allow therapy to drag on for months without any progress.* While many problems do require long-term therapy, there is usually some sense of progress after four to six sessions. Of course, progress will be slower for a person from a dysfunctional family who experienced much physical, emotional, or sexual abuse than it will be for a person from a reasonably healthy family with only one or two issues that need to be addressed. However, if you do not feel you have made any progress after six sessions, you may want to consider changing therapists. *Your time, money, and well being are at stake.* You are not obligated to a therapist simply because you started or have been with him or her for months or years.

When you feel that you want to either end therapy or change therapists, it is usually best to discuss this with your current therapist *before* you take action. The only exception to this would be if the therapist makes sexual advances towards you or does anything else that is clearly unprofessional. If this ever occurs, leave immediately and report what has happened to your state licensing agency. If there is no licensing of therapists in your state, report the incident to the professional organization to which the therapist belongs.

If you have changed therapists several times and have tried several different approaches with little progress, it may be that you have not made a real commitment to the therapeutic process or failed to give any one approach enough time. If this is the case, you may find it beneficial to resume work with the therapist who seemed most effective.

Locating a Local Self-Help Group

3

Appendix

Self-help groups provide a valuable resource for people with anxiety-related problems. If you are in therapy, you will find self-help groups can provide excellent supplement or follow-up to professional treatment. You will also find them valuable if professional treatment is either not available or not affordable. Even people who do not feel their anxiety-related problems are severe enough to warrant professional treatment find self-help groups a valuable resource.

There are many regional and local groups, many of which deal with specific anxiety-related issues. *Psychology Today* stated in its January 1988 issue that "An estimated 12 million people now help themselves and their neighbors by participating in roughly 500,000 self-help groups." With this large number of groups the chances of finding one in your area are very good. Some will be groups sponsored by a therapist in private practice or a mental health clinic. Others will be national, regional, or local self-help groups.

The first place to look when trying to find a local self-help group is your telephone book. Most telephone books now have a separate section titled, "Community Services", in either the white or yellow pages. This section is usually listed in the table of contents. Find this section and look under the heading titled, "Mental Health". This will list local agencies which can help you find a self-help group in your area. If you have a local chapter of the Mental Health Association listed there, you will find this organization especially helpful.

If you are unable to locate any agencies that know of local self-help groups, the next step is to look in the yellow pages under the headings of "mental health clinics," "psychiatrists," "psychologists," "marriage and family counselors," and "social workers." As you look under each heading, see if there are any clinics or therapists who specialize in anxiety-related problems. If there are, call them and ask if they know of any local self-help groups. You may also want to try calling the local professional organizations of the various types of therapists to see if they can help you.

After you have the names of several possible groups, it is time to identify the one that is best for you. As with selecting a therapist, it is important to find a group that matches your need. If there are several chapters of a particular group in your area, attend more than one so you get the flavor of each one. Attend at least three meetings before deciding whether or not a particular group is right for you.

If you are unable to locate a local self-help group, you may want to consider forming one in your area. The Anxiety Disorders Association of America is the foremost national organization specializing in anxiety-related problems. Their *National Treatment Directory for Phobias and Related Anxiety Disorders* lists people across the country who specialize in working with anxiety-related problems. They can provide help in organizing a local self-help group and may even be able to supply you with the telephone number and address a self-help group near you. They can be contacted at:

>Anxiety Disorders Association of America
>6000 Executive Boulevard, Suite 513
>Rockville, MD 20852
>(301) 231-9350

Another national organization that has many local chapters across the nation and which people with anxiety-related problems often find useful is Recovery, Inc. Check your local telephone directory for information on locations of Recovery meetings near you or write to:

>Recovery, Inc.
>802 North Dearborn Street
>Chicago, IL 60610
>(312) 337-5661

The *Self-Help Sourcebook* (see Recommended Reading for address) is another valuable resource. It lists contacts and descriptions of over 400 national and demonstrational model self-help groups along with extensive listings of self-help clearing houses. It also contains an excellent section on how to start an effective self-help group for people with panic disorder, agoraphobia, and simple phobias.

A free packet of information on how to use these lessons with a self-help group is also available. To receive this packet, send $1.00 to cover the cost of postage and handling to the following address:

>LifeSkills
>Self-Help Group Packet
>P.O. Box 7915
>Citrus Heights, CA 95621

People with anxiety-related problems often find it necessary to address non-anxiety-related issues in order to be successful with this program. Some of the most common ones are listed below. If any of these are part of your life, you may find that joining a self-help group that deals directly with it helpful.

Substance Abuse

Many people with anxiety-related problems develop substance abuse problems as a result of trying to use alcohol, tranquilizers, or other legal or illegal substances to overcome their anxiety symptoms. Whenever this is the case, it is always necessary to first deal with the substance abuse problem before progress can be made with the anxiety-related problems. If you are currently abusing any legal or illegal drug, you need to be in treatment. You also need to become active with Alcoholics Anonymous, Narcotics Anonymous, Pill Addicts Anonymous or one of the other groups for substance abusers.

Issues Concerning the Effects of Being Raised in a Dysfunctional Family

A dysfunctional family is one which is in some way an unhealthy place to live. Children in this type of family experience one or more of the six types of child abuse described in Lesson 1. The abuse of alcohol or some other legal or illegal drug is also common in these families. Some of the problems that can result from being raised in this type of family include problems with intimacy, an attraction to mates who have many of the qualities of the dysfunctional parent, poor communication skills, a limited ability to cope with stress, poor parenting skills, and low self-help esteem. Examples of national organizations that deal with these issues are National Association For Children of Alcoholics and V.O.I.C.E.S. In Action (Victims Of Incest Can Emerge Survivors).

Issues Concerning a Current Unhealthy Relationship

If you currently live with or have a close relationship with someone who is a substance abuser or who abuses you mentally or physically, you will probably need help to deal with the situation. This help may need to be in the form of professional therapy. In addition, self-help groups can provide you with both the strength and courage to act effectively, and practical suggestions for how to handle a difficult situation. Al-Anon, the companion organization to A.A. is a good example of a national organization. Most large communities have local shelters for battered women that sponsor regional and local groups.

Effects of a Major Illness or Physical Disability

If you have a major illness or physical disability, you may need to deal with the issues surrounding it before you will be able to effectively deal with your anxiety-related problems. Most major illnesses and physical disabilities have their own national or regional self-help organizations. These organizations can usually provide the latest information regarding the treatment of a particular problem and help a person accept and cope with the difficulties that problem might produce.

Suggestions for People with Sleep Problems

4

Appendix

Chronic loss of sleep can increase your symptoms of anxiety and interfere with your health, relationships, and overall ability to function effectively in life. Chronic sleep disturbance associated with sadness can also be a sign of major depression. Because chronic sleep problems can be due to either a medication or medical problem, it is always best to discuss sleep problems with your physician. Fortunately, sleep problems in people with anxiety-related problems are more often due to poor sleep habits or thinking patterns that interfere with sleep. Here are some general guidelines for practicing what is commonly called good *sleep hygiene*.

- Go to bed and get up at the *same time* each day and avoid making up for lost sleep on weekends or holidays. This helps set your biological clock if you have been going to bed and getting up at widely varying times. Naps are all right if they are taken on a fixed schedule and if adjustments are made in nighttime sleep.

- Reserve your bed for sleeping and sex. Do not read, watch television or do other activities in bed. If sleeping is very difficult, make the entire bedroom off limits to everything except sleep and sex. Do not make it an all-purpose room where you do many activities such as balance the checkbook, fight with your spouse, or exercise.

- Don't neglect the obvious: sleep is easiest in a dark, quiet, ventilated room.

- Follow an established routine for going to bed, such as brushing your hair and teeth, pulling down the sheets, and setting out clothes for the next day. These activities become a conditioned response trigger that tells your body, "It's time to fall asleep now."

- Do relaxing activities just prior to the time you are to go to sleep such as taking a hot bath or shower, reading, watching television, praying or meditating. Avoid anxiety-provoking activities like paying bills or arguing.
- Use any of the relaxation techniques described in Appendix 1 to help you fall asleep.
- Do not lie awake in bed for more than twenty minutes. If the relaxation response exercises in Appendix 1 do not induce sleep, get up and go to a different part of the house. Do a quiet relaxing activity like reading a book or watching television until you feel tired. At first, some people find they spend much of the night out of bed and get only four or five hours of sleep altogether. However, this is continuous, sound sleep, and gradually it expands to fill the night.
- Avoid caffeine, nicotine, heavy meals, and strenuous exercise for three to five hours before bedtime.
- Exercise during the day. Exercise just before sleeping will interfere with sleep. However, exercising in the late afternoon increases the amount of "deep-sleep" in the first half of the night. Even a brisk walk around the block may help.
- If noise in your surroundings makes it difficult to either go to sleep or wakes you up, place a radio next to your bed and tune it *between* stations to produce *white noise*. The white noise will serve as a cover for other distracting sounds.
- Stay away from alcohol. Drinking can actually make matters worse. Even moderate amounts of alcohol can disturb sleep or create a backlash of sleeplessness later in the night.
- Avoid the daily use of sleeping medications and only use when absolutely necessary. Over-the-counter remedies (usually antihistamines) are often not very effective. Prescription drugs can alter normal sleep patterns and suppress deep sleep or REM (the time when you are dreaming) sleep. They can also leave you groggy the next day. Because the body becomes tolerant of some drugs, higher and higher doses are needed leading to dependency. In fact, sleeping pills are often one of the main ingredients of long-term sleeplessness.
- When productivity lags during the day, change your activity pace. The most "natural" way to keep awake is to move: get up from your chair, pace the room and stretch. Try light rests and creative breaks instead of alcohol, cigarettes, or coffee.

When worrying about problems prevents you from falling asleep, get out of bed and go to another part of the house. Then, use the Four-Step Analysis described in Lesson 7 to develop a concrete plan for dealing with the problem. Summarize your plan into a simple coping self-statement as is described in Lesson 7. Then go to bed and use one of the relaxation techniques described in Appendix 1 to focus your mind on a neutral activity and relax your body. Many people find the technique called "breath counting" especially effective. When you begin thinking about the problem, repeat your coping self-statement and resume your relaxation exercise. If worry over problems prior to going to sleep is a recurring pattern, establish a regular time prior to your bedtime routine when you can use the Four-Step Analysis to develop concrete plans for dealing with your concerns.

If you often find that you wake up worrying about a problem and find it difficult to return to sleep, use the Four-Step Analysis described in the manner above. However, it is important to get out of bed first. When you are lying on your bed alternating between being awake and half asleep, you are probably in a light trance state. It is natural to slip into old, negative thinking patterns at a time like this. Often this takes the form of negative thoughts or images that repeat over and over in a circular pattern. Once you are fully awaken, you are able to use all your rational ability to carry out the problem-solving steps outlined above and challenge your irrational thoughts.

Some people with anxiety-related problems find they are sometimes awakened by a panic attack in the middle of the night. This often leaves them in a state of high anxiety. Current research now suggests that panic attacks that occur during sleep are *not* due to dreams. Instead, it is thought that they are due to some neurological mechanism that is not understood at the present. People who awaken with panic attacks probably have a genetic factor that, in some way, triggers the fight or flight response. If you experience these, but are able to return to sleep fairly easily then continue to do whatever you do to return to sleep. However, if you find that nighttime panic attacks trigger negative self-talk and high anxiety that makes it difficult to return to sleep, do the following.

- First, get out of bed and fully awaken yourself. This is easily done by washing your face. Once you are fully awake, use coping self-statements to state accurately what has just happened and calm yourself, such as, "This was just that neurological quirk that I have. It is *NOT* dangerous. These feelings are only uncomfortable and will diminish soon." If you have difficulty remembering your coping self-statements at night, write them on a card and post them in an easy to read place.
- Second, spend about ten minutes with a distracting and relaxing activity such as reading or having a cup of warm milk (cocoa has caffeine in it). This is essentially a decompression period that allows your body to settle down.
- Finally, go back to bed. If you find it difficult to go to sleep, use one of the relaxation response techniques in Appendix 1 to help you get back to sleep.

Developing Effective Listening Skills

Appendix

In our modern, busy world, taking time to listen is one of the greatest gifts you can give to someone. Listening shows you care about another person and is the key to effective problem-solving. Unfortunately, most people really don't know how to listen effectively. This appendix shows you how to use what is often referred to as "active listening" or "reflective listening."

□ *Acknowledgment Responses*

Acknowledgment responses refer to all the non-verbal and verbal responses you make which indicate to the speaker that you are listening. Common non-verbal responses include eye contact and nodding of the head. Common verbal responses include the various "empathetic grumblings" you make such as, "uh huh," "yes," and "mmmm." Acknowledgment responses are the simplest of the four basic active listening skills. Since they are probably already a part of your automatic behavior, they will not be dealt with in detail.

□ *Feeling Confirmation*

Feeling confirmation is the process of making guesses about another person's emotional response and commenting on it. Feeling confirmation has many uses and benefits. It provides you with a method for dissipating a person's strong emotions so this person can utilize his or her rational abilities more effectively. This is useful with problem-solving involving emotionally charged issues. It also makes you more effective by increasing your understanding of the person you are listening to and increases the overall amount of communication that takes place. In addition, it's an effective way to convey understanding and empathy to a person at the feeling level.

The first step in giving feeling confirmation is to make a guess about what the other person is experiencing on an emotional level. Next, comment on what you believe the other person is experiencing using one of the following three approaches:

Personal statements: Decide how you would feel if you were in the other person's situation and make a personal statement about it. This is the easiest approach for many people.

> Examples: "That would have really scared me." "I think I'd be angry if he said that to me."

"Seems" approach: Use words like "seem" to indicate it is your perception. This is seldom offensive to others. Never say how a person is feeling in a direct fashion (example: "You're angry") as the other person may resent it, especially if you're wrong.

> Examples: "You seem angry." "I guess that really scared you."

"Soft" questions: Comment using words like "weren't," "didn't," or "aren't."

> Examples: "Weren't you worried?" "Didn't that make you mad?"

☐ *Clarification Skills*

Clarification skills involve the use of questions or statements to obtain information from a person. The most common clarification approach is to use direct questions such as, "What do you want?" or "Where are you going?" While direct questions are fine in many situations, they tend to block communication and cause a person to become defensive or stop talking when the person is experiencing negative emotions. Any one of the following three approaches can be used to soften a direct question and obtain the same information.

Personal statements: Use phrases such as "I'd be interested in learning" or "I'd like to know" to change your question into a statement which expresses your interest in learning more about the information you want.

> Examples: "I'd be interested in learning more about what you want." "I'd like to know how you do that."

Confusion: State in a simple, direct sentence your confusion or inability to understand whatever it is you wish to learn. This is a very non-threatening approach which can be used whenever there is a high risk of the other person becoming defensive. A person is rarely threatened by your confusion. This is one approach that can usually be repeated if the other person continues to be vague. The only problem with this approach is that some people will not allow themselves to appear confused. If your level of self-esteem is high enough to allow you to appear confused, you will find this approach very useful.

Examples: "I don't quite understand what it is you want." "Boy, how you do that is a real mystery to me." "I'm still confused by that."

Incomplete sentence: Use an incomplete sentence that requires the information you want in order to be complete. This approach is like the fill-in-the-blank tests you took in school. It works best when used in the middle of a conversation and you want specific information.

Examples: "What you want is..." "You went to..."

□ *Paraphrasing*

Paraphrasing is summarizing key points and repeating them in your own words. This is different from parroting back the other person's exact words. The main use of paraphrasing is to verify that what you heard was accurate and to communicate that understanding to the other person. This allows the other person to correct any misunderstandings. Since paraphrasing can sound artificial and become distractive when only one form is used, become skilled with each of the following four forms.

"I statement": Begin with a phrase such as "I hear you saying..." or "As I understand it...,"

"You statement": Begin with a phrase such as, "So you think/feel/want/etc." or simply, "You think/believe/are going/etc."

Summary form: Begin with a statement that indicates you intend to summarize what has been said such as, "Let me see if I'm following you..." or "So what you are saying is...."

Question form: Any of the above forms can be transformed into a question by simply raising your voice at the end of the sentence. You can also use a direct question such as, "Are you saying...." While direct questions are often effective when commenting on implied messages or clarifying confused ideas, direct questions can make a person feeling strong negative emotions defensive if they are overused.

Examples:

Speaker: "I've had this flu for the last few days and haven't been feeling like putting in any more time than I have to... I know the meeting at six is going to drag on and not get much accomplished and I probably won't be much good in the shape I'm in anyway, and so I was kind of hoping I could stay home so I could take care of my flu and maybe even go to bed early.

"I statement":   "What I hear you saying is you want to skip the meeting and stay home so you can take care of yourself."

"You statement":   "Because you're sick, you want to skip the meeting and stay home."

| Summary form: | "Let me see if I'm following you; you want to skip the meeting and stay home." |
| Question form: | "Are you saying that you want to skip the meeting and stay home?" |

□ *Exercises*

Learning to develop the above listening skills is actually fairly simple. Begin by spending two days practicing feeling confirmation skills. Whenever you are talking with someone who is expressing emotions, comment on them using one of the feeling confirmation forms. You will be most successful if you start by commenting on strong *positive* emotions (example: "That must have really been exciting!"). After you have practiced feeling confirmation skills with positive emotions for two days, spend the next two days practicing clarification skills in neutral or positive situations. Then spend the next two days practicing paraphrasing skills in neutral or positive situations. If you feel you need more work, repeat the two day practice cycles all over. Do not use your new skills in situations where there are strong negative emotions until you feel skilled in neutral and positive situations.

Recommended Reading

Self-Help Books on Anxiety

Agras, Stewart. *Panic: Facing Fears, Phobias, and Anxiety.* An excellent book for people interested in the research behind our current understanding of phobias. Also a good description of exposure therapy.

Barlow, David H. and Craske, Michelle G. *Mastery of Your Anxiety and Panic.* A teaching manual originally designed for people working under clinical supervision. A detailed presentation of coping skills and desensitization techniques.

Clum, George A. *Coping with Panic: A Drug-Free Approach to Dealing with Anxiety Attacks.* A good book with lots of practical cognitive and behavioral techniques for dealing with anxiety.

Greist, John H.; Jefferson, James W.; Marks, Isaac M. *Anxiety and Its Treatment.* A good overview of anxiety disorders by three leading psychiatrists in the field. The chapter on the use of medications with anxiety disorders is one of the best among these books.

Neuman, Frederic. *Fighting Fear: The Eight Week Program for Treating Your Own Phobias.* One of the most detailed descriptons of how to use in vivo exposure with phobias available. Many practical skills are included.

Neziroglu, Fugen and Yarya-Tobias, Jose A. *Over and Over Again: Understanding Obsessive-Compulsive Disorder* Good discussion of the latest research and practical suggestions for self-help.

Peurifoy, Reneau. *Anxiety, Phobias & Panic: Taking Charge and Conquering Fear.* Designed as a series of fifteen easy-to-follow lessons, it is the most complete guide for overcoming anxiety-related problems currently available.

Rapoport, Judith. *The Boy Who Couldn't Stop Washing His Hands: The Experience & Treatment of Obsessive-Compulsive Disorder.* An excellent description of what is currently known about obsessive-compulsive disorder (OCD). An important supplement to this book for anyone with OCD.

Seagrave, Ann and Covington, Faison. *Free From Fears: New Help for Anxiety, Panic and Agoraphobia.* Useful skills for overcoming agoraphobia by two lay persons who themselves overcame this problem and are now directors of the Center for Help for Agoraphobia/Anxiety through New Growth Experiences (CHAANGE).

Wilson, R. Reid. *Don't Panic: Taking Control of Anxiety Attacks.* Excellent sections on the role of hyperventilation and panic attacks. Also has extensive sections on the physiological causes of panic and techniques for producing what Wilson calles cue controlled deep muscle relaxation.

Wilson, R. Reid. *Breaking the Panic Cycle.* A short but concise booklet put together for the Phobia Society of America. Outlines a seven step approach to overcoming panic attacks.

Books on Anxiety for Professionals

Beck, Aaron T., and Emery, Gary. *Anxiety Disorders and Phobias: A Cognitive Perspective.* The first truly comprehensive book outlining both the cognitive view of anxiety and cognitive techniques.

Michelson, Larry and Ascher, L. Michael, editors. *Anxiety and Stress Disorders, Cognitive-Behavioral Assessment and Treatment.* An excellent overview of cognitive-behavioral theory, assessment, and treatment of anxiety disorders. Extensive references in each area.

Ochberg, Frank M., *Post-Traumatic Therapy and Victims of Violence.* The most recent addition to the Brunner/Mazel Psychosocial Stress Series. An excellent overview of how to work with victims of violence. Previous volumes deal with other types of PTSD.

Walker, John R., Norton, G. Ron, Ross, Colin A. *Panic Disorder and Agoraphobia: A Comprehensive Guide for the Practitioner.* An excellent overview of panic disorder and agoraphobia that covers etiology, research, and both psychological and pharmacological treatment. Extensive references in each area.

Self-Help Resources

National Phobia Treatment Directory. Lists therapists working with anxiety-related problems throughout the U.S. Call or write Anxiety Disorders Association of America, 6000 Executive Boulevard, Suite 513, Rockville, MD 20852; (301) 231-9350

The Self-Help Sourcebook. Contains a listing of over 400 national and demonstrational self-help groups along with national toll-free 800 helplines, and guidelines for starting a self-help group. Call or write Self-Help Clearinghouse, Attn: Sourcebook, St. Clares-Riverside Medical Center, Pocono Road, Denville, New Jersey 07834; (201) 625-7101.

Additional Self-Help Books

Rational Thinking and Positive Self-Talk

Backus, William and Chapian, Marie. *Telling Yourself the Truth.* (Christian)

Burns, David. *Feeling Good and Intimate Connections: How To Get More Love In Your Life.*

Butler, Pamela E. *Talking To Yourself.*

Dyer, Wayne W. *Your Erroneous Zones.*

Ellis, Albert, and Harper, Robert. *A New Guide To Rational Living.*

Lazarus, Arnold and Fay, Allen. *I Can If I Want To.*

Stoop, David. *Self-Talk: Key To Personal Growth.* (Christian)

Depression

Burns, David D. *Feeling Good: The New Mood Therapy.*
DeRosis, Helen and Pellegrino, Victoria. *The Book of Hope: How Women Can Overcome Depression.*
Papolos, Demitri F. and Papolos, Janice. *Overcoming Depression.*

Social Phobia

Burns, David D. *Intimate Connections.*
Zimbardo, Philip. *Shyness: What It Is, What to Do About It.*

Adults Who Were Physically, Sexually, or Mentally Abused as Children

Brown, Stephanie. *Safe Passages: Recovery for Adult Children of Alcoholics.* (Physical, sexual or mental abuse)
Davis, Laura and Bass, Ellen. *The Courage to Heal.* (Incest, molestation)
Forward, Susan and Buck, Craig. *Betrayal of Innocence: Incest And Its Devastation.*
Miller, Alice. *Drama of the Gifted Child.* (Emotional abuse, narcissism in parents)
Whitfield, Charles. *Healing the Child Within: Discovery and Recovery For Adult Children of Dysfunctional Families.*
Woititz, Janet Geringer. *Adult Children of Alcoholics.*

Substance Abuse

Black, Claudia. *It Will Never Happen To Me.* (for ACAs)
Gorski, Terence. *Passages Through Recovery.*
Kinney, Jean and Leaton, Gwen. *Loosening the Grip.*
Johnson, Vernon. *I'll Quit Tomorrow.*
Milam, James and Ketcham, Katherine. *Under the Influence: A Guide To Myths and Realities of Alcoholism.*

Relationships with Substance Abusers

Beattie, Melody. *Co-Dependent No More.*
Drews, Toby Rice. *Getting Them Sober.*
Wegscheider, Sharon. *Another Chance: Hope and Health for the Alcoholic Family.*
Zink, Muriel. *Ways To Live More Comfortably With Your Alcoholic.*

Positive Self-Image, Self-Esteem, and Self-Acceptance

James, Muriel. *Breaking Free.*
Kalellis, Peter M. *A New Self-Image.*
Maltz, Maxwell. *Psychocybernetics.*
McKay, Matthew, and Fanning, Patrick. *Self-Esteem.*
Peale, Norman V. *The Power of Positive Thinking.*

Relaxation Techniques

Benson, Herbert. *the Relaxation Response and Beyond the Relaxation Response.*
Carrington, Patricia. *Freedom In Meditation.*
Davis, Martha, Eshelman, Elizabeth Robbins, and McKay, Matthew. *the Relaxation and Stress Reduction Workbook.*
Jacobson, Edmund. *Progressive Relaxation.*
Le Shan, Laurence. *How To Meditate.*

Assertiveness

Alberti, R. E., and Emmons, M. L. *Your Perfect Right: A Guide To Assertive Behavior.*
Baer, Jean. *How To Be An Assertive (Not Aggressive) Woman In Life, In Love, and On the Job.*
Bower, S. A. and G. H. Bower. *Asserting Yourself: A Practical Guide for Positive Change.*
Smith, Manual. *When I Say No, I Feel Guilty.*

Anger

Gaylin, Willard. *the Rage Within.*
Hauck, Paul A. *Overcoming Frustration and Anger.*
Lerner, Harriet G. *the Dance of Anger.*
Tavris, Carol. *Anger, the Misunderstood Emotion.*

Relationships

Forward, Susan. *Men Who Hate Women and the Women Who Love them.*
Missildine, Hugh W. *Your Inner Child of the Past.*
Norwood, Robin. *Women Who Love Too Much.*
Sheehy, Gail. *Passages and Pathfinders.*
Viscott, David. *How To Live With Another Person, the Language of Feelings, and Risking.*

Marital Issues

Beck, Aaron T. *Love Is Never Enough: How Couples Can Overcome Misunderstandings, Resolve Conflicts, and Solve Relationship Problems Through Cognitive therapy.*
Campbell, Susan M. *the Couple's Journey: Intimacy as a Path to Wholeness.*
Neil, Merrily and Tangedahl, Joanne. *A New Blueprint for Marriage.*
Rock, Maxine. *the Marriage Map: Understanding and Surviving the States of Marriage.*
Scarf, Maggie. *Intimate Partners, Patterns in Love and Marriage.*

Grief and Loss

Bozarth-Campbell, Alla. *Life Is Goodbye, Life Is Hello: Grieving Well Through All Kinds of Loss.*

Kubler-Ross, Elisabeth. *On Death and Dying.*

Kushner, Harold S. *When Bad Things Happen To Good People.*

Staudacher, Carol. *Beyond Grief: A Guide For Recovering From the Death of A Loved One.*

Sexuality

Barbach, Lonnie G. *For Yourself: the Fulfillment of Female Sexuality and For Each Other.*

Zilbergeld, Bernie. *Male Sexuality.*

Communication Skills

Bolton, Robert H. *People Skills.*

Egan, G. *the Skilled Helper.*

Gordon, Thomas. *Leader Effectiveness Training and P.E.T. In Action.*

Martin, Robert J. *A Skills and Strategies Handbook for Working With People.*

Parenting Skills

Briggs, Dorothy. *Your Child's Self-Esteem: the Key To His Life.*

Dodson, Fitzhugh. *How To Discipline With Love.*

Dreikurs, Rudolf. *Children the Challenge.*

Ginott, Haim. *Between Parent And Child and Between Parent and Teenager.*

Other Topics

Fiore, Neil A. *The Now Habit: Overcoming Procrastination Through Quality Work and Guilt-Free Play.*

Fulghum, Robert. *All I Really Need to Know I Learned in Kindergarten; It Was On Fire When I Lay Down On It; Uh Oh.*

Frankl, Viktor. *Man's Search for Meaning.*

Lakein, Alan. *How To Get Control of Your Time and Your Life.*

McKenzie, Robin. *Treat Your Own Neck; Treat Your Own Back.*

Index

Supplemental Materials

This book has been designed to be used by itself. However, depending upon your personality and individual needs, you may want to consider obtaining one or more of the following supplemental materials:

The Relaxation Response Series

This series contains four programs on two audio cassette tapes. These programs help you develop cue-controlled relaxation—the ability to trigger the relaxation response by simply placing two fingers together. These programs also help make relaxed diaphragmatic breathing, externalization, and basic stress management skills automatic behaviors.

The Changing Attitudes Series

This series contains ten programs on five audio cassette tapes. These programs are designed to be used just before you go to sleep. They communicate directly to your subconscious mind and reinforce the information and skills presented in the lessons.

Taking Charge and Conquering Fear

On this set of eight audio cassette tapes you meet the author of *Anxiety, Phobias & Panic* as he talks about the ideas and skills presented in each of the lessons. It's almost like having Mr. Peurifoy right there with you. There are also interviews with people who have used the program successfully. The discussion tapes can be played while you drive, work, or relax. These programs are especially useful for people who find the material difficult, who learn best when information is explained verbally, or who just find it difficult to stick with a set of written lessons. This series was revised when the new edition of *Anxiety, Phobias & Panic* was released so it now follows the revised lessons.

A Spiritual Guide Through Anxiety: A Supplement to Anxiety, Phobias & Panic

by Marjorie Working

The chapters in this book parallel the lessons in *Anxiety, Phobias & Panic* and are designed to be used in conjunction with the lessons. Marjorie Working explores anxiety-related issues that are of special interest to Christians and provides Biblical references for key points in each lesson. In this way, the reader is shown how to add a spiritual dimension to the techniques described in the lessons and make spiritual renewal the basis for overcoming an anxiety-dominated existence.

Price List

Individual Tapes (Two programs on each tape)

101	RR-1:	Developing a Relaxation Response	$ 9.95
	RR-2:	Increased Relaxation with Relaxed Breathing	
102	RR-3:	Externalization	9.95
	RR-4:	Increasing Your Stress Management Skills	
201	CA-1:	Replacing Should/Must Thinking .... With Positive Problem-Solving	9.95
	CA-2:	Increasing Your Rational Self-Talk Skills	
202	CA-3:	Accepting Errors and Imperfection	9.95
	CA-4:	Facing Life as a Positive Realist	
203	CA-5:	Approval	9.95
	CA-6:	Self-Esteem and Self-Acceptance	
204	CA-7:	Transforming Anger into a Positive, ... Constructive Force	9.95
	CA-8:	Releasing Resentments and Accepting Change	
205	CA-9:	Positive Assertiveness	9.95
	CA-10:	Overcoming resistance from Others	

Multiple Tape Sets

901 The Relaxation Response Series 17.95
(all four Relaxation Response programs on two cassettes)

902 The Changing Attitudes Series 41.95
(all ten Changing Attitudes programs on five cassettes)

903 The Relaxation Response/Changing Attitudes Combinded Set 55.95
*(all Relaxation Response and Changing Attitude
programs on seven cassettes)*

904 Taking Charge and Conquering Fear 63.95
*(an individual discussion of each of the fifteen lessons in
ANXIETY, PHOBIAS & PANIC plus interviews on eight cassettes)*

905 The Complete Set 98.95
*(all Relaxation Response, Changing Attitudes and
Discussion programs on fifteen cassettes)*

Books

B06 A Spiritual Guide Through Anxiety 6.95

B07 Anxiety, Phobias & Panic: Taking Charge and Conquering Fear 12.95

Order Form

Name:_____

Street Address:_____

City:_____ State:_____ Zip:_____

Telephone: (_____)_____

Please send the following:

Quant	Item No	Description	Unit Price	Total Cost
	901	Relaxation Response Series (2 tapes)	$17.95	
	902	Changing Attitude Series (5 tapes)	$41.95	
	903	Complete Relaxation Response and Changing Attitude Series (7 tapes)	$55.95	
	904	Taking Charge (8 discussion tapes)	$63.95	
	905	The Complete Set (all the above Programs - 15 tapes at over 1/3 off)	$98.95	
	BO6	A Spiritual Guide Through Anxiety: A Supplement to Anxiety, Phobias & Panic	$6.95	
	BO7	Anxiety, Phobias & Panic: Taking Charge and Conquering Fear	$12.95	

Shipping & Handling Charges
$0.00 - $9.99 = $1.50
$10.00 - $19.99 = $2.50
$20.00 - $29.99 = $3.50
$30.00 - $49.99 = $4.50
over $50 = $5.50

Total Order	
California Residents add 7.75% Sales Tax	
Shipping & Handling	
Grand Total	

Add $4.00 for COD

Please make your check or money order payable to: LIFESKILLS

Mail your order to: LIFESKILLS
P.O. Box 7915
Citrus Heights, CA 95621-7915

Order Form

Name:_____

Street Address:_____

City:_____ State:_____ Zip: _____

Telephone: (_____)_____

Please send the following:

Quant	Item No	Description	Unit Price	Total Cost
	901	Relaxation Response Series (2 tapes)	$17.95	
	902	Changing Attitude Series (5 tapes)	$41.95	
	903	Complete Relaxation Response and Changing Attitude Series (7 tapes)	$55.95	
	904	Taking Charge (8 discussion tapes)	$63.95	
	905	The Complete Set (all the above Programs - 15 tapes at over 1/3 off)	$98.95	
	BO6	A Spiritual Guide Through Anxiety: A Supplement to Anxiety, Phobias & Panic	$6.95	
	BO7	Anxiety, Phobias & Panic: Taking Charge and Conquering Fear	$12.95	

Shipping & Handling Charges
$0.00 - $9.99 = $1.50
$10.00 - $19.99 = $2.50
$20.00 - $29.99 = $3.50
$30.00 - $49.99 = $4.50
over $50 = $5.50

Total Order ____

California Residents add 7.75% Sales Tax ____

Shipping & Handling ____

Grand Total ____

Add $4.00 for COD

Please make your check or money order payable to: LIFESKILLS

Mail your order to: LIFESKILLS
P.O. Box 7915
Citrus Heights, CA 95621-7915

AR1